T0406990

Silent Partners

STUDIES IN CANADIAN MILITARY HISTORY

Series editor: Tim Cook, Canadian War Museum

The Canadian War Museum, Canada's national museum of military history, has a threefold mandate: to remember, to preserve, and to educate. Studies in Canadian Military History, published by UBC Press in association with the Museum, extends this mandate by presenting the best of contemporary scholarship to provide new insights into all aspects of Canadian military history, from earliest times to recent events. The work of a new generation of scholars is especially encouraged, and the books employ a variety of approaches – cultural, social, intellectual, economic, political, and comparative – to investigate gaps in the existing historiography. The books in the series feed immediately into future exhibitions, programs, and outreach efforts by the Canadian War Museum. A list of the titles in the series appears at the end of the book.

CANADIAN WAR MUSEUM
MUSÉE CANADIEN DE LA GUERRE

Silent Partners
The Origins and Influence of Canada's Military-Industrial Complex

Edited by Alex Souchen and Matthew S. Wiseman

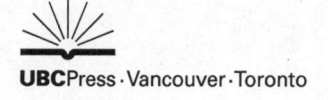

UBCPress · Vancouver · Toronto

32 31 30 29 28 27 26 25 24 23   5 4 3 2 1

Printed in Canada on FSC-certified ancient-forest-free paper (100% post-consumer recycled) that is processed chlorine- and acid-free.

Library and Archives Canada Cataloguing in Publication

Title: Silent partners : the origins and influence of Canada's military-industrial complex / edited by Alex Souchen and Matthew S. Wiseman.
Names: Souchen, Alex, editor. | Wiseman, Matthew S., editor.
Series: Studies in Canadian military history.
Description: Series statement: Studies in Canadian military history | Includes bibliographical references and index.
Identifiers: Canadiana (print) 20230216269 | Canadiana (ebook) 20230216315 | ISBN 9780774868952 (hardcover) | ISBN 9780774868969 (softcover) | ISBN 9780774868983 (EPUB) | ISBN 9780774868976 (PDF)
Subjects: LCSH: Military-industrial complex—Canada—History—20th century. | LCSH: Military research—Canada—History—20th century. | LCSH: Canada—Military policy—20th century.
Classification: LCC HC120.D4 S55 2023 | DDC 355/.07097109045—dc23

UBC Press gratefully acknowledges the financial support for our publishing program of the Government of Canada, the Canada Council for the Arts, and the British Columbia Arts Council.

This book has been published with the help of a grant from the Canadian Federation for the Humanities and Social Sciences, through the Awards to Scholarly Publications Program, using funds provided by the Social Sciences and Humanities Research Council of Canada.

Publication of this book has been financially supported by the Canadian War Museum.

UBC Press
The University of British Columbia
2029 West Mall
Vancouver, BC V6T 1Z2
www.ubcpress.ca

For our PhD supervisors
Jonathan F. Vance and Kevin A. Spooner

Contents

Abbreviations

ACAMR	Associate Committee on Aviation Medical Research (Canada)
ACMR	Associate Committee on Medical Research (Canada)
AVGP	armoured vehicle general purpose
AVM	air vice marshal
AWSC	Allied War Supplies Corporation (Canada)
CAC	conduct after capture
CAF	Canadian Armed Forces
CAL	Canadian Arsenals Limited
CAS	chief of the air staff (Canada)
CBW	chemical and biological weapons
CCC	Canadian Commercial Corporation
CCF	Co-operative Commonwealth Federation
CFB	Canadian Forces Base
CIA	Central Intelligence Agency (United States)
CIL	Canadian Industries Limited
CIPA	Canadian Industrial Preparedness Association
CIU	No. 1 Clinical Investigation Unit (Canada)
CMHC	Central Mortgage and Housing Corporation (Canada)
DDGM	Diesel Division General Motors
DDP	Department of Defence Production (Canada)
DEA	Department of External Affairs (Canada)
DHC	de Havilland Canada
DIL	Defence Industries Limited (Canada)
DMS	Department of Munitions and Supply (Canada)
DND	Department of National Defence (Canada)
DOD	Department of Defense (United States)
DPSA	Defence Production Sharing Agreement (Canada–United States)
DRB	Defence Research Board (Canada)
DRML	Defence Research Medical Laboratories (Canada)
DRNL	Defence Research Northern Laboratory (Canada)
DSS	Department of Supply and Services (Canada)
DTC	Department of Trade and Commerce (Canada)

GECO	General Engineering Company (Canada)
HRRAC	Human Resources Research Advisory Committee (Canada)
IAM	Institute of Aviation Medicine (Canada)
IRB	Industrial and Regional Benefit
ITC	Department of Industry, Trade and Commerce (Canada)
LAV	light armoured vehicle
MAP	Mutual Aid Program (Canada)
MIC	military-industrial complex
MRAC	Medical Research Advisory Committee (Canada)
NATO	North Atlantic Treaty Organization
NORAD	North American Aerospace Defence Command (note: changed from North American Air Defence Command in 1981)
NRC	National Research Council (Canada)
PDC	Plant Decontamination Committee (Canada)
POW	prisoner of war
RAF	Royal Air Force (United Kingdom)
R&D	research and development
RCAF	Royal Canadian Air Force
RCMP	Royal Canadian Mounted Police
RCNAS	Royal Canadian Naval Air Service
RDF	Rapid Deployment Force (United States)
RTI	resistance to interrogation
SES	Suffield Experimental Station
STOL	short take-off and landing
TACOM	Tank-Automotive and Armaments Command (United States)
U of T	University of Toronto
UN	United Nations
UNEF	United Nations Emergency Force
USAF	United States Air Force
USSEA	Under-secretary of state for external affairs (Canada)
WAC	War Assets Corporation (Canada)

Acknowledgments

THE IDEA FOR THIS BOOK started when Alex passed a note across the table to Matthew at the 2019 Canadian Military History Colloquium at Wilfrid Laurier University. The note read something to the effect of, "Do you want to coedit a book on Canada's military-industrial complex with me? Circle: Yes or No." Later, during a break between sessions, we sketched out potential topics and discussed the value of adding historical perspectives to ongoing conversations and debates in a field largely dominated by political scientists, economists, and defence analysts. Following the conference, we drafted a call for papers and circulated it throughout our networks, and the response we received was very encouraging.

Over the next few years, our contributors worked diligently to produce outstanding chapter drafts, under very difficult and stressful circumstances brought about by the COVID-19 pandemic. With archives closed, cities locked down, and uncertainty everywhere, we turned to the historical sources we could access online and the documents we had already collected during "the before times." Others circled back to subjects that had been extensions of previous projects or shortened something new that was meant to be part of their next book. Whatever the case, our contributors did amazing work, and for that we, as editors, would like to acknowledge their efforts and thank them for sharing their research with us and for being so receptive to our feedback and timelines. It was a pleasure to work with each of you, and we hope this project will pave the way for other collaborations in the future.

Several other people deserve special mention for helping us cross the finish line. At UBC Press, Randy Schmidt supported the project from the very beginning, and Katrina Petrik and the entire production team were so helpful throughout the whole publication process. It was a pleasure working with you; thank you for your guidance and contributions to this project. We are thrilled that this book is part of UBC Press's Studies in Canadian Military History series, joining the nearly sixty other books in the series, many written by our friends and colleagues. We would also like to acknowledge the partnership between UBC Press and the Canadian War Museum, which has sustained this prestigious series for the past twenty years, and thank Tim Cook, Chief Historian and Director of Research at the Canadian War Museum, who supported our project at every turn.

We all owe an enormous debt to the many archivists and librarians at several different research institutions, including Archives and Special Collections at the University of Manitoba, the Directorate of History and Heritage, Library and Archives Canada, the McGill University Archives, the Military History Research Centre at the Canadian War Museum, the National Archives, and the University of Toronto Archives and Records Management Services. For providing permissions to use the illustrations and maps appearing in this collection, we thank the Ajax Public Library, Defence Research and Development Canada, Library and Archives Canada, the National Archives and Records Administration, the *Winnipeg Free Press*, and Eric Leinberger. We would also like to acknowledge the financial support of the Canadian War Museum and the Awards to Scholarly Publishing Program of the Social Sciences and Humanities Research Council of Canada (SSHRC), which graciously provided the funds for publishing this book.

Alex would like to thank Doug Delaney for his sage advice and encouragement throughout this project, as well as his colleagues at the University of Guelph who have been so welcoming and supportive since he joined the Department of History and Bachelor of Arts and Science Program in July 2022. He would also like to thank Matthew for his dedication, attention to detail, teamwork, and good sense of humour – all of which made writing and editing this book a more enjoyable and meaningful experience. Few people know more about the Cold War and defence science than Matthew, so it was a privilege working together. Hopefully, this is the first of many collaborations.

Matthew wishes to acknowledge Timothy Sayle, John English, and his former colleagues at the Bill Graham Centre for Contemporary International History at the University of Toronto, where he completed a SSHRC Postdoctoral Fellowship between 2017 and 2019 on the history of the military-industrial complex in Canada. Matthew also thanks Alex for spearheading this book project, facilitating with UBC Press, and tirelessly reading, editing, and revising drafts along the way. Alex's commitment to historical research and writing is outdone only by his kindness and generosity, and this volume exists because of his qualities as a historian and his determination to push the bounds of the field.

Finally, and most importantly, we want to share our deep appreciation for our partners, Sara and Alycia. You put up with our bad jokes, complaints about research, and anecdotal references to bizarre facts about Canadian history. For your unwavering interest through it all, you mean more to us than words could ever express. Thank you for your love and support.

Silent Partners

Introduction
A Canadian Military-Industrial Complex?

Alex Souchen and Matthew S. Wiseman

ON REMEMBRANCE DAY IN 1982, Canada's former minister of national defence, Barnett Danson, delivered an address to a privileged audience at the Empire Club of Canada in Toronto. A distinguished veteran, politician, and industrialist, Danson stood before his peers as a respected and highly qualified authority on a curious and seemingly unlikely Canadian issue, something he called "Canada's military-industrial complex."[1] In his speech, he outlined the current security challenges facing the country and delved into recent trends in military and strategic affairs to examine the balance of power between the world's two super-powers, the United States and the Soviet Union, and the many implications for Canada. He listed facts and figures on Canada's defence spending and discussed some of Ottawa's procurement policies to illustrate the critical importance of international cooperation with other allies in the North Atlantic Treaty Organization (NATO). He argued that "a reasonable state of preparedness" was essential to the maintenance of national sovereignty and security. "We cannot afford to bury our heads in the sand like the ostrich," he analogized, "if we do, the family of free nations could well become an endangered species."[2] Above all, Danson made clear to his audience that, for Canada, a strong military required a strong economy and that the relationship between the two was symbiotic and mutually beneficial.

Born in 1921 to Jewish parents, Barnett Jerome "Barney" Danson grew up in Toronto's Parkdale neighbourhood. He came from humble origins: his family struggled through the Great Depression, but he learned the value of hard work and the importance of family from his parents and siblings. His life changed dramatically at the outbreak of war in 1939, and at the age of eighteen, he enlisted with the Queen's Own Rifles of Canada. Like many others in his unit, Danson was disappointed when they were not put on active service with the 1st or 2nd Canadian Infantry Divisions, but they eventually sailed for England with the rest of the 3rd Division in 1941. During the war, he was promoted to lieutenant and married the love of his life, Isobel Bull, while overseas in February 1943, before landing at Bernières-sur-Mer on D-Day, 6 June 1944. In Normandy, he survived the early hell of the bridgehead battles and the capture of Caen, but in late August he was severely wounded by shrapnel from a mortar bomb that struck him in the head and blinded him in one eye.[3] Undaunted by his grievous injuries, Danson's war experience later "propelled" him, to use his own words, into the "political arena" because it instilled the confidence and determination to pursue a long and distinguished career in public service.[4]

Danson returned home in December 1944 and built a successful career as an entrepreneur and esteemed member of Toronto's expanding business community. He became an advocate for the Canadian National Institute for the Blind and, in his later years, for the establishment of the new Canadian War Museum. In 1953, he founded the Danson Corporation, which specialized in the design, manufacture, and distribution of production machinery for the booming postwar plastics industry – an industry that owed its existence to wartime spending and defence policies.[5] Danson's political career took root some years later, in 1968, when he was elected to Parliament as a Liberal MP representing the constituency of York North, and he later joined Cabinet as minister of urban affairs in 1974, maintaining that file for two years before Prime Minister Pierre Elliott Trudeau shuffled him into the defence portfolio. He served as minister of national defence for three years until losing his seat in the 1979 election. He left Ottawa as a well-connected politician with strong ties to Canadian industry, fostering close professional associations with de Havilland Aircraft of Canada, Methon Energy Corporation, and Scintrex, among other major industrial players. He also directed the Ontario Safety League, the Canadian Council of Christians and Jews, and the Canadian Institute of Strategic Studies, working and socializing among influential leaders with high standings in both political and economic affairs.

By the time Danson stepped to the podium to address the Empire Club in 1982, his military background, business savvy, and political experience provided him intimate, first-hand knowledge of the inner workings of Canada's defence procurement policies. Perhaps more than anyone in the country, he was primed to speak with confidence and expertise about the size and substance of the past, present, and future of Canadian defence industries. Danson became defence minister at a low point for the recently unified Canadian Armed Forces (CAF), as successive Liberal governments under Lester B. Pearson and Pierre Trudeau relegated defence spending and sought to revise Canada's contributions to the NATO alliance. The quagmire of Pearson's budget cuts in the 1960s was compounded by Trudeau's defence policy reviews in the early 1970s. The result was a long period of decline, as Pearson shut down procurement programs for major weapons systems and Trudeau initially sought to downsize the NATO garrison in West Germany and to eliminate heavy armoured vehicles from Canada's arsenals.[6]

Under pressure from NATO allies, Trudeau relented and put Danson at the helm to navigate the Department of National Defence (DND) through the late

1970s, spearheading a period of significant growth. Between 1976 and 1984, the DND budget doubled and there was a modest boost in procurement, as the CAF received new hardware that replaced its rusting and outdated kit in the 1980s.[7] Even after leaving office, Danson continued to advocate for procurement and national defence, using his speech at the Empire Club as an opportunity to further address these issues head on. His speech argued for a reversal of earlier budgetary constraints and stronger investments in the CAF to meet Canada's evolving military and strategic needs. He spoke from first-hand experience, as he was acutely aware of Canada's unique security and defence problems, in both domestic and international affairs. His pragmatic views on defence preparedness and spending were shaped by the real-world circumstances of the Cold War, a period marred by rapid advances in weapons technology and strategic issues. "We have just voted overwhelmingly to express our deep desire for [nuclear] disarmament," Danson told his audience in closing, "we are prepared to preserve our values; prepared to seriously seek every path to mutual and balanced arms reduction. But we are also determined that in doing our share we are not exposed to the blackmail which, in the past, has cost those precious lives which we remember with love, reverence, and sadness today."[8] To Danson, therefore, Canada's military-industrial base did not represent a problematic or evil entity; rather, it was a national necessity, born out of a commitment to collective security and events transpiring far beyond Canada's international borders.

The Military-Industrial Complex

By the 1980s, the term "military-industrial complex" (MIC) was a well-known and heavily debated concept, having entered the popular lexicon and imagination more than two decades earlier thanks in part to President Dwight D. Eisenhower. In January 1961, during his farewell address, he warned Americans about the powerful "conjunction of an immense military establishment and a large arms industry" and its potential for acquiring "unwarranted influence" in the councils of government. The outgoing president, himself a highly decorated soldier and retired five-star general, emphasized the need to guard against this "misplaced power" and its "grave implications" for the future structure of American society. His remarks struck a chord with many concerned Americans, but the statement was also something of a caveat to the main thesis and one quite similar to Danson's position years later: the large American arms industry and military establishment had become necessary for the survival of the free, democratic world. As Eisenhower put it, shortly before his warning, "we can no longer risk emergency improvisation of national defense; we have been compelled to create a permanent armaments industry of vast proportions." The MIC was "new" to the American experience, but it was now an "imperative need" in the great geopolitical struggle of the Cold War and nuclear stand-off with the Soviet Union. The unpreparedness with which the United States had greeted the First and Second World Wars could not be replicated in the atomic age.[9]

Although the contexts of the two speeches were different, they bear some resemblance in their interpretation of the MIC's necessity. Eisenhower understood the critical importance of military spending to defence preparedness, national security, economic power, and international relations. Therefore, he supported a strong defence-industrial base as sound policy, in both domestic and foreign affairs, and followed through on a vision for the future that saw the continued expansion of the US arms industry and its corollary boost to American power. When "Ike" took office in January 1953, the American defence budget consumed about 14.5 percent of the GNP, and although spending dipped over the next decade, his "New Look" foreign policy reduced reliance on conventional arms while simultaneously increasing America's nuclear arsenals and first strike capabilities to deter Soviet aggression.[10] By the time he left office, that arsenal stood at roughly twenty-three thousand warheads, up from the thousand at President Harry S. Truman's disposal in 1952.[11] Recognizing and accepting the necessity of defence and industrial cooperation, however, forced Eisenhower to acknowledge the increasing power and influence of industrialists, lobbyists, military officers, and politicians who benefitted from rising investment in munitions, equipment, science, and military technology. The president, who was by all accounts a leading figure in the MIC, worried about possible corruption and the undue influence garnered by the growing defence-industrial relationship, so he offered his famous warning – however ironic or hypocritical – to be cautious of this new dynamic in American life.[12]

Twenty years later, Danson shared a similar view about the necessity of investing in national defence, but unlike Eisenhower, he was not particularly concerned with the political and economic influence of the businesspeople, military officers, and politicians who were associated with Canada's defence industries. The years of political interference and indifference to the defence portfolio before and during his time in Cabinet had shown that military influences were thinner in the halls of government in Canada. In fact, he offered little worry about any insidious distortions in policymaking, economics, and military affairs. Instead, Danson welcomed expanding investments in Canada's defence-industrial base and argued for the prioritization of military spending on the federal agenda.[13] Above all, he saw a positive and productive meaning to the MIC: its potential could be harnessed for profitable ends, as something to leverage economic growth and technological development in Canada, provide well-paying jobs for workers, secure income and contracts for businesses, expand infrastructure, and defend national borders and interests. In effect, there was a strong connection to defence spending and effective public policy.

The similarities and differences between the two speeches signal the importance of studying the MIC on its own terms, and with a view toward understanding its national peculiarities and wider political, economic, social, and environmental impacts. Since Eisenhower's farewell address, generations of scholars have investigated the MIC in the United States, whereas others have examined its various incarnations in Brazil, Britain, Japan, France, the Soviet Union, and other countries.[14] Taking inspiration from this international literature and ongoing debates about the MIC in modern states, *Silent Partners* explores the ways in which the Canadian military, defence industries, and the federal government have influenced the country and its citizenry, whether directly or indirectly, through the procurement of weapons, defence spending, and military research and development (R&D). We argue that a Canadian MIC exists, with roots deeply embedded in the historical and contemporary fabric of the nation-state. We call attention to the depth and complexity of military, industrial, academic, and bureaucratic relationships to better understand and interrogate the MIC and its implications for Canada's political economy and Canadian society more generally.

Defining and Theorizing the MIC

The robust field of literature on the MIC, as well as the wide-ranging public debates about private military contractors, offers many definitions and interpretations to digest. Some of those definitions are interchangeable and complementary terms that highlight the synergy of military and industrial power, whereas others differ in their scale and national contexts or adopt pejorative meanings in describing the MIC and its influential elites. As American author and editor James Ledbetter puts it, "There is no military-industrial complex, but many military-industrial complexes – all of them defined by someone other than Dwight D. Eisenhower."[15] Ledbetter's work traces the intellectual and cultural origins of the term, revealing how the MIC's meaning fluctuated over time, as various critiques of the insidious alliances between arms manufacturers and the state evolved throughout the twentieth century.

In other words, the MIC is a powerful and evocative term that evades simple definitions. It can mean different things in different contexts, as scholars and writers emphasize various aspects over others, but several key themes and characteristics are worthy of closer scrutiny: collusion, political economy, experts, technology, and environment.[16] The theme of collusion underlies most accounts of the MIC, even predating the term's first usage and popularity. In *The Power Elite*, sociologist C. Wright Mills charted one of the first intellectual frameworks for understanding the integration and concentration of military and corporate power in American society.[17] Often considered a departure point for academic investigations, his 1956 study built on Harold Lasswell's earlier work and theories about the "garrison state." A prominent political scientist, Lasswell argued in 1941 that the garrison state was a "developmental construct" that emerges when political and military elites take control of the government to direct the economy toward their own objectives – much like what was to happen during the Second World War.[18]

Mills's book gave Lasswell's theory some added credibility by examining the legacies of military mobilizations and the ascendency of military and corporate officials within the US government's executive and legislative branches during the war and following the National Security Act of 1947, which created the Department of Defense (DOD). According to Mills, the rise of military influence in the halls of power dovetailed with the increasing wealth of major businesses and the corporate elites that supplied the armed forces. Mills called this collusion "military capitalism," and most studies that followed in the Vietnam era examined various elements and incarnations of his thesis, criticizing the emergence of a warfare state in the United States and the corporate profiteering generated by close ties to the Pentagon. In most cases, the MIC was portrayed as an insulated clique and corrupt enterprise that was dangerous to democracy and that distorted traditional American values.[19]

Closely related to the theme of collusion is that of political economy. Most accounts of the American MIC demonstrate the political and strategic necessities of defence and its significance to economic policy, industry, and infrastructure development. In the decades following Mills's study, public interest in the MIC moved largely to the periphery as the growth of social movements for civil rights, feminism, and environmentalism brought other issues to the fore.[20] Through the 1960s and 1970s, only a small cadre of historians and social scientists remained attentive to the political economy of defence spending and its role in the projection of American power during the Cold War, while furthering (and sometimes thwarting) political and economic agendas at home.[21] However, the Cold War's sudden end in the early 1990s rejuvenated inquiries and investigations into the MIC, as different theories and interpretations emerged from earlier explorations.

Economist Ann R. Markusen, along with several coauthors, offered a new and convincing analytical framework for understanding the MIC and its political and economic influences. Together, they coined the term "defense dependence" to explain how the MIC had reshaped American society over time. According to the theory, defense dependence arises when the state invests in procuring weapons and equipment for the military: the influx of capital spurs research and innovation in science and engineering, while also stimulating the reorganization of private businesses to accept defence dollars, and the relocation of jobs and production facilities for political and strategic purposes – as opposed to the normal patterns of supply and demand in civilian markets. Consequently, military spending creates major demographic changes, urban development, and economic disparities when skilled and non-skilled labourers migrate for job opportunities. Workers bring their families and consumer-spending power along with them, thereby precipitating spin-off developments in infrastructure, schooling, housing, and other commercial amenities.[22]

According to this framework, the cycle of defense dependence in the United States developed over successive decades and fundamentally "remapped" the industrial bedrock of the country, exerting an uneven impact on regional economies and populations. For instance, in the 1950s, defence contracts were increasingly awarded to companies in the South, West, and Northeast, as the military's insatiable need for advanced technologies, electronics, aircraft, nuclear weapons, bases, and testing sites brought unprecedented growth and prosperity to a new "gunbelt" that stretched around the nation's perimeter.[23] The country's old industrial heartland in the Midwest – Michigan, Illinois, and Pennsylvania – faded into a "rustbelt" as defence dollars left the region and brought prosperity elsewhere, particularly out West, where the federal government spent over $50 billion in California alone between 1950 and 1960.[24] The lure of federal investment and defence contracts centralized a well-paid and educated workforce within a large network of western businesses, specializing in communications, satellites, aerospace, computers, and other military technologies, thereby paving the way for the rise of several high-tech giants in today's Silicon Valley.[25] Indeed, the patterns of federal and military investments shaped the contours of economic growth and decline in Cold War America.

Inexorably entwined within the political economy of defence spending are the other three themes of expertise, technology, and the environment. The Second World War had given new meaning to the term "total war," as the mobilization of science, technology, and natural resources yielded terrifying new weapons and destructive forces. As the Cold War emerged, the US government and military became increasingly dependent on the intellectual resources of scientists, engineers, psychologists, and other experts to weaponize the latest technologies and to better understand the human mind, overcome the limitations of human anatomy, and harness the power and riches of the natural world for military purposes.[26] Across almost every academic discipline, money flowed into universities and research centres throughout the United States. During the earliest decades of the Cold War, American funding agencies spent more on national security and defence than Canada's entire GNP.[27] For instance, in 1963, the number of people directly employed or funded by the DOD equalled the entire Canadian labour force, while up to 90 percent of Washington's R&D budget was funnelled into the national defence economy.[28] With such financial backing, scientists, engineers, and other experts were pulled into the military's orbit, where they completed their important work and furthered military objectives by accumulating data about the earth and oceans, monitoring climates and weather, designing more deadly weapons systems, and developing new cutting-edge technologies.[29]

Of course, the state's dependency on experts predated the 1940s. As political scientist James Scott reminds us, the power of the state stems from its ability to defend its borders, feed its people, encourage economic growth, and manage natural resources, all of which brought high-modernist state planning into conflict with local customs, human agency, and nature itself.[30] The state needs its experts to function, and military preparedness, tactics, and technologies have always held special prominence stretching back well beyond the mid-twentieth century. In fact, historian Katherine C. Epstein pushes the periodization of the MIC's origins back over fifty years before Eisenhower's farewell address. Her analysis locates the MIC's starting point near the end of the nineteenth century, when American and British governments adopted a "new paradigm for procuring weapons" amid the growing arms race and naval buildup prior to the First World War. Industrial naval technologies – such as the self-propelled torpedo – became so technologically advanced and expensive that increasing public investment in research, development, and production was unavoidable, thereby bringing scientists and engineers into collaboration with government, corporate, and military officials.[31]

The reach of the state's influence in science and technology has certainly not gone unnoticed or unchallenged. By the mid-1990s, many scholars started re-examining the impact of defence spending on the nature and direction of scientific and engineering research throughout the twentieth century. Largely spurred by the gradual opening of Cold War–era archives, heated debates over the impartiality and integrity of science raged as new research uncovered the depths of collaboration in what historian Stuart Leslie terms the "military-industrial-academic complex."[32] Leslie's critical views kicked off the so-called science wars, as other historians and humanists revealed the depths of financial and political ties among scientists, doctors, engineers, industrialists, and defence officials, while the accused responded to the scathing criticism and defended their reputations and dependency on DOD funds.[33] More recently, other scholars, some with formal training in the physical sciences, have contributed new perspectives that further debunk the myths surrounding scientific objectivity and independence, demonstrating how the MIC became embedded in the work of leading scientists and engineers, some of whom helped design more destructive and deadly weapons.[34]

The critical reappraisal of science and the MIC over the last few decades has also vaulted the role and significance of the environment into clearer focus. Modern militaries are some of the largest organizations and institutions created by humans, and they are responsible for generating diverse environmental and ecological changes. During the twentieth century, the impact of war and military activities grew to such a pervasive extent that some scientists have argued for the creation of a new interdisciplinary field called "warfare ecology." Research in this area aims to quantify, understand, and address the immediate and long-term environmental implications of military activities. In 2008, scientists Gary Machlis and Thor Hanson published a theoretical framework for the field that integrates the environment into the MIC by focusing on the consequences of mobilization, combat, and demobilization.[35] Such an approach helps to synthesize the outpouring of research on related topics, such as chemical weapons and insecticides, weapons testing, natural resources, infrastructure, unexploded ordnance, atomic weapons and fallout, base closures, wildlife conservation, and climate change.[36] These perspectives have enriched our understanding of the MIC in new ways, but they also affirm the interrelationship and influences between the experts who develop new technologies and the places and spaces in which those assets are used and perfected. They also document, to some extent, the "spill over" and "spin-off" effects of military technologies in civilian and non-military contexts. Although the tactical-to-practical transition is not possible with every military technology, many have become indispensable in contemporary society, such as the internet.[37]

The twentieth century witnessed an unprecedented expansion of military-funded R&D, with drastic environmental implications. Although the push for new products was not restricted to the military realm, industrial activity that sought to generate new products for both military and civilian use often reflected wider social and technological changes. During the 1950s and 1960s, for instance, American chemical giant DuPont, British Imperial Chemical Industries, and other large industrial firms with ties to military funding started mass producing and distributing synthetic polymers. As historians J.R. McNeill and Peter Engelke point out, the technical mastery of rubber and plastics represented social progress, and the relative affordability of synthetics fuelled world production to some 6 million tons by the start of the 1960s.[38] Yet, much of the factory infrastructure and scientific breakthroughs enabling this growth owed their origins to wartime events, especially the fall of Singapore in February 1942 and the loss of rubber plantations in Malaysia. In one of the darkest moments of the Second World War, desperate Allied governments invested millions into a new but unproven product: synthetic rubber had never been manufactured outside of laboratories in North America or mass produced anywhere before the war.[39] In the end, they built some fifty synthetic rubber plants across North America (including the Polymer Corporation in Sarnia, Ontario), which greatly diversified the fossil fuel industry and paved the way for all the synthetic polymers that dominate our lives today. Indeed, the legacies of military, industrial, and political cooperation are on full display in Sarnia's "Chemical Valley" – as are the health and environmental effects of emissions and pollution on surrounding communities.[40]

Although public dissent toward the American MIC manifested during the Vietnam War, it was the publication of Rachel Carson's *Silent Spring* in 1962 that catalyzed environmental activism and concerns about the effects of chemical residues in environments and human bodies. Carson argued that DDT – a product of the Second World War and economic cooperation between the US military and private industry – was derived from an ideological belief in the superiority of science and technology over the environment. To governments and militaries, DDT and other pesticides appeared safe, affordable, and necessary for controlling environments.[41] Thus, science and technology were championed as a means for humans to conquer nature and better organize their lives; and when combined with capitalism and democracy, they could revolutionize domestic life in ways that communism could not match.[42] However, Carson challenged these worldviews by highlighting the ominous health and environmental risks posed by chemical industries and major scientific advancements.

Following Carson's lead, over the last several decades, scholars, journalists, and activists have documented the harmful social and environmental consequences. Among others, historian Kate Brown has shown that the same chemical companies that produced ammonia for explosives and DDT during the war used mass marketing campaigns to sell wartime chemical surpluses for everyday domestic use in the 1950s.[43] More recently, historian Bartow Elmore chronicled the rise of Monsanto to show how the company used profits from the manufacture of toxic products (Agent Orange, DDT, and PCBs) to create the glyphosate-based herbicide Roundup and to pioneer genetically modified agriculture.[44] Unfortunately, Canadian historians have been slower to address related themes and the "enviro-tech" implications and legacies of military R&D in Canada. Historian Joy Parr's *Sensing Changes* offers one exception, as she explores the history of the Canadian Forces Base at Gagetown, New Brunswick, and the testing of Agent Orange and other herbicides by the American military in the 1960s.[45] Historian P. Whitney Lackenbauer's extensive research on military activity and civil-military affairs in northern Canada and the Arctic is another focal point, integrating and confronting important issues surrounding colonialism, state power, national defence, and environmental change.[46] Outside the spatial and conceptual frame of Canada's northern regions, however, the environmental and demographic impacts of military, industrial, and technological development across Canada's extensive geography remain largely unexplored.

The Canadian Context

As the existing scholarship on the American MIC makes clear, documenting the history and ongoing participation of firms and institutions with financial ties to the military is only the first step in a larger analytical process that aims to quantify and qualify the political and economic power they possess over society and the environment. The issue at the heart of the debate is not whether firms undertook military R&D in the past, but whether military and corporate interests colluded to exert influence on favourable federal policies. Under this broad theoretical interpretation, to qualify as having a discernable and identifiable MIC analogous to that of the United States, Canada would need to have a clear track record of firms or institutions leveraging defence spending and political power to further their interests. This is the basis of the warning expressed in Eisenhower's farewell address, and it is fundamental to examining the impact of military and industrial interests on Canada's economic, foreign, and defence policies.

Yet the American example is only partially applicable to the Canadian context. In Canada, collusion takes place but on a vastly smaller scale, and it operates differently than in the United States. If or when it takes place, it is often at the initiative of federal departments tasked with procurement, industry, trade, and defence. In other words, the bureaucrats and policymakers inside these administrative entities act as intermediaries for corporate and military interests, bringing them together but also buffering direct partnerships with a level of political interference, control, and patronage that can help – as much as hinder – the acquisition of weapons and military equipment. Oftentimes, these officials and institutions bring their own agendas and objectives into procurement processes, meaning that wider public policy and non-military considerations can get appended to defence spending, sometimes changing equipment preferences and final selections. In fact, sometimes the military must settle on compromise options if the others were not politically viable. Indeed, whether defined as an alliance, a constituency, or a network, the collection of organizations and individuals in Canada that constitute a MIC are bound together by a common interest in the promotion of industrial production and national defence (as well as their financial interests), but there have always been limitations on the political power they possess. Thus, the word *influence* is key to understanding the structure, scope, and implications of Canada's MIC because defence spending and procurement have remained firmly under the civilian purview – for better or worse.

In Canada, the intersections of political, military, and industrial interests have not always been productive, as competing priorities, budget cuts, deferments, cancellations, political posturing, and civilian oversight have plagued the history of the MIC. Such stumbling blocks have stunted the lobbying influence of corporate and military interests in Ottawa, prompting some experts to conclude that Canada does not have a MIC, as defined by the American example.[47] This is certainly true: Canada's defence economy pales in comparison to the colossus south of the border, but that does not mean that Canada lacks a MIC entirely. Instead, such statements suggest a need to re-examine the shape and characteristics of the Canadian MIC on their own terms.

Placing Canadian procurement, defence spending, and military R&D at the centre of our analyses, the following chapters explore some of the developments and consequences of Canada's MIC during the second half of the twentieth century. In so doing, several important and interrelated themes emerge, about not only the origins and evolution of military-industrial relations in Canada, but also the implications of militarization for Canada, its population, and its position in world affairs. Taken collectively, the chapters in *Silent Partners* demonstrate that the Canadian state has a long and complicated history of leveraging military and defence expenditures to fund domestic industries, bolster employment, and support science and technology; at the same time, this sponsorship has influenced Canada's demography, geography, institutions, urban areas, trade, and industry in uneven patterns. By profiling, specifically, the environmental impact of military activities and defence spending, the ethical issues of human experimentation and military testing, and the economic and political implications of procurement and arms exports, the authors in this volume refocus attention on the historical roots of a symbiotic relationship among Canada's military, political, economic, and research institutions.

The shape and characteristics of Canada's MIC took root before Confederation. As historian Aaron Plamondon explains, in the 1860s tensions between Britain and the United States incited fears of an American invasion and increased pressure to improve Canada's militia and defence. A Militia Commission was formed in 1862, and John A. Macdonald, who was responsible for the militia portfolio at the time, used its recommendations as the basis of a new bill calling for a trained force of fifty thousand and a large investment of $500,000. The bill was soundly defeated, however, and Macdonald's government was forced to resign. The situation left Canada in a vulnerable position, but it also signalled to political leaders that defence spending was risky business. Canadians were not interested in paying for their own defence, so procurement had to be approached cautiously and with ample political tact. In the 1880s, when the government-owned arsenal in Quebec City was first established, politicians found it "politically healthier" to avoid competitive bidding and "reserve the small number of contracts for industrial friends."[48] This hands-on political favouritism worked to limit the scope of military and industrial influences by stifling free-market competition and removing military officials from decision-making processes.

Political patronage defined much of Canada's defence-industrial base well into the twentieth century. As historian Ronald Haycock shows, the military's influence in procurement was relatively negligible until the 1940s; before then, politicians closely vetted civilian contractors for an "acceptable political persuasion" before awarding contracts, regardless of experience or capability. Such tactics explain the origins of the infamous Ross rifle and its politically well-connected designer, Charles Ross.[49] The notoriety of the Ross rifle and its utter failure on the battlefields of the First World War were emblematic of the patronage in procurement, but they were also a sign of worse things to come. At the outbreak of war in 1914, the bombastic and temperamental militia minister, Sam Hughes, barged forward in mobilizing the country. With a mounting need for more munitions and supplies for the army he recruited, Hughes turned to his trusted cronies and Tory friends in industry for help. Most businesses had little experience or desire to convert over to munitions production, though they welcomed the contracts, money, and titles from Hughes's office. The result was a disaster. In the first year of the war, Hughes's ill-fated Shell Committee distributed over $170 million in contracts to manufacturers, but only $5.5 million worth of shells were delivered by May 1915.[50] Profiteering, scandal, and inefficiency eventually led to his downfall in 1916, though Canada's production record for artillery shells dramatically improved in 1917 and 1918 after Joseph Flavelle, a successful businessman in the meatpacking industry, took over the newly formed Imperial Munitions Board.[51]

Following the war, confidence in Canada's defence-industrial base was shaken, and the financial strain of the Great Depression eroded many prospects for long-term survival. During the interwar period, the Canadian military survived on meagre budgets that greatly affected operational capabilities, while the angst and bereavement for those lost or permanently scarred by the war cast dark shadows over the so-called merchants of death – the arms manufacturers and other companies that had profited from the killing and suffering.[52] In the social climate of the interwar period, support for domestic munitions procurement was political suicide, and Ottawa avoided investing in Canadian-made designs and instead relied on foreign (British) purchases. The Bren Gun Scandal in the late 1930s served as a further catalyst for maintaining strict civilian oversight and control of procurement through the Defence Purchasing Board.[53] On the eve of the Second World War, Canada's military and defence-industrial base had been starved of funding for political expedience, leaving the country's feeble armed forces ill-prepared for the coming emergency, forcing the state to make drastic interventions into the economy.

Part 1: Origins and Environments

In Chapters 1 and 2, Alex Souchen and Brandon Davis, respectively, explore the origins of Canada's MIC and the environmental changes caused by munitions production and testing across Canada. Although the exact start date for the MIC is difficult to pinpoint, it was profoundly changed by the Second World War. As Souchen shows, the momentous defeats in Europe and Asia between June 1940 and February 1942 shook the Allied cause to its foundations.[54] As a result, the Liberal government of Prime Minister William Lyon Mackenzie King was compelled to mobilize the nation's military, financial, and industrial resources for total war. Thus, the emergency spurred the unprecedented integration of public and private enterprise through the newly formed Department of Munitions and Supply (DMS) and its powerful Cabinet minister C.D. Howe.

The DMS gained a wide and pervasive mandate to mobilize, ration, and regulate the entire economy to sustain a large military force and munitions industry. For the duration of hostilities, it aligned political and economic interests behind victory: it funded industrial expansion, expropriation, and development; it acquired technologies and resources for production; it recruited expertise from businesses and universities; it hired a workforce as large as the Canadian armed services; and it managed an empire of war contractors that made the business of war as productive as possible. These achievements were as impressive as they were impactful: between 1939 and 1945, Canada's so-called industrial front churned out mountains of munitions and supplies, including roughly 4.6 billion rounds of ammunition and artillery shells.[55]

This immediate and drastic rise in national productivity caused sweeping environmental changes, in addition to myriad other political, economic, and social developments. Using the production of chemicals, explosives, and ammunition as a case study, Souchen dissects the environmental history of Canada's fledgling MIC. Geographic and demographic factors – such as logistics, energy, natural resources, land, and labour supply – refined site selections for new munitions plants, and the factories themselves reshaped their surrounding environments. The construction of new railways, roads, buildings, amenities, and accommodations for workers altered landscapes across the country, and the production of explosives and the filling of ammunition also brought serious contamination and safety hazards for workers and local communities.

Munitions factories were enormous establishments that swallowed up swaths of territory, thereby hinting at another important element of Canada's MIC: land use. Arguably, Canada's most important contribution to the Allied war effort was its vast tracts of land and low population density. Indeed, modern militaries and defence contractors, both during the war and long afterward, had insatiable appetites for land. As Davis shows, during the war, thousands of acres were expropriated or otherwise taken over by the federal government under the War Measures Act. This opened space for the Canadian and Allied armed services, as well as their industrial partners, to repurpose land for training troops and aircrew or to manufacture and test weapons systems. The legacies of this expansion are still felt today, as the DND occupies over 2 million hectares and owns almost forty thousand structures and buildings, making it one of the largest landowners in the country.[56]

In recounting the history of the Suffield Experimental Station (SES) in southern Alberta, Davis explores the connections between land use, national security, and the legacies of militarization. Early in the war, Ottawa welcomed British overtures about establishing a major field-testing site on the Canadian prairies to better develop defences against air power and chemical weapons. After some deliberation, officials selected the Suffield site, and the government and military quickly moved to expropriate the roughly 700,000 acres. When acquiring the land, officials took the view that it was barren and agriculturally unproductive, and that the present emergency required sacrifices from everyone, which overrode any prior usage and farming in the area. Thus, the establishment of one of the world's largest and most active military proving grounds followed a pattern of dispossession and resettlement that had marked the region for decades.[57] Prior to the 1940s, Indigenous communities on the western plains were displaced by disease, violence, the eradication of the bison, and the treaty and reserve systems imposed by the dominion government. During the war, however, the Canadian state displaced about six hundred white-settler families from their homesteads in the Suffield Block. These "Suffield evacuees" – as they were called – were compensated for their relocation and loss of lands, but the payments were hardly adequate, and some sought recognition and redress after the war, though to no avail.

Together, Souchen and Davis demonstrate that Canada's MIC was shaped by wartime necessity and defined by the Canadian environment. The mobilization of resources, labour, and landscapes for war purposes carried forward dynamic and permanent consequences for society. Calls to close the SES after the war were easily dismissed as a state of permanent war-readiness descended with the ever-increasing threat of radiological, chemical, and biological warfare during the Cold War. Although Suffield's continued existence was justified, the massive network of explosive, ammunition, and shell-filling factories was not. The war had drastically inflated global demand, and Canadian factories responded by increasing outputs and supplying the nation's allies, especially the British, ahead of its own military.[58] However, postwar retrenchments in the size of military forces and shifting economic priorities in Britain and the United States abruptly curtailed international outlets and left the shrinking Canadian military as the only legitimate customer. As a result, a small nucleus of factories was retained under the auspices of a new Crown company, Canadian Arsenals Limited (CAL), formed in September 1945 to maintain a postwar armaments industry in Canada. Under CAL's umbrella, the supply of weapons and explosives continued over the next few decades, until the government opted for privatization, and a new generation of companies moved in toward the end of the twentieth century.

The boom of wartime expenditures and development was followed by a sudden bust. Thousands of workers were forced to find new jobs in a fragile economy locked in a turbulent peacetime transition. Surplus factories and installations were demolished or repurposed, and lands and buildings were decontaminated, while the DMS was rebranded as the Department of Reconstruction and Supply in December 1945. The boom/bust pattern of defence spending during the Second World War certainly bears some resemblance to the "defense dependence" identified by American scholars at the end of the Cold War. In Canada, wartime spending brought unparalleled expansion to urban areas – especially Toronto and Montreal – and in towns that lay close to new factories or military installations. Thousands of people migrated for work, which precipitated a major accommodation crisis, as the DMS struggled to build housing, infrastructure, and amenities for employees and their families.[59] In some cases, the investments prompted permanent environmental and demographic changes, as whole new towns sprang up in places such as Ajax, Ontario, and Ralston, Alberta.

In other cases, the war boom caused development in areas without much chance for long-term survival. Thus, when governments stopped footing the bill or strategic priorities shifted, the rushed development left behind a mixed legacy of militarization, ecological degradation, and economic decline. This is particularly evident in northern Canada and Arctic regions, where defence, strategic, and technological imperatives necessitated a whole host of military operations and training, as well as the construction of the Alaska Highway, research installations, air bases, and radar stations. As P. Whitney Lackenbauer and Matthew Farish argue, the "lens of military modernization" helps scholars to understand the environmental impact of militarization in the

North. Initiatives such as the Distant Early Warning (DEW) Line were born from particular geopolitical and geostrategic considerations in Washington and Ottawa but were later rendered obsolete by the pace of other technological and scientific breakthroughs funded by the MIC.[60] In the end, the DEW Line facilities, like other places around the country, left behind a legacy of pollution and environmental change that is still being cleaned up today.[61]

Part 2: Ethics and Experts

In late 1945, a new global struggle emerged between the United States and the Soviet Union, both vaunted to superpower status by virtue of their materiel, financial, technological, ideological, and strategic supremacy. Canada's emergence as a middle power and junior ally in world affairs was a product of its wartime military-industrial juggernaut, but Prime Minister Mackenzie King harboured deep misgivings about the prospects of maintaining a large, permanent military force. As a result, postwar defence budgets were gutted, and by 1948, the year King left office, the armed forces numbered about fifty-five thousand and survived on a paltry budget of about $400 million.[62] Yet despite these setbacks, a truncated military establishment persisted in Canada, and a few years later, it received a tremendous boost when communist North Korea invaded South Korea in June 1950. Under pressure from the Americans, the new Liberal government of Louis St-Laurent decided to send an infantry brigade to Korea and substantially increase defence expenditures, especially in R&D.

Large sums of money were funnelled through the Defence Research Board (DRB), formed by an Order-in-Council in April 1947. The DRB was accorded a powerful position in the DND hierarchy, on par with the navy, air force, and army branches, thereby affirming the centrality of scientific and technological expertise in military affairs and operational effectiveness. Through the DRB, senior officials and defence scientists distributed funding for military R&D projects that were designed to support the Cold War armed forces in all theatres and operational contexts. Between 1947 and the mid-1970s, hundreds of scientists, engineers, technicians, graduate students, and other experts working in dozens of public and private research facilities received DRB funding to help prepare the armed forces for the battlefields of tomorrow. In both the physical and social sciences, defence funding paid for research projects ranging from atomic, biological, and chemical warfare studies to jet engines, rocket propulsion, psychological warfare, recruitment, and morale. Throughout the 1950s, approximately 18 percent of Canada's total annual defence budget was earmarked for military research, representing a significant sum that ultimately shaped the scope and character of university research in Canada, as scientists embraced defence projects to further their professional careers during a critical period in world affairs.[63]

Chapters 3 and 4 trace these themes in Canada, as Matthew Wiseman, Matthew Farish, and Meghan Fitzpatrick peel back the shroud of secrecy surrounding Canada's Cold War–era defence research activities and expand upon the growing body of scholarship that places the DRB and its pool of so-called experts at the centre of scientific and technological breakthroughs in the post-1945 period.[64] Together, these chapters interrogate the significance and repercussions of defence-funded research and question its impact on research ethics and institutions by exploring the personal, political, financial, and strategic relationships that brought scientific expertise into an evolving military-industrial-academic complex in Canada. Above all, these chapters demonstrate that military sponsorship and the militarization of science during the Cold War was extensive, pervasive, and sometimes morally questionable. In Chapter 3, Wiseman and Farish delve into this history by "placing" early Cold War–era Canadian defence research in a particular time and space to explore the networks of people and institutions that operated a major research centre at Downsview in the suburbs of Toronto, then Canada's second-largest city. From the opening of the University of Toronto's Institute of Aerophysics at Downsview in September 1950 to the expansion of the Royal Canadian Air Force's (RCAF) Institute of Aviation Medicine (IAM), Toronto was home to many of the country's most advanced defence research facilities of the era. Central to this history was the Defence Research Medical Laboratories (DRML) at Downsview, a unique establishment built with DRB funds in the early 1950s and populated in part by scientists and engineers from the University of Toronto (U of T).

The ties between the DRML and U of T were mutually beneficial. On the one hand, senior DRB officials tapped into the networks of expertise at U of T to further their mandate while supporting a new and robust research agenda involving human subjects. At Downsview, scientists were paid to conduct detailed studies on the operational problems of healthy and physically fit soldiers working in "extreme" environmental conditions. On the other hand, scientists and engineers at U of T gained access to significant government research contracts and funding, as well as to the state-of-the-art laboratories at Downsview. In tracing this history, Wiseman and Farish shed important light on the geography of defence research in a major metropolitan area while raising new questions about the ethics of military sponsorship of scientific, technological, and material developments during the early Cold War.

Scientists and engineers at Downsview conducted a variety of experiments on human subjects, using what one observer later called "modern torture gadgets."[65] Their goal was to test the limits of human abilities in extreme climates and environmental conditions, with the intent of better understanding human fragility and developing new technologies to compensate for or overcome the limits of human endurance in the body and mind. Human experimentation is a major (and disconcerting) element of Canada's MIC. The work conducted at Downsview fit into the military's long-standing practice of using soldiers and civilians as research subjects, most of whom had little knowledge of the tests' possible side effects. At Suffield, for instance, trials involving mustard gas and new protective equipment intentionally exposed approximately three thousand Canadian soldiers to this dangerous blistering agent and weapon of mass destruction, whereas other military-sponsored scientific experiments involving civilians were conducted in Indigenous and northern communities during the early Cold War.[66]

Students at McGill University and the University of Manitoba were also used as subjects. In a startling account of DRB-funded research on sensory deprivation, isolation, and experimental mind control, Fitzpatrick's chapter further illustrates how far academics went to produce results for senior political and military leaders. Concerned that scientists in China and the Soviet Union had developed and applied mind control techniques against the roughly 13,500 UN troops captured during the Korean War, senior DND and DRB officials financed a long-running series of psychological experiments to determine the impact of sensory and auditory isolation on human subjects. As Fitzpatrick argues in Chapter 4, their dramatic findings left a lasting impact on the field of psychology and future investigations on the role of social and physical environments in shaping personality and behaviours. In fact, Canadian researchers and their findings played a pivotal and pioneering role in this field during the 1950s and beyond.

Fitzpatrick's chapter shows, unequivocally, how a series of "brainwashing" experiments conducted at McGill and the University of Manitoba entwined academic and military interests. At these institutions, a variety of scientists, psychiatrists, and psychologists performed experimental tests on human subjects that were designed to explore the defensive and offensive potential of mind control. Their findings revealed how vulnerable and compliant human beings became when deprived of sensory stimuli, which proved to be a major turning point for the nascent discipline of psychology, as concerned military officials decided to make prolonged investments in the field to bolster the psychological resiliency of soldiers. Thus, Canadian academics and their military sponsors were firmly embedded in many morally dubious and questionable research projects on human subjects, which further illuminates the MIC's pervasive influences over the direction of scientific research, the integrity of research institutions, and the ethical conduct of officials and experts.

Chapters 3 and 4 also fit into a new and growing debate in Canadian history about the role of political patronage in science and technology, and its incumbent ethical and moral dilemmas. As historians Edward Jones-Imhotep and Tina Adcock argue, the Canadian state is less peaceful and more militant than stereotypical and nationalistic tropes might suggest.[67] Therefore, investigating the history of Canada's MIC illustrates the state's involvement in the development of science and technology, and offers an important opportunity to reflect upon and question the social, political, environmental, and ethical impacts of Western scientific epistemology and related research activity in mid-century Canada. Interrogating the ethical and material implications of state-sponsored research and military activities, in particular, is useful for highlighting the social power of the MIC and its impact on the public institutions that Canadian citizens trusted in the twentieth century.

Part 3: Politics and Procurement

The final three chapters of *Silent Partners* explore the political economy of military procurement and production during the Cold War. Together, the chapters by Asa McKercher, Frank Maas, and Randall Wakelam delve into the inner workings of Canada's procurement processes and policies to elucidate more on the conflicts and cooperation that have existed between federal departments, the armed forces, defence contractors, and foreign governments over time. The political and economic reach of Canada's MIC has always been fraught – rightly or wrongly – by obstacles and limitations tied to Canada's unique geo-strategic position as a junior ally and middle-ranked power in international and continental affairs. Moreover, the federal government has inconsistently prioritized spending on national security and defence. Budgetary controls and political interference over procurement have redirected or restrained the growth of a colossal MIC like the American example. At the same time, the financial capital and industrial capacities of Canadian manufacturers have ebbed and flowed over time, limiting their ability to meet every materiel requirement of the Canadian forces. Yet, even if industry satisfied demand, the Canadian military has never been large enough to sustain dynamic and profitable defence industries alone, meaning that Canada's MIC contains a modest network of private and public interests that depend on international markets for arms exports and imports to survive.[68]

When the Cold War entered its second decade in the mid-1950s, Canada's defence-industrial base underwent substantial and lasting transformations. The steep cuts to defence after the Second World War corresponded with the diffusion of military procurement and production between several federal agencies. In the late 1940s, CAL and the Industrial Defence Board were transferred from the Department of Reconstruction and Supply to the Department of Trade and Commerce (DTC), while the Canadian Commercial Corporation took over exports.[69] However, the rising Cold War tensions throughout the 1950s forced the St-Laurent government to fund a major rearmament program and to establish the new Department of Defence Production (DDP) in April 1951. The second coming of C.D. Howe's DMS, the DDP recentralized defence procurement to become the focal point of all military and industrial relations for the next decade. In the late 1960s, another round of changes reorganized procurement once again: CAL was progressively privatized, and the Department of Supply and Services (DSS) superseded the DDP, following the Glassco Commission's recommendations for creating one centralized purchasing agency for the federal government. Today's Public Services and Procurement Canada is thus a distant relative of these earlier institutions.[70]

The DDP oversaw a golden age of sorts in Canada's MIC, as defence expenditures soared to new heights in the early 1950s. Often symbolized by the famed Avro Arrow, the influx of capital and contracts for military R&D sustained a period of prosperity that reinvigorated Canada's arms industry. Money flowed into aircraft and engine designs, rocketry, communications, and other DRB-related initiatives, while the production of conventional weapons, explosives, and ammunition at CAL also expanded. So, too, did the search for potential customers, though success here proved more elusive. Purchases of Canadian-made kit were always small, and the domestic requirements of the Canadian military were never enough to sustain the high R&D costs alone. Therefore, arms manufacturers needed to secure export markets to thrive. In Chapter 5, McKercher provides a tour-de-force in the history of Canadian arms sales from the late 1940s to the late 1950s and clearly demonstrates how narrow economic and strategic interests prevailed in Cabinet deliberations that fundamentally counter national myths about Canada and peacekeeping. Canada was an active arms dealer during the Cold War, selling all manner of small arms, ammunition, weapons systems, and military kit to governments on every continent: Nationalist China, India, Pakistan, Israel, Egypt, Colombia, and every NATO ally. Not only were these sales an important element of Canadian foreign and defence policies, but they were vital to the nation's defence-industrial base since the proceeds from transactions helped offset high production expenses with economies of scale and by creating stable manufacturing jobs for Canadians.

Canada's MIC could not survive without export markets and arms sales. As McKercher shows, initially there was some caution in the Department of External Affairs, as officials were concerned by the political and diplomatic complications of exacerbating regional instability. They were cognizant of Canada's international position and considered the role of arms trader to be reserved for great powers only. As a result of their recommendations, Cabinet decided to restrict sales to a case-by-case basis. However, attitudes shifted as the Cold War deepened and Canada's alliance networks expanded through NATO, which provided a wider network of friendly customers who were eager to acquire Canadian-made products. By the early 1950s, the commercial justifications and economic benefits had won out over political objections and moral qualms about end usage. Ultimately, Canada's middle-power position in world affairs proved to be rather advantageous for arms trading: if sales were balanced between regional rivals, Canadian officials saw no harm in aiding the domestic economy, and since sales were always modest in size, they could deflect any criticism levied by opponents.

At the turn of the next decade, however, the golden age came to crashing halt when domestic R&D programs (such as the Avro Arrow) were cut in favour of more cost-effective alternatives (such as the Bomarc missile) and the bilateral Defence Production Sharing Agreement (DPSA), signed by Canada and the United States in the late 1950s. The DPSA built upon the Ogdensburg Agreement of August 1940 and the Hyde Park Declaration of April 1941, which, respectively, established a Permanent Joint Board on Defence and balanced payments and trade in defence procurement, to usher in a new era of Canadian and American relations. The DPSA brought Canada further into the American orbit by creating mechanisms to offset imbalances caused by cross-border purchases of military equipment and to increase the interoperability of the two nations' armed forces. In addition, it sought to better deploy scientific and technical resources, thereby allowing both countries to specialize in areas and share the results.[71] It also further integrated the North American defence economies by exempting Canadian firms from "Buy American" provisions (permitting them to bid on American defence contracts) and by allowing US firms to establish factories in Canada. However, in practice, the DPSA effectively ended major Canadian R&D programs for new weapons systems, leaving this expensive task to American companies and entrenching Canada as a destination for subcontractors and component suppliers for American prime contractors.[72] As a result, the Americanization of defence procurement (and the economy more generally) increased throughout the Cold War, thereby irking Canadian nationalists who saw Canada's sovereignty under threat, while Canadian leaders faced criticism when Canadian-made parts and materiel were shipped across the border in the 1960s and sent to Vietnam despite an official ban on weapons exports to conflict regions.[73]

Foreign dominance in Canada's defence-industrial base was nothing new, but the emergence of American ownership and export markets during the Cold War departed from the traditional dependence on the British, who had owned or subsidized great portions of the Canadian defence industry since the conquest of New France in 1759. The long-term effects of the DPSA have led various economists, political scientists, and defence analysts to identify foreign owner- ship, export dependence, and continental integration as core tenets of Canada's MIC. For instance, in 1983, British economist Gavin Kennedy defined a MIC as "an interacting relationship between the military as an institution and the part of industry that supplies the military hardware," and six years later, fellow economists Lynne M. Pepall and Daniel M. Shapiro applied Kennedy's definition to Canada in one of the most cited studies on the topic.[74] Using data compiled from government and public sources in both Canada and the United States, Pepall and Shapiro identified a high concentration of prime contracts awarded to a small number of defence contractors, the majority of whom were foreign- owned companies (mostly American) with Canadian subsidiaries. Their study concluded that Canada has "a well-defined industrial component of a Military- Industrial Complex" but one that is distinguished by a high level of American ownership, continental integration, and a significant dependency on export markets. This prompted them to conclude that Canada "is really a part of a North American MIC."[75]

Other scholars writing near the end of the Cold War drew similar conclusions about Canada's military-industrial base and the interconnectedness of Canadian and American defence interests. For instance, after studying the international arms trade and Canadian military exports, Ernie Regehr, a security studies scholar and disarmament advocate, concluded in 1987 that Canada's arms industry operates on principles similar to the military-industrial enterprise in the United States, except on a smaller scale.[76] Three years later, Howard Peter Langille, an expert in peace and conflict studies, reiterated the same point: "Canada's complex is a far smaller version, or branch plant, of the U.S. military- industrial complex."[77] Langille argued that an identifiable MIC emerged in Canada during the middle decades of the Cold War, and he contended that several influential constituencies, including DND officials, federal bureaucrats, Canadian defence industrialists, and lobbyists, exerted political and economic influence over Canadian procurement and bids on American contracts.[78] In 1995, political scientists Alistair D. Edgar and David G. Haglund published *The Canadian Defence Industry in the New Global Environment,* which surveyed the problems and prospects facing Canada's post–Cold War industrial base, as government funding declined, and international markets shifted after the Soviet Union's collapse. They echoed similar conclusions to those of Regehr and Langille while also highlighting the steep costs of weapons development, Can- ada's dependence on foreign markets and technologies, and the cooperation and conflicts between public and private interests coping with changing security contexts.[79]

In particular, Edgar and Haglund identified how export dependence shaped the political economy of Canada's defence-industrial base, as the demand for armaments from the Canadian military has never been sufficient to sustain the industry. This has left it vulnerable to external influences that can have direct or indirect impacts on economic viability and private investment, thereby bringing the profitability of the Canadian MIC into question. In their analysis, Pepall and Shapiro found "no systematic evidence suggesting that defence contractors are highly profitable," and they concluded that foreign-controlled firms are more profitable than Canadian-controlled ones. In the end, the limitations on profits and influence, as well as the high degree of foreign control, shape the political economy of defence procurement in Canada, almost to the point where one might question why Canadian firms even bid on defence contracts in the first place.[80] The issue of profitability has been a consistent focal point in the history of Canada's MIC, and scholars have traced the ebbs and flows of defence spending, showing that it is consistently about producing tangible outputs with limited financial resources. With such modest and sporadic investments, it is clear that Canada's MIC marches to the beat of a different drum and that the drumsticks are held firmly by the federal government. Success for defence contractors, therefore, depends on how well they adapt to the government's changing drumbeats.

In Chapter 6, Maas follows up on related themes by examining the procurement and production of a new lightly armoured wheeled vehicle for the Canadian Army: first, the armoured vehicle general purpose (AVGP), and then later, the light armoured vehicle (LAV). In the 1970s and 1980s, the LAV became a mainstay of mechanization in the Canadian Army, when political choices in Ottawa phased out – for better or worse – the main battle tank from service. As a result, the army had to procure a replacement and decided on a new, dynamic "family" of armoured vehicles that could provide fire support, personnel transport, and maintenance. After a competitive process marked by distinct and sometimes conflicting political, economic, and strategic considerations, it selected the Piranha design from Mowag, a Swiss firm. An excellent choice, the Piranha fared extremely well in the field tests of prototypes, but before the transaction could be completed Mowag had to fulfill new policies introduced by the DSS.

With public attitudes shifting during the later Cold War, investments in national security, defence industries, and R&D were cast in more positive ways. Couched in the language of creating good manufacturing jobs across the country and developing expertise in the production of new technologies, defence spending became valuable as an economic lever. In the mid-1970s, the DSS established the Industrial and Regional Benefit (IRB) requirements as part of all procurement decisions. The IRB formalized earlier "offset" policy iterations that were designed to support the domestic economy and protect Canada's industrial base. As Maas explains, IRB requirements ensured that any major purchase from foreign companies by the federal government came with strings attached: some of the contract's value had to be spent in Canada on manufacturing components or fulfilled through licences and technology transfers to Canadian firms. The IRBs were designed to help lower production and development costs, create jobs, and allow the CAF to benefit from economies of scale by tacking on orders for additional units to existing contracts. IRBs have also resulted in Canada gaining significant expertise in niche areas involving components and subsystems in the aerospace, electronics, and communication sectors, though the regional dividends have been predominantly consolidated in Ontario and Quebec.[81] Thus, to finalize the deal, Mowag found a Canadian company to partner with in London, Ontario: Diesel Division General Motors (DDGM). The forebear of today's General Dynamics Land Systems, DDGM eventually became the prime contractor in the production of the Canadian Piranha variants: the Cougar, Grizzly, and Husky.

By exploring the procurement of a new weapons system, Maas shines important light on the unique circumstances that shaped the birth of a new industry in Canada. It was a product of diverse factors that were at once global and local, military and civilian, and international and national. The Piranha competed against American and Brazilian designs, each of which was accompanied by political and diplomatic baggage that swayed officials behind the scenes, but a surprise visit to London by Mowag's CEO solidified the partnership with DDGM. Moreover, DDGM was a well-managed branch plant of the American automotive giant that succeeded in merging an international supply chain of parts and materials, while its employees overcame engineering and manufacturing obstacles that allowed it to produce an excellent final product. Coming at a time when political choices shifted the Canadian Army away from heavy armoured vehicles, DDGM capitalized on the opportunity and then doubled down on its success when the US Marine Corps enhanced its mobility and firepower with LAV purchases. The prolonged success of DDGM into the late Cold War period and beyond translated into more than just corporate profits, as employment opportunities opened for many Londoners, while new tax revenues were generated for all levels of government. Yet, at the same time, its success would not have been possible without export markets that recouped high production costs or the integration of American and Canadian defence interests through the DPSA that allowed DDGM to bid on American contracts.

In Chapter 7, Wakelam provides an overview of the trials and tribulations of fighter aircraft procurement throughout the twentieth century, whose history differs markedly from that of the AVGP and LAV. From the birth of the RCAF in the years after the First World War to the replacement of the venerable CF-18 Hornet today, the history of fighter aircraft procurement has been marred by politics. As Wakelam shows, civilian leaders hold all the power in this sector because they approve budgets and dictate acquisition strategies based on input from RCAF leaders. Consequently, air force officials have had few opportunities to negotiate directly with industry, and the steep procurement and R&D costs for fighter aircraft have prompted a consistent pattern of program cancellations and technical compromises. As a result, the RCAF has made do with stop-gap measures and gently used aircraft to maintain operational and alliance commitments, while government officials negotiated for made-in-Canada parts and servicing capacities through IRBs in the Canadian aerospace industry. However, given the sporadic interactions of industry and air force leaders, as well as the propensity for acquiring second-hand aircraft, Wakelam concludes that a MIC did not exist in the Canadian aerospace sector.

Such conclusions stand as an important counterpoint to the other chapters. Rife with compromises that eroded the influence of industry and the air force in the halls of government, politicians and bureaucrats sometimes procured their own solutions by relying on inferior arms imports and foreign purchases to maintain the RCAF. International markets were thus a two-way street: without profits from exports, defence industries could not survive, whereas, inversely, the military could not survive without arms imports to shore up supply chains and kit deficiencies during a period of rapid technological evolution in rocketry, jet propulsion, and aircraft design. Wakelam's chapter resists generalizations about Canada's MIC by demonstrating that military, political, and economic cooperation does not always yield satisfactory results – a theme that has only recently come under scrutiny in the United States.[82] Wakelam hints at the need for more nuanced critiques, with inquiries focused on specific industries and technologies or the way in which business, political, and military interests comingle in the councils of government. Indeed, for a MIC to exist, and gain the unwarranted influences that Eisenhower feared, a concerted and coordinated pattern of interaction and mutual profit must be discernible. If anything, Wakelam's chapter suggests that pecuniary interests reign supreme in Canada, and in the absence of great-power status, political leaders were less enthused by expensive state-of-the-art solutions and more interested in using Canada's military-industrial base as a means for economic stimulus and targeted growth in particular sectors.

In the Conclusion, Wiseman provides a retrospective analysis of Canada's MIC and bookends several of the themes and issues explored throughout this volume. Highlighting a large 1953 convention of the Canadian Industrial

Preparedness Association, he recounts the tense and escalating international security circumstances of the early Cold War that led many powerful political and corporate leaders in Canada to believe that military-industrial cooperation was the crucial backbone of national defence. Building on the political and economic partnerships established during the Second World War, hundreds of top industry executives worked with senior politicians and bureaucrats to bolster Canada's industrial capabilities for the benefit of both the armed services and the national economy. This pattern continued throughout the Cold War, without much dissent or objections from the public. In many respects, therefore, the MIC remained a silent partner in Canada's political, economic, and academic institutions that influenced Canadian society in myriad ways during the twentieth century. Yet, as Wiseman points out, that influence is further silenced by Canada's feeble and problematic access-to-information laws, which obstruct transparency and impede archival and historical investigations into military and defence topics. Without unfettered access to information, the full extent of political, economic, academic, and military relationships will remain shrouded behind veils of national security, access restrictions, and privacy concerns. It is our hope that *Silent Partners* makes this history louder by opening new conversations about military-industrial relationships in Canada and by shifting more attention to understanding the foundations and historical evolution of Canada's MIC.

Notes

1 Barnett J. Danson, "Canada's Military Industrial Complex: An Address by the Honourable Barnett J. Danson," in *The Empire Club of Canada Addresses* (Toronto: Empire Club of Canada, 1982), 92–104, https://speeches.empireclub.org/61457/data?n=1.
2 Danson, "Canada's Military Industrial Complex."
3 Barney Danson and Curtis Fahey, *Not Bad for a Sergeant: The Memoirs of Barney Danson* (Toronto: Dundurn Press, 2002), 17–58.
4 Danson and Fahey, *Not Bad for a Sergeant*, 10.
5 Matthew J. Bellamy, *Profiting the Crown: Canada's Polymer Corporation, 1942–1990* (Montreal and Kingston: McGill-Queen's University Press, 2005).
6 Frank Maas, *The Price of Alliance: The Politics and Procurement of Leopard Tanks for Canada's NATO Brigade* (Vancouver: UBC Press, 2017); J.L. Granatstein, *Who Killed the Canadian Military?* (Toronto: HarperFlamingoCanada, 2004); Alistair D. Edgar and David G. Haglund, *The Canadian Defence Industry in the New Global Environment* (Montreal and Kingston: McGill-Queen's University Press, 1995).
7 Maas, *The Price of Alliance*, 130–32; J.L. Granatstein, *Canada's Army: Waging War and Keeping the Peace* (Toronto: University of Toronto Press, 2002), 374–76.
8 Danson, "Canada's Military Industrial Complex." Voters in more than eighty Ontario municipalities went to the polls on 8 November 1982 with the additional question of nuclear disarmament on the ballot. The referendum was a test of public opinion, with disarmament advocates calling for a world-wide vote on the issue. See "Support for Disarmament Tested

in Ontario Vote," *United Press International*, 8 November 1982, https://www.upi.com/Archives/1982/11/08/Support-for-disarmament-tested-in-Ontario-vote/5695405579600/.

9 Dwight D. Eisenhower, "President Dwight D. Eisenhower's Farewell Address (1961)," Final TV Talk 1/17/61 (1), box 38, Speech Series, Papers of Dwight D. Eisenhower as President, 1953–61, Eisenhower Library, National Archives and Records Administration, https://www.archives.gov/milestone-documents/president-dwight-d-eisenhowers-farewell-address.

10 Julian E. Zelizer, *Arsenal of Democracy: The Politics of National Security – From World War II to the War on Terrorism* (New York: Basic Books, 2010), 124–28.

11 James Ledbetter, *Unwarranted Influence: Dwight D. Eisenhower and the Military-Industrial Complex* (New Haven: Yale University Press, 2011), 4.

12 Ledbetter, *Unwarranted Influence*, 10.

13 For an example, see Danson and Fahey, *Not Bad for a Sergeant*, 218–22.

14 For some examples, see Michael J. Green, *Arming Japan: Defense Production, Alliance Politics, and the Postwar Search for Autonomy* (New York: Columbia University Press, 1995); Ken Conca, *Manufacturing Insecurity: The Rise and Fall of Brazil's Military-Industrial Complex* (Boulder: L. Rienner, 1997); Rachel Woodward, *Military Geographies* (Oxford: Blackwell, 2004); David Edgerton, *Warfare State: Britain, 1920–1970* (New York: Cambridge University Press, 2006); Adam Tooze, *Wages of Destruction: The Making and Breaking of the Nazi Economy* (New York: Viking, 2006); Chris Pearson, *Mobilizing Nature: The Environmental History of War and Militarization in Modern France* (Manchester: Manchester University Press, 2012).

15 Ledbetter, *Unwarranted Influence*, 6.

16 For a good synopsis, see Alex Roland, *Delta of Power: The Military-Industrial Complex* (Baltimore: Johns Hopkins University Press, 2021).

17 C. Wright Mills, *The Power Elite* (New York: Oxford University Press, 1956).

18 Harold D. Lasswell, "The Garrison State," *American Journal of Sociology* 46, 4 (1941): 455–68.

19 David Horowitz, ed., *Corporations and the Cold War* (New York: Monthly Review Press, 1969); Seymour Melman, *The Defense Economy: Conversion of Industries and Occupations to Civilian Needs* (New York: Praeger, 1970); Seymour Melman, *Pentagon Capitalism: The Political Economy of War* (New York: McGraw-Hill, 1971); Seymour Melman, *The Permanent War Economy: American Capitalism in Decline* (New York: Simon and Schuster, 1974). See also Michael A. Bernstein and Mark R. Wilson, "New Perspectives on the History of the Military-Industrial Complex," *Enterprise and Society* 12, 1 (2011): 2–3.

20 Bernstein and Wilson, "New Perspectives on the History," 2–3.

21 B.F. Cooling, *War, Business, and American Society: Historical Perspectives on the Military-Industrial Complex* (Port Washington: Kennikat Press, 1977); Paul A.C. Koistinen, *The Military-Industrial Complex: A Historical Perspective* (New York: Praeger, 1980); Bartholomew H. Sparrow, *From the Outside In: World War II and the American State* (Princeton: Princeton University Press, 1996); Benjamin O. Fordham, *Building the Cold War Consensus: The Political Economy of U.S. National Security Policy, 1949–51* (Ann Arbor: University of Michigan Press, 1998). See also Edmund F. Wehrle, "'Aid Where It Is Needed Most': American Labor's Military-Industrial Complex," *Enterprise and Society* 12, 1 (2011): 96–119; Mark R. Wilson, *Destructive Creation: American Business and the Winning of World War II* (Philadelphia: University of Pennsylvania Press, 2016).

22 Ann Markusen et al., *The Rise of the Gunbelt: The Military Remapping of Industrial America* (New York: Oxford University Press, 1991); Ann Markusen and Joel Yudken, *Dismantling the Cold War Economy* (New York: Basic Books, 1992); Gordon Gauchat et al.,

"The Military Metropolis: Defense Dependence in U.S. Metropolitan Areas," *City and Community* 10, 1 (2011): 25–48.

23 Markusen et al., *The Rise of the Gunbelt*, 3. See also Ryan H. Edgington, *Range Wars: The Environmental Contest for White Sands Missile Range* (Lincoln: University of Nebraska Press, 2014); Edwin A. Martini, ed., *Proving Grounds: Militarized Landscapes, Weapons Testing, and the Environmental Impact of U.S. Bases* (Seattle: University of Washington Press, 2015).

24 Zelizer, *Arsenal of Democracy*, 126. See also Steven High, *Industrial Sunset: The Making of North America's Rustbelt, 1969–1984* (Toronto: University of Toronto Press, 2003).

25 Margaret Pugh O'Mara, *Cities of Knowledge: Cold War Science and the Search for the Next Silicon Valley* (Princeton: Princeton University Press, 2005); Lisa McGirr, *Suburban Warriors: The Origins of the New American Right* (Princeton: Princeton University Press, 2001); Roger W. Lotchin, *Fortress California, 1910–1961: From Warfare to Welfare* (New York: Oxford University Press, 1992).

26 For examples, see Daniel Lee Kleinman, *Politics on the Endless Frontier: Postwar Research Policy in the United States* (Durham: Duke University Press, 1995); Mark Solovey and Hamilton Cravens, *Cold War Social Science: Knowledge Production, Liberal Democracy, and Human Nature* (New York: Springer, 2012); Jacob Darwin Hamblin, *Arming Mother Nature: The Birth of Catastrophic Environmentalism* (New York: Oxford University Press, 2013); Joy Rhode, *Armed with Expertise: The Militarization of American Social Research during the Cold War* (Ithaca: Cornell University Press, 2013).

27 Matthew S. Wiseman, "Canadian Scientists and Military Research in the Cold War, 1947–60," *Canadian Historical Review* 100, 3 (September 2019): 445–46.

28 Jonathan Turner, "The Defence Research Board of Canada, 1947 to 1977" (PhD diss., University of Toronto, 2012), 122.

29 For examples, see Roland, *Delta of Power*, 67–83; Joanna Bourke, *Deep Violence: Military Violence, War Play, and the Social Life of Weapons* (Berkeley, CA: Counterpoint, 2015); Naomi Oreskes, *Science on a Mission: How Military Funding Shaped What We Do and Don't Know about the Ocean* (Chicago: University of Chicago Press, 2021).

30 James C. Scott, *Seeing Like a State: How Certain Schemes to Improve the Human Condition Have Failed* (New Haven: Yale University Press, 1998).

31 Katherine C. Epstein, *Torpedo: Inventing the Military-Industrial Complex in the United States and Great Britain* (Cambridge: Harvard University Press, 2014).

32 Stuart W. Leslie, *The Cold War and American Science: The Military-Industrial-Academic Complex at MIT and Stanford* (New York: Columbia University Press, 1993).

33 N. David Mermin, "Science Wars Revisited," *Nature* 454 (2008): 276–77.

34 For examples, see Mark Solovey, *Shaky Foundations: The Politics-Patronage-Social Science Nexus in Cold War America* (New York: Rutgers University Press, 2015); Audra J. Wolfe, *Freedom's Laboratory: The Cold War Struggle for the Soul of Science* (Baltimore: Johns Hopkins University Press, 2018).

35 Gary E. Machlis and Thor Hanson, "Warfare Ecology," *BioScience* 58, 8 (2008): 729–36.

36 For examples, see Edmund Russell, *War and Nature: Fighting Humans and Insects with Chemicals from World War I to Silent Spring* (Cambridge: Cambridge University Press, 2001); Richard Tucker et al., eds., *Environmental Histories of the First World War* (Cambridge: Cambridge University Press, 2018); J.R. McNeill and Corinna R. Unger, eds., *Environmental Histories of the Cold War* (Cambridge: Cambridge University Press, 2010); David G. Havlick, *Bombs Away: Militarization, Conservation, and Ecological Restoration* (Chicago: University of Chicago Press, 2018); Stuart Parkinson, "The Carbon Boot-Print of the Military," *Responsible Science* 2 (March 2020): 18–20; Benjamin Neimark, Oliver Belcher, and Patrick Bigger, "US Military Is a Bigger Polluter than as Many

as 140 Countries – Shrinking This War Machine Is a Must," *The Conversation*, 24 June 2019, https://theconversation.com/us-military-is-a-bigger-polluter-than-as-many-as-140-countries-shrinking-this-war-machine-is-a-must-119269.

37 John Naughton, "The Evolution of the Internet: From Military Experiment to General Purpose Technology," *Journal of Cyber Policy* 1, 1 (2016): 5–28.

38 J.R. McNeill and Peter Engelke, *The Great Acceleration: An Environmental History of the Anthropocene since 1945* (Cambridge: Belknap Press of Harvard University Press, 2014), 137.

39 Bellamy, *Profiting the Crown*, 33–87; William M. Tuttle Jr., "The Birth of an Industry: The Synthetic Rubber 'Mess' in World War II," *Technology and Culture* 22, 1 (1981): 35–67.

40 For more, see Sarah Marie Wiebe, *Everyday Exposure: Indigenous Mobilization and Environmental Justice in Canada's Chemical Valley* (Vancouver: UBC Press, 2016).

41 Rachel Carson, *Silent Spring* (New York: Houghton Mifflin, 1962); Russell, *War and Nature*, 145–83.

42 For more, see the Nixon-Khrushchev "kitchen debate" in Elaine Tyler May, *Homeward Bound: American Families in the Cold War Era* (New York: Basic Books, 2008), 19–25.

43 Kate Brown, *Plutopia: Nuclear Families, Atomic Cities, and the Great Soviet and American Plutonium Disasters* (New York: Oxford University Press, 2013), 224.

44 Bartow J. Elmore, *Seed Money: Monsanto's Past and Our Food Future* (New York: W.W. Norton, 2021).

45 Joy Parr, *Sensing Changes: Technologies, Environments, and the Everyday, 1953–2003* (Vancouver: UBC Press, 2010).

46 P. Whitney Lackenbauer, *Battle Grounds: The Canadian Military and Aboriginal Lands* (Vancouver: UBC Press, 2006); P. Whitney Lackenbauer and Matthew Farish, "The Cold War on Canadian Soil: Militarizing a Northern Environment," *Environmental History* 12, 4 (2007): 920–50; P. Whitney Lackenbauer, *The Canadian Rangers: A Living History* (Vancouver: UBC Press, 2013).

47 Edgar and Haglund, *The Canadian Defence Industry*, 75–76.

48 Aaron Plamondon, *The Politics of Procurement: Military Acquisition in Canada and the Sea King Helicopter* (Vancouver: UBC Press, 2010), 18.

49 Ronald Haycock, "Policy, Patronage, and Production: Canada's Public and Private Munitions Industry in Peacetime, 1867–1939," in *Canada's Defence Industrial Base: The Political Economy of Preparedness and Procurement*, ed. David G. Haglund (Kingston: R.P. Frye, 1988), 72.

50 Tim Cook, *The Madman and the Butcher: The Sensational Wars of Sam Hughes and General Arthur Currie* (Toronto: Penguin, 2010), 108.

51 For more, see Michael Bliss, *A Canadian Millionaire: The Life and Business Times of Sir Joseph Flavelle, Bart., 1858–1939* (Toronto: Macmillan of Canada, 1978); David Carnegie, *The History of Munitions Supply in Canada, 1914–1918* (London: Longmans, Green, 1925).

52 H.C. Engelbrecht and F.C. Hanighen, *Merchants of Death: A Study of the International Armaments Industry* (New York: Dodd, Mead, 1934); John Edward Wiltz, "The Nye Committee Revisited," *Historian* 23, 2 (1961): 211–33.

53 Corruption allegations plagued the procurement of Bren guns in Canada before the start of the Second World War, leading to a royal commission that ultimately found no evidence of corruption. See D. McKenzie, "The Bren Gun Scandal and the Maclean Publishing Company's Investigation of Canadian Defence Contracts, 1938–1940," *Journal of Canadian Studies* 26, 3 (1991): 140–62.

54 Jonathan Fennel, *Fighting the People's War: The British and Commonwealth Armies and the Second World War* (Cambridge: Cambridge University Press, 2019).

55 Alex Souchen, *War Junk: Munitions Disposal and Postwar Reconstruction in Canada* (Vancouver: UBC Press, 2020), 6–7.

56 Canada, Department of National Defence, "Transfer or Sale of Defence Properties: Modernizing Defence Infrastructure," 26 April 2021, https://www.canada.ca/en/department-national-defence/services/transfer-sale-defence-properties.html.

57 James Daschuk, *Clearing the Plains: Disease, Politics of Starvation, and the Loss of Aboriginal Life* (Regina: University of Regina Press, 2013).

58 C.P. Stacey, *Arms, Men, and Governments: The War Policies of Canada, 1939–1945* (Ottawa: Queen's Printer, 1970), 488–89.

59 O.J. Firestone, *Locations and Effects of Wartime Industrial Expansion in Canada, 1939–1944* (Ottawa: Department of Reconstruction, 1945), 35–48; Jeffrey Keshen, *Saints, Sinners, and Soldiers: Canada's Second World War* (Vancouver: UBC Press, 2004).

60 Lackenbauer and Farish, "The Cold War on Canadian Soil," 924.

61 Canada, "The Department of National Defence Completes Largest Environmental Remediation Project in Government of Canada History," 7 March 2014, https://www.canada.ca/en/news/archive/2014/03/department-national-defence-completes-largest-environmental-remediation-project-government-canada-history.html.

62 For exact personnel numbers and defence budgetary figures, see Brooke Claxton, "Canada's Defence 1947: Information on Canada's Defence Achievements and Organization," in *Canada's National Defence*, vol. 1, *Defence Policy*, ed. Douglas L. Bland (Kingston: School of Policy Studies, Queen's University, 1997), 22. See also Granatstein, *Canada's Army*, 315–16; Andrew Godefroy, *In Peace Prepared: Innovation and Adaptation in Canada's Cold War Army* (Vancouver: UBC Press, 2014), 47–74.

63 Wiseman, "Canadian Scientists and Military Research," 441. See also Jocelyn Wills, *Tug of War: Surveillance Capitalism, Military Contracting, and the Rise of the Security State* (Montreal and Kingston: McGill-Queen's University Press, 2017); Donald Avery, *Pathogens for War: Biological Weapons, Canadian Life Scientists, and North American Biodefence* (Toronto: University of Toronto Press, 2013); Donald Avery, *The Science of War: Canadian Scientists and Allied Military Technology during the Second World War* (Toronto: University of Toronto Press, 1998).

64 Turner, "The Defence Research Board," 120–29; Wills, *Tug of War*, 33–35.

65 Ron Kenyon, "Modern 'Torture' Gadgets Test Human Endurance," *Toronto Telegram*, 12 February 1954, RG 24, vol. 10341, file August 28/[19]53 to August 14/[19]54, Library and Archives Canada (LAC).

66 Susan L. Smith, *Toxic Exposures: Mustard Gas and the Health Consequences of World War II in the United States* (New Brunswick, NJ: Rutgers University Press, 2017), 15–41; Ian Mosby, "Administering Colonial Science: Nutrition Research and Human Biomedical Experimentation in Aboriginal Communities and Residential Schools, 1942–1952," *Histoire Sociale/Social History* 46, 91 (May 2013): 145–72; Matthew S. Wiseman, "Unlocking the 'Eskimo Secret': Defence Science in the Cold War Canadian Arctic, 1947–1954," *Journal of the Canadian Historical Association* 26, 1 (2015): 191–223; Matthew S. Wiseman, "Frontier Footage: Science and Colonial Attitudes on Film in Northern Canada, 1948–1954," in *Cold Science: Environmental Knowledge in the North American Arctic during the Cold War*, ed. Stephen Bocking and Daniel Heidt (New York: Routledge, 2019), 61–74.

67 Edward Jones-Imhotep and Tina Adcock, "Science, Technology, and the Modern in Canada," in *Made Modern: Science and Technology in Canadian History*, ed. Edward Jones-Imhotep and Tina Adcock (Vancouver: UBC Press, 2018), 18.

68 Edgar and Haglund, *The Canadian Defence Industry*, 61–80; Lynne M. Pepall and Daniel M. Shapiro, "The Military-Industrial Complex in Canada," *Canadian Public Policy* 15, 3 (1989): 277–78.

69 Martin Auger, *The Evolution of Defence Procurement in Canada: Background Paper* (Ottawa: Library of Parliament, 2016), 4–6.

70 Auger, *The Evolution of Defence Procurement*, 4–6.

71 Edgar and Haglund, *The Canadian Defence Industry*, 62–69; Plamondon, *The Politics of Procurement*, 15–31.

72 Edgar and Haglund, *The Canadian Defence Industry*, 64.

73 John W. Warnock, *Partner to Behemoth: The Military Policy of a Satellite Canada* (Toronto: New Press, 1970), 246–60; Philip Resnick, "Canadian Defence Policy and the American Empire," in *The Americanization of Canada*, ed. Ian Lumsden (Toronto: University of Toronto Press, 1970), 93–117.

74 Gavin Kennedy, *Defense Economics* (New York: St. Martin's Press, 1983), 149.

75 Pepall and Shapiro, "The Military-Industrial Complex," 277.

76 Ernie Regehr, *Arms Canada: The Deadly Business of Military Exports* (Toronto: James Lorimer, 1987), 69.

77 Howard Peter Langille, *Changing the Guard: Canada's Defence in a World in Transition* (Toronto: University of Toronto Press, 1990), 122.

78 Langille, *Changing the Guard*, 122–23.

79 Edgar and Haglund, *The Canadian Defence Industry*, 61–103.

80 Pepall and Shapiro, "The Military-Industrial Complex," 277–78.

81 Edgar and Haglund, *The Canadian Defence Industry*, 75–78; Pepall and Shapiro, "The Military-Industrial Complex," 266–67.

82 Eugene Gholz, "Eisenhower versus the Spin-off Story: Did the Rise of the Military-Industrial Complex Hurt or Help America's Commercial Aircraft Industry?" *Enterprise and Society* 12, 1 (2011): 45–95.

Part 1
Origins and Environments

1

Victory at All Costs
Canada's Munitions Industry and the Environment during the Second World War

Alex Souchen

THE SUMMER OF 1949 was marred by many forest fires. In August, roughly 230 were reported throughout Ontario and Quebec, where firefighters battled desperately to save homes, farms, and businesses.[1] In Quebec, residents in the villages of Terrebonne Heights and Pincourt, outside Montreal, prepared to evacuate while firefighters mounted a "last-ditch touch-and-go battle" against the conflagration. Fortunately, the winds shifted and they managed to contain the blaze on the outskirts of Terrebonne.[2] A few kilometres away, another fire threatened the town of Sainte-Thérèse, but here the efforts to extinguish the inferno were complicated by a special type of hazard left over from the Second World War: unexploded ordnance.

As the fire inched closer to Sainte-Thérèse, it engulfed some of the lands that had been home to one of the largest munitions factories in Canada during the war. Situated on over five thousand acres outside the town, and known as the Bouchard plant, the factory was operated by a private military contractor, Defence Industries Limited (DIL), and entirely funded by the federal government's Department of Munitions and Supply (DMS). The Bouchard plant was exceptionally productive: it filled more than 76 million projectiles between September 1941 and June 1945.[3] Yet the final output tells only part of the story, because munitions production was a complex and dangerous undertaking. Each shell was a self-contained technological system comprised of a variety of working parts and energetic materials that had to be manufactured and calibrated according to precise specifications or else they would fail to detonate on target. Quality controls were stringent and sample batches were tested regularly at the nearby St. Maurice proof range; but many failed to explode, especially early in the war, when the DMS rapidly expanded capacity with inexperienced workers. As a result, the St. Maurice proof range became littered with "thousands of dud shells" that were set off by the forest fires in 1949. According to one *Globe and Mail* report, the explosions were visible ten miles away.[4]

Over two hundred soldiers-turned-firefighters battled the blaze near Sainte-Thérèse, but shrapnel and a lack of water slowed their efforts. Fortunately, though, changing weather patterns eased the situation, and by 25 August the fires near the old Bouchard plant and proof range were under control. The incident, however, highlights a significant but under-appreciated element in the history of Canada's military-industrial complex (MIC): the environment. Notwithstanding Matthew Evenden's work on aluminum production and hydroelectricity in Canada, Canadian historians have generally overlooked the environmental impact of Canada's industrial front during the Second World War.[5] Instead, their focus gravitates to other important subjects, such as women, consumerism, labour, and material outputs.[6] As a consequence, this has obscured appreciation for the central role of the environment in industrial mobilization and planning, as well as for the ecological changes wrought by munitions production and its associated commodity chains. This chapter seeks to uncover and untangle this history within the Canadian context, and in doing so, it draws inspiration and perspective from ongoing scholarly explorations of the environmental history of warfare and militarization in the Global North.[7]

This chapter makes two interrelated arguments. First, following the string of Allied defeats in Europe and Asia between June 1940 and February 1942, the federal government was forced to take drastic emergency actions to mobilize the nation's entire military, financial, and industrial resources for war. This emergency spurred an unprecedented integration of public and private enterprise, through the DMS's wide and pervasive mandate, to support and sustain a large military force and munitions industry, no matter the cost or obstacle. For the duration of hostilities, the DMS made the business of war as productive as possible for its empire of war contractors. Using the production of chemicals, explosives, and ammunition filling as an example, this chapter shows how political, economic, scientific, and military interests intersected to forge the foundations of Canada's MIC.

The chapter's second argument delves into the environmental history of Canada's industrial front by exploring how the environment shaped – and was reshaped by – munitions production. When locating new war factories, officials were limited by geographic, resource, and logistical factors. To expedite production, planners were primarily confined to Ontario and Quebec because ordnance factories needed access to pre-existing transportation infrastructures and manufacturing capacities, a steady labour supply, and underdeveloped land. As a result, they built factories around Montreal and Toronto or on the outskirts of nearby towns, where land was cheaper to expropriate and public safety hazards were minimal. Site selection was further refined by another environmental factor that scholars have not adequately addressed: access to water. Water was crucial to every stage in the production of chemicals, explosives, and ammunition, so it was no coincidence that every munitions factory was located close to a major body of water: millions of gallons were piped into production every day, while the effluents and emissions were discharged into the nearby lakes, rivers, soil, and air. Thus, Canada's MIC tapped into the nation's immense freshwater reserves to expedite production and simplify disposal.

Once production sites were selected, the factories themselves reshaped the surrounding environments in myriad ways. The construction of new railways and roads, buildings and storehouses, dormitories and amenities, and drains and proof ranges permanently altered landscapes and environments. What had once been fallow fields, forests, farmlands, or traditional hunting grounds were rapidly developed for industrial purposes and armaments production, no matter their impact on Indigenous and settler communities. Throughout the war, the volume of chemicals, acids, explosives, and other toxic substances flowing through these sites not only posed serious health and safety hazards for workers, but also contaminated the buildings, machinery, and adjacent ecosystems. At the end of hostilities, when the boom of wartime expenditures dried up and the DMS orchestrated the shutdown of its factories, the ecological consequences of munitions production transcended the availability of funds and the sometimes porous decontamination efforts, the lasting scars of which were cast in sharp relief by the forest fires of 1949. Yet, in other cases, the boom of wartime investments established new cities or towns that sprang up around factories and survived the bust of postwar budget cuts, job loss, and demobilization. Thus, what had been conceived of as a temporary emergency and wartime necessity carried forward tangible legacies and permanent environment changes.

Forging a Military-Industrial Complex

When Canada declared war on Nazi Germany on 10 September 1939, its armed forces were ill-prepared to fight. The interwar period had not been kind to the Canadian military, as political leaders slashed budgets and spent money elsewhere to relieve the social and economic dislocation of the Great Depression. When Germany invaded Poland on 1 September, the Canadian Army and part-time militia numbered fewer than fifty thousand troops, and they trained with weaponry left over from the First World War. The situation was no better in the other services, as the Royal Canadian Navy had ten barely modern warships, and the Royal Canadian Air Force could muster only 92 aircraft and 120 trainers.[8] The prospects of Canada making major military contributions to the Allied cause seemed remote, especially given its stagnant economy and deficits in technical expertise in defence production. These deficits made officials in the British War Office leery of awarding major contracts to Canadian firms early in the war, save for several "educational" orders for Bren guns, 25-pounder field guns, 3.7-inch shells, and 800,000 pounds of trinitrotoluene (TNT).[9]

At first, the war policies of Prime Minister William Lyon Mackenzie King's Liberal government mirrored the nation's military and industrial feebleness. Ottawa intended to limit its liabilities for overseas military deployments, not only because it lacked a well-armed military to send, but also because such commitments could result in mass casualties, conscription, and financial debts, thereby endangering national unity, as it had a generation earlier.[10] However, the haunting legacies of the First World War's conscription crisis soon gave way to new traumas, as the string of Allied defeats – stretching from the Fall of France in June 1940 to the Japanese conquest of Southeast Asia in early 1942 – shook the British Empire and the Allied cause to their very foundations.[11] The deteriorating situation necessitated drastic political, economic, and strategic interventions to facilitate the rapid emergence of a military-industrial complex in Canada. The emergency compelled the King government to mobilize for total war, the end results of which were astounding by comparison to their meagre prewar origins. By 1945, Canada possessed one of the largest air forces and navies in the world, and an army of over five infantry and armoured divisions serving overseas. Out of a total population of about 11.5 million, approximately 1.1 million Canadians enlisted in the armed forces, and over 1 million others worked in a bustling wartime economy, brought back to life by the seemingly endless stream of war contracts and federal funding for weaponry and equipment.[12]

At the heart of this "rags to riches" transformation in military and industrial fortunes was the DMS. A civilian agency, formed in early 1940 and headed by C.D. Howe, a fifty-five-year-old American-born engineer and Liberal MP for Port Arthur, Ontario, the DMS gained extraordinary powers to mobilize, ration, and coordinate all production inputs, expertise, materials, and machinery in the Canadian economy. Under Howe's leadership, and backed by the War Measures Act, the DMS redirected the flow of goods and resources away from normal civilian consumption patterns, pouring nearly everything into munitions procurement, especially after Japan's onslaught in December 1941. Government intervention ensured that military needs reigned supreme for the duration of hostilities. Through a myriad of resource controllers for coal, steel, electricity, timber, chemicals, rubber, and other essential industries, along with commodity and price administrators in the Wartime Prices and Trade Board, Canada's MIC took root across the country.[13]

The scale and speed of industrial mobilization would not have been possible without the sudden infusion of experts who populated the growing number of programs, committees, and controls. Their recruitment was a central dynamic of Canada's fledgling MIC, since they would otherwise have remained employed at universities or private companies had the DMS not needed their immediate services. Whether hand-picked by Howe and his advisors or recruited by reputation and other personal connections, the scientists, economists, engineers, lawyers, technocrats, and business executives who joined the DMS played an instrumental role in expediting production programs, many of which were highly technical in nature and beset by numerous start-up challenges and obstacles unique to the Canadian situation. This group of professionals quickly gained the moniker "dollar-a-year men" because wartime propaganda celebrated their contributions and service, supposedly rendered for the token fee of one dollar per year. However, in reality, the talent was loaned to the government while parent companies paid most of their salaries.[14]

To better acclimate his new army of experts, with little experience in governmental procedures, Howe formed an "executive committee" composed of an inner circle of advisors whom he trusted implicitly. This select group oversaw much of the department's daily operations, staffing, and policymaking. In other words, the so-called minister of everything was a master delegator, who relied on trusted subordinates to worry about the details and get results, while he concentrated on high-level decision making and smoothed over any jurisdictional conflicts that resulted from his department's expanding operations and unusual structure.[15] With businessmen-turned-bureaucrats running the show, their experiences, attitudes, and approaches were brought to bear on the seemingly infinite assortment of tasks and challenges involved with industrial mobilization. In the end, they designed the administrative and procurement branches of the DMS to function more like corporations than government agencies, so they could better integrate into the free-market economy and harness the dormant capacity of private industry, especially during the war's early phases.[16]

Howe and his dollar-a-year men did everything possible to make the business of war profitable and productive. Through various direct and indirect investment programs, roughly $3.5 billion was funnelled into the economy. To incentivize war production for private industry, special depreciation allowances were offered to companies with defence contracts, so they could write off conversion expenses, such as plant expansions, renovations, or purchases of single-purpose machinery with low postwar value.[17] Moreover, the DMS opted for "cost-plus" contracts in its dealings with private industries, in which it agreed to guarantee loans or directly finance the "cost" of production and pay contractors a little extra for completed work. This "plus" took the form of a fixed management fee, award-per-item, or a percentage of the total.[18] These measures prompted the private sector to invest roughly $1 billion into war production or about a third of total expenditures on Canada's industrial front.[19]

However, the cost-plus system was also open to abuse, as contractors could inflate their start-up and production expenses to turn a larger profit or double up on other conversion incentives. In 1941, an investigative report written by the Special Committee on War Expenditures and Economies concluded that cost-plus contracts were the most expensive type to issue. Despite this fact, DMS officials saw little alternative but to sacrifice cost efficiency given the deficient capacities of Canadian defence industries and the mounting Allied defeats.[20] As Howe boldly proclaimed in June 1940, when instructing his staff to take all necessary actions to increase production, "We have no idea of the cost but before this war is over everything will be needed so let's go ahead anyway. If we lose the war nothing will matter ... If we win the war the cost will still have been of no consequence and will have been forgotten."[21]

As the war progressed, the DMS shifted from covering start-up costs and pump-priming industrial expansion to sustaining an economic juggernaut. By March 1943, the government took over almost all of Britain's wartime investments in Canada and funded production through its Mutual Aid Program, Canada's version of Lend-Lease. Unlike in the 1930s and early war years, when the British government largely bankrolled Canada's defence-industrial base, the Mutual Aid Program fully nationalized procurement: Ottawa now paid for all Allied orders in Canada, allocating over $2 billion worth of production through the DMS by war's end.[22] The net results of this public-private partnership were staggering. By 1945, the DMS stood atop an empire of war contractors that manufactured enough "bits and pieces" to mass produce 800 naval and cargo vessels, 16,000 aircraft, 800,000 vehicles, 50,000 armoured vehicles, 1.5 million firearms, and approximately 4.6 billion rounds of ammunition and shells.[23]

Mobilizing Explosives Production

When private industry could not or would not meet the demands of the war effort, Howe's DMS increasingly took the lead and directly subsidized expansion by establishing over twenty-five Crown companies to produce or regulate essential materials. DMS officials also established the War Industrial Expansion Program, investing $700 million into the purchase of machine tools and other precision instruments and financing the construction of 33.5 million square feet of floor space at roughly 170 locations across the country, including almost 12.4 million square feet for chemicals, explosives, and ammunition-filling plants.[24] These initiatives and subsidies were important to Canada's early MIC, as Crown companies were formed across many important sectors of the economy. Some birthed entirely new industries in Canada, such as the Polymer Corporation and synthetic rubber in Sarnia, Ontario, but others greatly expanded and diversified existing industries.[25] The chemicals and explosives program organized by the DMS is one such example. Although Canada's meagre armaments industry had survived the austerity of the interwar years, its expertise and capacity were woefully inadequate despite the nucleus provided by British educational orders.[26] Nevertheless, the war emergency forced a rapid expansion in an industry composed of only a small number of companies that were capable of manufacturing and filling ordnance on such a large scale.

As a result, the DMS took more assertive actions through its Chemicals and Explosives Production Branch. This branch predated the formation of the DMS and was originally conceived and funded by the British to supplement production needs early in the war. When the DMS took over in 1940, the branch's responsibilities steadily expanded over a range of important duties, including the distribution of contracts and orders, research and development, logistics and storage, and machinery and chemicals.[27] The branch also coordinated production and research programs with its American and British counterparts, as well as with scientists and engineers employed by the National Research Council (NRC) and Canadian universities working on defence projects.[28]

This close cooperation yielded many dividends, as Canadian deficits in expertise and machinery were ameliorated by training secondments to Britain and the United States, and by loans of equipment and production techniques, made available through the increasing integration of Allied armaments programs.[29] Moreover, as historian Donald Avery shows, scientists and academics at Canadian universities mobilized their expertise, as funding for military research and development brought major technological breakthroughs in radar and proximity fuses, as well as in the development of chemicals and explosives. Canadian scientists were instrumental in the development of RDX, an explosive compound more powerful than TNT, and according to the official history of the DMS they also pioneered the prilling of ammonium nitrate, a powerful explosive and artificial fertilizer.[30] Prilling, or transforming ammonium nitrate into small pellets, made it ideal for transportation and explosives production, and later as a fertilizer in agriculture – thereby signalling an exponential boom in postwar food production.

The war's deepening crisis in 1940 and 1941, when German and Japanese victories mounted across all fronts, prompted an unavoidable expansion in plant capacities. However, this added considerably to the branch's already enormous portfolio, so it became necessary to create another organization. On 23 July 1940, the Allied War Supplies Corporation (AWSC) was formed by the DMS to supervise the construction, management, and operation of new government-run factories. Based in Montreal and headed by Harold Crabtree, a wealthy businessman and president of Howard Smith Paper Mills, AWSC quickly became a critical nerve centre in Canada's industrial war effort. Staffed by many lawyers, engineers, business executives, and other experts, it worked in tandem with the Chemicals and Explosives Production Branch by managing the operational elements of production: it oversaw the network of factories that manufactured almost all the contents and components needed to fill shells, detonators, bombs, and ammunition.[31]

By the end of 1943, AWSC had grown into a formidable empire of forty-one government-owned or -operated plants occupying over 12 million square feet of industrial floor space, stretched across five provinces. The factories financed through AWSC totalled seventeen chemical plants, five military explosive and propellant plants, nine ammunition-filling plants, nine ammunition storage magazines, and one bomb plant. Another ten commercially owned factories were also involved in the program.[32] The total output was diverse and substantial. By war's end, AWSC factories had produced four types of propellants, four types of explosives, and twenty-five types of chemicals. They also filled several types of fuses and detonators, six types of mortar bombs, five types of grenades, four types of 20 mm small-arms ammunition, three types of depth charges, and twenty-four types of artillery shells (complete with cartridges, primers, caps, and detonators).[33] At its peak, the whole chemicals and explosives program employed about fifty thousand workers and produced approximately ten thousand tons of chemicals and explosives per week. By June 1945, over 2 million tons were manufactured in total.[34]

In creating an empire of chemicals and explosives factories, AWSC officials relied on a network of subcontractors to manage all daily operations at each facility. The single-most important subcontractor was DIL, a subsidiary of the chemicals and explosives company Canadian Industries Limited (CIL), formed in September 1939 to separate military and commercial orders. Ottawa's relationship with CIL, which was itself a subsidiary of the American company DuPont and the British Imperial Chemical Industries, was one of necessity and circumstance: apart from Dominion Arsenals in Quebec City and Lindsay, Ontario, CIL was the only firm in Canada with the experience and potential capacity to meet the war's heavy demands.[35]

At the confluence of political, economic, and defence interests, DIL became the posterchild of a wildly prolific production program, born from the close cooperation of public and private enterprises. Through the DMS and AWSC, the federal government paid for everything related to production (the lands, facilities, machinery, resources, supplies, worker salaries, and everything else), so it owned the means of production and did not pay to acquire the finished products from DIL. Instead, DIL made its money through management fees: the state paid it to design, construct, and operate the factories, hire the labour force, monitor health and safety protocols, and fill production quotas outlined in its contracts.[36] Not only did DIL operate some of the largest and most productive factories in the Canadian war effort, it integrated all the commodity chains necessary to sustain munitions production at a high level. Throughout the war, and with the government's financial backing, DIL built up logistical networks to feed resources, products, and expertise into every stage of production.

At its heart were the factories in Nobel, Ontario, de Salaberry and Beloeil, Quebec, and Transcona, Manitoba, which manufactured the chemicals needed to produce explosives (such as nitric and sulphuric acid), as well as the explosives and propellants themselves. By the end of hostilities, these factories produced over 144,000 tons of TNT, 120,000 tons of cordite, 66,000 tons of nitrocellulose powders, and 4,400 tons of Tetryl.[37] Furthermore, ammonium nitrate was manufactured at three other government-subsidized plants across the country, though the factory operated by the private corporation Consolidated Mining and Smelting in Trail, British Columbia, was the largest. Thanks to generous government subsidies and contract provisions (that allowed Consolidated to retain ownership of all plant expansions after the war), it increased production to over 150 tons per day, and collectively, ammonium nitrate manufacturers churned out more than 475,000 tons for explosives and another 314,000 tons for agriculture.[38] The output from chemical factories was directed into Canada's network of ammunition-filling plants, and DIL operated several in Ontario and Quebec, including one in Pickering, Sainte-Thérèse, Montreal, and Saint-Paul l'Ermite (known as the Cherrier plant and taken over by DIL in 1944). All told, DIL produced 346,000 tons of military explosives, 71,000 tons of chemicals, 2.889 billion rounds of ammunition, and filled almost 183 million projectiles during the Second World War.[39]

Locating Production Sites

Canadian historians have long argued that the distribution of war contracts and the geography of Canada's industrial front, more generally, were shaped by Liberal political and economic priorities, as well as by Howe's personality and ideology. Prior to the war, defence procurement was stunted by a lack of political will, scandals, and virtually no funding, which left Canada unprepared and set the stage for unprecedented state interventionism. Consequently, when mobilizing the war economy and awarding contracts, Howe and his dollar-a-year men had little choice but to experiment with what they had on hand, and they justified concentrating production facilities in Ontario and Quebec on the basis of the war emergency and the expediency of using established businesses and pre-existing infrastructure. In effect, it was easiest to rely on the know-how and capacity of the private sector across many different industries, while simultaneously using public funds to kick-start economic recovery from the Great Depression.[40]

However, not everyone was convinced. As historian Ernest Forbes showed in his work on industrialization in the Maritimes, the actions of the DMS "consolidated disparities" across Canada's many regions, which disproportionately favoured Ontario and Quebec, the key electoral districts in federal politics. Using the distribution of contracts for shipbuilding and government assistance in the steel industry as examples, Forbes uncovered a distinct pattern of preferences for businesses in central Canada over the Maritimes and its strategic position in the Battle of the Atlantic.[41] Forbes's findings echo earlier complaints from critics, who decried central Canada's prominence over other regions and its unfair advantages in federal investments and defence contracts. During the 1940s, conservatives, social democrats, and provincial authorities grew uneasy about the encroachment of federal powers in provincial affairs, the assimilation of prominent Tory industrialists into government, and the use of public funds to expand corporate monopolies.[42]

Although an undeniable corporate and regional favouritism was ingrained in the way that Howe conducted DMS affairs, we must be cautious in generalizing uniform patterns and applying them equally to every industry. Some industrial sectors were outliers and deserve more nuanced critiques, as the chemicals and explosives production example clearly demonstrates. In effect, the manufacture of these death-dealing instruments depended more on logistical and environmental factors than on partisan politics. In fact, as historian Pierrick Labbé points out, the DMS never sought to distribute contracts and production sites fairly. Instead, its chemicals and explosives program was conceived with various pragmatic considerations in mind that were linked to short-term increases in productivity, while any concerns for long-term economic consolidation and political advantage were negated by the supposedly temporary nature of wartime necessities. Indeed, according to J.R. Donald, the director of Canada's Chemicals and Explosives Production Branch, the need for such a large-scale ammunition and explosives program would evaporate once victory was achieved, thereby implying that this impermanent creation was devoid of long-term utility.[43]

In the case of ammunition and explosives production, considerations for transportation, geography, labour supply, costs, and pre-existing capacities reigned supreme. When locating and constructing munitions factories, AWSC and DIL officials were confined to regions with well-developed transportation networks. Expansive and continuous access to local and national railways and roads was essential because large shipments of resources and finished products would move in and out of war factories, and also across the American border. Since these networks were already built near Canada's major industrial hubs, officials narrowed their site selections to the regions surrounding Montreal and Toronto. Locating factories near these metropolitan areas also offered ready access to Canada's steel and chemical industries, other manufacturing capacities, abundant energy sources, and a steady supply of labour.

All of these factors incentivized the distribution of ammunition and explosives production in Ontario and Quebec, especially since some factories were already established in those provinces prior to the war. By the end of 1939, British funds had paid for orders and plant expansions at CIL's ammunition plant in Browns-burg, Quebec, and chemical plant in Beloeil.[44] Moreover, the British government originally contracted DIL to build and operate the de Salaberry and Nobel plants early in the war, the latter of which was particularly advantageous since CIL's predecessor had produced explosives there during the First World War, and some of the old foundations were still viable and incorporated into the design of the new facility.[45]

Yet access to transportation infrastructures, industrial capacities, and labour markets was tempered by other financial and geographic considerations that further refined site selection. Given the spatial requirements for each factory and the dangerous nature of their outputs, planners had to be mindful of wider public safety concerns and on-site security requirements, as well as the costs for acquiring title to the land. This meant that it was not preferable to locate production sites directly in urban centres or to fully integrate them into major transportation arteries. Instead, it was best to construct the factories in the suburbs of major cities or the outskirts of small towns, where connections to transportation and resource networks could be built and monitored. For instance, one of DIL's competitors, the General Engineering Company (Canada) (GECO), which established a specialized factory for filling detonators and fuses in Scarborough, Ontario, operated a public transit system to bring workers to the plant. Four main bus routes linked the factory to Toronto, with terminal stops at Yonge Street and St. Clair Avenue, Bloor and Church Streets, and Victoria Park Avenue and Danforth Road. In March 1943, to relieve congestion on buses, a fifth route was added between the plant and Eglinton Avenue and Yonge Street.[46]

Land was cheapest to expropriate outside urban centres. This was crucial given the spatial needs of munitions factories. The Nobel site was originally situated on 975 acres north of Parry Sound, which were purchased from CIL at a bargain price of $10 per acre.[47] Four of the major filling plants sprawled for thousands of acres and comprised hundreds of structures and amenities, predominately erected as temporary buildings between 1940 and 1942. For instance, the Bouchard plant spanned over 470 buildings across 5,111 acres, whereas the Cherrier plant occupied 1,350 acres and had 345 buildings. The GECO plant was situated on 332 acres with 162 buildings. DIL's Pickering Works eventually consisted of over 440 buildings on 2,500 acres that were expropriated from local farming families at an average price of $125 per acre. The families were not happy about the small return for their land, but the needs of the war effort outweighed their protests.[48] Those families, though, made out far better than others. Outside Sarnia, some of the traditional lands of the Aamjiwnaang First Nation were taken over by the Polymer Corporation and other petrochemical companies and converted into Canada's "Chemical Valley." The resulting pollution and persistent health hazards have scarred generations since the war.[49]

Furthermore, underdeveloped land on the edges of cities and towns provided a natural spatial and security buffer that limited any collateral damage from accidental explosions or incursions from spies and saboteurs. Although fears of enemy agents were largely exaggerated, the dangers from explosions were always present at filling plants and, especially, at the chemical plants. On 18 November 1940, just two months into operations, three workers at the Nobel plant were killed when an explosion ripped through two buildings used for acid treatment in the manufacture of TNT.[50] The disaster was the first in Ontario and set production back a few weeks, but it was far from unique. Ammunition-filling plants also housed many energetic hazards and mechanical dangers that proved especially perilous to inexperienced workers. At the Bouchard factory, approximately 36,000 minor injuries (such as strains, cuts, bruises) occurred throughout its operational life, from August 1941 to December 1945. The frequency of accidents involving major injuries (lacerations, amputations, burns, fractures, and fatalities) was brought under control after the first eight months of operations when 111 incidents occurred. By contrast, 169 major injuries took place over the following forty-five months.[51] Similar trends were found in other factories. At Brownsburg, there were 90 major injuries during the war, though most were concentrated in 1941 and 1942 when production expanded considerably.[52]

By far the most decisive consideration in site selection was access to water. This fact, however, has not been adequately addressed in the historiography, as scholars studying Canada's industrial front make only tangential references to the environment. This obscures the centrality of water (and the environment more generally) to Canada's MIC. Water was an essential input at all stages of production. At the chemical and explosives plants, it was needed in the manufacture of sulphuric and nitric acids, and it was used to control the temperature of chemical reactions during the production process. Moreover, the purity of TNT depended on a thorough washing of the final product with a sulfite solution. Washing TNT removed unwanted isomers and residual dinitrated toluene that stabilized the explosive compound. Without this final washing, the crude TNT was liable to detonate spontaneously.[53] Given these requirements, it is no small wonder that every chemical and explosive factory was located near a source of water.[54]

Water was also omnipresent in the filling plants. Although statistics are not available for every site, Pickering Works, on the shores of Lake Ontario, consumed over 1 million gallons per day for all operational purposes, including drinking water, toilets, and for cleaning shells, machinery, and facilities.[55] Water was also integral to workplace safety, as employees were surrounded by toxic chemicals and combustible hazards. All were subject to stringent safety protocols that were designed to prevent accidents. Before entering the "clean" side of factories (where explosives were filled), they left their clothes and possessions in locker rooms and donned special coveralls, rubber shoes, and headscarves. They were not allowed to wear jewellery, to smoke, or to carry metallic objects and anything else that might cause a spark on the clean side.[56] When handling TNT and other high explosives, workers were trained to limit contact with masks, goggles, and gloves, as the toxic dust, fumes, and residues could be inhaled, ingested, or absorbed through the skin, causing sickness, skin irritations, liver damage, and in fatal exposures, toxic jaundice.[57] However, photographic evidence suggests that some of these precautions were not always followed (Figure 1.1). After each shift, foremen and supervisors ensured that all workers showered on-site to rinse off the contaminants and explosive residues that had collected on their bodies and hair. The uniforms were then laundered on-site and readied for the next shift.[58]

These health and safety protocols were augmented by the factory's layout and equipment. In rooms where TNT was handled, fans improved ventilation, and dust-proof hoods were installed on the transfer hopper, a machine that broke down clumps of TNT into flakes before they were melted and poured into shell casings.[59] Moreover, every building had water piped throughout its rooms for fire prevention, and emergency showers were always located adjacent to acid treatment areas and other danger zones. Water was needed for production purposes as well. Rooms and equipment were constantly washed with cleaning solutions, not only to protect staff, but to maintain machinery in peak working condition and minimize cross-contamination from foreign substances.[60] Particular attention was devoted to the TNT melter and ammonium nitrate incorporator. Every day at noon, both machines were shut down for a thorough

Figure 1.1 Assembly-line staff use pouring pots to fill shells with liquid TNT. Note the large storage kettle operated by two men at the left. This was where the TNT was kept warm before pouring. Few workers are wearing goggles or masks, and the ventilation comes from the windows at the right. | Provided by the Town of Ajax – P070-000-281, Ajax Archives.

flushing with hot water. Workers were careful not to create too much extra steam when hosing down the melter's interior since that would activate the emergency safeguards controlling temperature and "trip the water deluge valve ... and flood the entire building."[61] These safeguards were designed to prevent accidents or malfunctions from spiralling out of control, but it should not go unstated here that water was always considered the primary countermeasure in emergency situations.

Aftermath

Since munitions factories consumed such large volumes of water, they required a "sink" or drain for the resulting wastewater. Contamination was the inevitable by-product of production, and it carried a heavy environmental toll. Each stage of production introduced many toxic chemicals, acids, explosive residues, and other types of hazards into the water flowing through the facilities and then into the environment. When locating and building factories, DIL and AWSC planners sought to harness the proximity of rivers and lakes, not only for production purposes, but also for their dilution capacities. Therefore, Canada's MIC tapped into the nation's immense freshwater resources to engineer a convenient solution for effluent disposal while simultaneously expediting wartime production. In doing so, it militarized landscapes and reshaped environments at production facilities.

Effluent disposal was a key part of operational efficiency: factories could produce munitions only as fast as they could discharge the wastewater. TNT and cordite were particular concerns. The manufacture of TNT is water-intensive at both ends of production, and the effluent from purification and washing is called "red water," whereas "pink water" is generated by washing facilities and machinery. Both terms refer to the varying shades of red created by the complex mixture of organic constituents, non-symmetrical isomers, and nitroaromatic compounds and associated salts. The darker the red, the higher the concentration of contamination. Red water, in particular, is toxic, carcinogenic, and mutagenic, and it does not biodegrade easily. If left untreated, its contents will persist in the environment, contaminating soil and groundwater and causing long-term ecological and public health problems.[62]

To deal with TNT effluent, Canadian planners followed American and British precedents by constructing a series of interconnected drains and ditches at each site. The drains took in wastewater and other production runoff from inside the buildings and piped it to outfalls that emptied into several "tributary ditches" that flowed into a larger "main" ditch. These outdoor sewers were not enclosed. Instead, they were left open-faced so that the effluent was exposed to sunlight, which aided in decomposition as the polluted water traversed through the tributaries and main ditches that criss-crossed the site. Each ditch had baffles, catchment tanks, and holding ponds that collected the heavier particles and residues in the sediment; scientific experts and technicians expected the remaining contaminants to be diluted by the main ditch before emptying into the closest body of water.[63] At the de Salaberry plant, the ditches flowed directly into the St. Lawrence River. At Nobel, effluent from TNT, nitroglycerine, and cordite production flowed through practically the entire site before draining into either Simmes Lake or toward the holding pond, aptly named "Guncotton Swamp," before flowing down "Guncotton Creek" into "Guncotton Bay" on Parry Sound.[64]

Some munitions factories required more elaborate arrangements. The Transcona facility, located on eight hundred acres southwest of Winnipeg, is one example. It was situated on the outskirts of town, in an area devoid of major waterways, so engineers had first to connect the plant to the Greater Winnipeg Water District aqueduct, which allowed it to take in approximately 10 million gallons of water every day for manufacturing sulphuric acid, nitric acid, and cordite (some of its main outputs). However, this one-way system did not allow for effluent disposal. Thus, before production could even start, a massive ditch was dug to connect the facility to the Red River, over twelve kilometres away. By the spring of 1941, approximately 188,000 cubic yards of dirt was excavated through the North Transcona and East Kildonan neighbourhoods.[65] To shorten construction, engineers designed the ditch to empty into Bunn's Creek, which took the effluent the rest of the way to the Red River. In 2010, the Winnipeg Trails Association seized upon the popularity of the Second World War and opened the "Cordite Ditch" hiking trail bordering a portion of the old effluent channel, just south of the Transcona Railyards.[66] The project celebrated Winnipeg's wartime contributions and, ironically, provided a space for wildlife conservation next to a former sewer, which had moved an enormous volume of wastewater, laced with toxic substances and explosive residues, through residential and industrial areas.

Although the scale of development at Transcona was unique, effluent and water pollution were common issues at every factory. For instance, CIL commissioned a pollution study at the Brownsburg ammunition plant in 1956 to document the state of the West River, adjacent to the property. The report concluded unequivocally that the river was "polluted and unfit for aquatic life."[67] The deleterious situation, however, originated from wartime practices, as the report surmised that the river was at its worst in 1944–45, when a combination of low water levels and a lack of environmental regulations caused high concentrations of lead and acids to be discharged into the river. According to historical data on the river's flow and estimated production outputs at the plant, the amount of water was not sufficient to dilute the contamination: the concentration of lead in 1944–45 probably reached 2.4 ppm or about twenty-four times the "allowable concentration" according to the 1956 standards for safe drinking water (which the report's author used as a benchmark in his study).[68]

In the decade after the war, little was done to modify disposal methods, though staff monitored the river's flow to ensure that discharges were at least nominally proportional to expected dilution thresholds. As historian Jamie Benidickson shows, until the 1970s there was considerable reluctance and laxity on the part of federal and provincial governments to regulate water pollution, and since many municipalities pumped untreated sewage into nearby rivers without recourse, the effects of industrial wastes hardly merited more stringent oversights.[69] The engineers, scientists, and explosives experts who designed the drainage systems and perfected production processes showed little regard for the ecological consequences and contamination of explosives production. Instead, they were confident in their systems and reliance on dilution, though the end of hostilities exposed the limitations of their thinking.

The wartime emergency had overridden all considerations and prioritized rapid expansion, but as the volume of production increased, so, too, did the pollution. By 1945, most factories had been in operation for over thirty-six months, churning out chemicals, acids, explosives, and complete munitions every day. As a result, entire buildings and areas were "impregnated" by explosive residues lodged in the wood, piping, panelling, and concrete. Thus, before any factory could be shut down, converted, or dismantled, its building materials, machinery, equipment, and landscapes had to be decontaminated. In July 1945, Howe created the Plant Decontamination Committee (PDC) to oversee the postwar cleanup at surplus factories. Under the supervision of the PDC, war contractors and experts from the ammunition and explosives production branches in the DMS desensitized facilities and equipment before turning the properties over to the War Assets Corporation (WAC) for final disposal.[70]

To decontaminate the buildings and equipment inside factories, workers followed strict protocols. At the GECO plant, they used a combination of vacuums, high-pressure water hoses, and cleaning solutions of sodium sulphite and acetone.[71] After every room was thoroughly scrubbed from floor to ceiling, the metallic equipment was relocated and steamed to remove any remaining residues, the plumbing and airducts were flushed or removed for incineration, and the linoleum floors were upturned and systematically washed. Spot tests were made using matches or small controlled fires (called "flashing"), which could be dangerous depending on the level of leftover residues.[72] Anything that could not be cleaned or was too forgone was brought to the factory's burning ground. At every production site in Canada, certain areas were reserved for the destruction of production wastes and waste explosives by incineration.[73] Following the war, these burning grounds were used for destroying the cleaning solutions, wood, flooring, brick, topsoils, filters, piping, and any other contaminated materials. At the GECO plant, more than 6,800 tons of contaminated materials were set on fire in its proofing yard, and the polluted soil was later removed by bulldozers and trucked to a nearby garbage dump.[74]

At DIL factories, the advent of peace signalled a rush to downsize and demobilize – much to the consternation of the PDC. DIL employees showed little interest in desensitizing materials and equipment, as the company was not enthused about salvage and recovery costs. Therefore, it moved swiftly to tear down surplus factories and often resorted to area burning and other inexpensive shortcuts. At the Pickering plant, area burning included whole buildings, and any unneeded structures with thick concrete walls were toppled over and buried in large pits.[75] Similar tactics were used at the Bouchard factory, where DIL requested blanket permission to demolish or burn entire buildings and to destroy contaminated equipment. The PDC refused, citing opportunities for salvaging lumber and building supplies for resale, but DIL proved less than accommodating. In September 1945, it reported the destruction of $192,000 worth of assets from Production Line No. 1, and subsequent reports from company officials recommended destroying another $700,000 worth of materials and equipment from the other three lines. In October, a special meeting was arranged between PDC and DIL officials to clarify the testing standards for contamination levels, cost estimates for salvage work, and acceptable justifications for destroying Crown property.[76]

Outside the munitions factories, the landscapes were also polluted, but the dangers could be difficult to locate. Lax record keeping and personnel turnover deprived technicians of first-hand knowledge of problem spots, and toxic residues were often difficult to remove or were hidden by years of neglect or by brush that sprouted back over time. Unexpected discoveries were not uncommon, such as when fifteen to twenty pounds of Tetryl pellets (a toxic yellow crystalline powder used in detonators) exploded during a burn at the GECO proofing yard in July 1945.[77] Area burning was a useful strategy for locating the invisible hazards, but it was not universally applicable. In those instances where burning was too dangerous, such as near the storage magazines or the entrances to production lines, war contractors resorted to excavating the topsoils with bulldozers and shovels to avoid missing anything.[78]

Unexploded ordnance was another concern, especially at proof ranges, since a dud shell's velocity could bury it deeply underground, rendering it inaccessible to clearance technicians years later. The St. Maurice proof range was a particular problem for the PDC. The costs to clear it by area burning were estimated to be about $50 to $65 per acre, leaving the final price tag somewhere between $100,000 and $125,000. The cost was high because personnel had to prepare the whole two-thousand-acre site "for an ordinary farmers' slash," and once the fires died out, a shielded bulldozer was needed to plow the charred ground to unearth buried ammunition.[79] Given the steep costs, the PDC chairman referred the matter to his superior, G.K. Sheils, deputy minister of the DMS, who recommended foregoing "fuller decontamination" and limiting clearance to the building area, roads, and other access points. This left most of the range and its many unexploded bombs untouched, until the forest fires swept through in 1949.[80]

The drainage systems at Nobel and Transcona were the largest and most expensive problems for the PDC, as both plants were shuttered and scheduled for disposal after the war. At Nobel, technicians had difficulty decontaminating the solvent and acid storage tanks, so eventually they resorted to packing them with combustible materials and lighting a controlled burn to clean them out. Similar improvisation characterized the treatment of the nearby effluent ditches for TNT, nitroglycerine, and nitrocellulose. In early 1946, the PDC ordered the "flushing out" of the entire drainage system, as well as the additional precautions of extensive area burning, the dredging of contaminated soils and sediments, and the use of prima cord to detonate any hidden explosive materials. In the spring, the site was handed over to the WAC and its contractors finished up the work.[81] At Transcona, DIL implemented its experiences from Nobel, with the result that operations moved more smoothly as its personnel worked quickly to blast out and burn the ditches. To save time and money, DIL recommended filling in the nitrocellulose settling pond with loads of dirt, but the PDC concluded that this would not bury the explosive residues at a depth preventing future recoveries or accidents. Instead, it ordered the pond drained and the sediment "treated [burnt] to remove the hazard" before it was filled in.[82]

Despite these measures, the PDC was well aware that its remediation tactics were untested over the long term. Therefore, it could not guarantee that DIL and other contractors had cleaned up every explosive hazard or iota of contamination. In February 1946, its officials noted that any future construction located near munitions factories, and especially the Transcona and Nobel sites, was liable to encounter residual explosive materials.[83] As an additional precaution, it paid for the installation of fences and warning signs on the shores of Parry Sound at Guncotton Bay after technicians made a final sweep in the spring of 1946.[84] More recently, anecdotal evidence collected by concerned citizens has confirmed the PDC's earlier predictions. In the Nobel area, it is not uncommon for grenades and shells to appear on the beaches of Parry Sound and Georgian Bay, hunters share stories about deformed animals, and parents frequently warn their children about the dangers of swimming and fishing in the nearby Simmes Lake.[85]

In other cases, decontamination efforts achieved different objectives. For instance, three large munitions plants (the Villeray and Verdun Works in Montreal, and the John Inglis plant expansion in Toronto) were decontaminated, cleared, and renovated to offer small and medium businesses industrial floor space for manufacturing civilian goods. During a time of severe economic dislocation and steep rental prices in major cities, these low-rent "multiple tenancy" initiatives (operated through the WAC) provided important opportunities for over eighty companies and generated over six thousand jobs producing a host of new goods, from electrical equipment and glassware to clothing and processed foods.[86] Such tactical-to-practical conversions of old munitions factories demonstrate a tangible legacy of Canada's MIC, as defence dollars had built up an infrastructure and capacity that yielded spin-off civilian benefits in peacetime.

These spin-off benefits also extended beyond the confines of the factory buildings, as the wartime influx of labour, capital, and development spurred lasting environmental changes in surrounding regions. For example, the DIL Pickering plant brought an influx of over nine thousand workers to the area during the war, but initially the region was almost entirely devoid of accommodations and amenities. Therefore, defence expenditures stimulated the construction of more than just railroads, ditches, magazines, pumping stations, and production lines: homes, dormitories, cafeterias, recreation centres, hospitals, parks, stores, schools, and other amenities followed. By the midsummer of 1941, so much mail was flowing in and out of the small prewar Pickering post office that DIL established a satellite branch inside the factory. A naming competition was organized, and though most workers referred to the sprawling facility colloquially as "Dilco" or "Dilville," these popular nicknames lost out to the famed exploits of HMS *Ajax* during the Battle of the River Plate in December 1939. Henceforth, the region would be known as Ajax.[87]

Defence expenditures remapped more than just placenames in Canada, as military spending spawned permanent development, urbanization, and industry. By 1942, in Ajax, roughly six hundred families had moved into the housing built near the factory, and the number of children steadily increased. As a result, DIL established the Lord Elgin School and paid its staff of one principal and eight teachers. The school was completed in October 1942, just after the first church was erected, and in May 1943, the first grocery store opened its doors. Following the war, a large portion of the Ajax plant was taken over by the University of Toronto's Faculty of Applied Sciences, where it trained veterans for civilian careers (see Figure 1.2).[88] In 1948, the federal government's new Central Mortgage and Housing Corporation (CMHC) took over development in the area, acting as the de facto municipal government until the province established one in 1950. Through the CMHC's efforts, several Canadian, British, American, and Swedish companies moved to Ajax in the late 1940s, which sustained employment in a region that "would otherwise be a ghost town" following the end of munitions production.[89] Ajax managed to navigate the boom-and-bust pattern of wartime expansion better than other places, as a more balanced economy emerged from a near total dependency on defence spending and war contracts. Such a transition demonstrates, not only how a cycle of "defense dependence" emerged in Canada, but also how the nation's MIC profoundly affected the environment.[90] The confluence of political, military, and financial resources altered landscapes and demographic patterns to fundamentally reshape the ecological history of many regions across the country.

Figure 1.2 Aerial photograph of the University of Toronto's Ajax Campus after the war. The wartime houses are on the left. The DIL buildings-turned-classrooms are near the centre. | Provided by the Town of Ajax – P230-001-040, Ajax Archives.

Conclusion

Between 1940 and 1945, the DMS established a productive munitions industry that added considerably to Allied arsenals. The deteriorating military situation from 1940 to 1942 necessitated radical political, economic, and strategic interventions to facilitate the rapid emergence of what O.J. Firestone, deputy director-general of the Economic Research Branch in the DMS, later termed Canada's "wartime industrial structure."[91] The symbiotic partnership between private and public enterprise entwined political, military, industrial, and academic interests to forge the foundations of Canada's MIC during the 1940s.

The remarkable achievements of Canada's industrial front materially aided the Allied cause, as approximately 70 percent of all output went to other countries, with the British receiving the largest share.[92] Canadian factories were key contributors to the global arms trade and imperial supply channels, but they were almost entirely dependent on export markets and artificially high wartime demands. Canadian defence production was thus far in excess of future military and domestic requirements. This imbalance was thrown into sharp relief once hostilities ended and Mackenzie King ordered a rapid demobilization, deep cuts to defence spending, and widespread disposal operations for surplus munitions and supplies. The postwar retrenchment of the armed forces made large-scale munitions manufacture in Canada unsustainable over the long term, particularly as the American and British governments shifted focus to domestic production.[93]

When Germany and Japan were defeated, the vast empire of munitions plants operated through the DMS was shut down or converted into peacetime production. A small rump of plants, technology, and expertise was consolidated under the mandate of a new Crown company, Canadian Arsenals Limited (CAL), founded in September 1945, which oversaw a truncated postwar armaments industry until it was privatized completely in the 1980s. The de Salaberry and Cherrier plants, among others, were transferred to CAL, as a smaller but permanent defence-industrial base took root in Canada to supply the ongoing needs of the Canadian military and international clients – a theme discussed by other chapters in this collection. The environmental impact of Canada's munitions industry remains an open question, despite the increasing scope of government regulations against pollution over the latter half of the twentieth century. The ecological degradation and disruptions, as well as the contamination and public safety risks caused by munitions factories, were the by-products of wartime necessities and key elements of Canada's home front contributions to Allied victory; but they also left hazardous legacies for all Canadians growing up in the long shadow of the Second World War.

Notes

1 "Forest Firefighters Battle Desperately to Save Villages," *Globe and Mail*, 23 August 1949, 13; "230 Bush Fires Rage in Ontario and Quebec, Menace Several Villages," *Globe and Mail*, 24 August 1949, 5; "Bulldozers, Plane Help Firefighters in Ontario Battling 113 Outbreaks," *Globe and Mail*, 23 August 1949, 1.

2 "Quebec Villagers Flee Roaring Forest Flames," *Globe and Mail*, 23 August 1949, 1.

3 "Bouchard Works Finished Goods Produced," vol. 1, section 2 Production, Defence Industries Limited Shell Filling Department: Bouchard Works Plant History (DIL Bouchard Works Plant History), 55B 1 1, Canadian War Museum (CWM).

4 "Munitions Dump Fire by Quebec Bush Blaze," *Globe and Mail*, 22 August 1949, 1.

5 Matthew Evenden, "Aluminum, Commodity Chains, and the Environmental History of the Second World War," *Environmental History* 16, 1 (2011): 69–93; Matthew Evenden, *Allied Power: Mobilizing Hydro-electricity during Canada's Second World War* (Toronto: University of Toronto Press, 2015).

6 For examples, see Jennifer Stephen, *Pick One Intelligent Girl: Employability, Domesticity, and the Gendering of Canada's Welfare State, 1939–1947* (Toronto: University of Toronto Press, 2007); James Pritchard, *A Bridge of Ships: Canadian Shipbuilding during the Second World War* (Montreal and Kingston: McGill-Queen's University Press, 2011); Michael Stevenson, *Canada's Greatest Wartime Muddle: National Selective Service and the Mobilization of Human Resources during World War II* (Montreal and Kingston: McGill-Queen's University Press, 2001); Graham Broad, *A Small Price to Pay: Consumer Culture on the Canadian Home Front, 1939–1945* (Vancouver: UBC Press, 2013).

7 Richard P. Tucker et al., eds., *Environmental Histories of the First World War* (Cambridge: Cambridge University Press, 2018); Simo Laakkonen, Richard P. Tucker, and Timo Vuorisalo, eds., *The Long Shadows: A Global Environmental History of the Second World War* (Corvallis: Oregon State University Press, 2017).

8 C.P. Stacey, *Six Years of War: The Army in Canada, Britain, and the Pacific* (Ottawa: HMSO, 1966), 34; C.P. Stacey, *Arms, Men, and Governments: The War Policies of Canada, 1939-1945* (Ottawa: HMSO, 1970), 106; J.L. Granatstein, *Canada's Army: Waging War and Keeping the Peace* (Toronto: University of Toronto Press, 2002), 172-73; W.A.B. Douglas, Roger Sarty, and Michael Whitby, *No Higher Purpose: The Official Operational History of the Royal Canadian Navy in the Second World War, 1939-1943, vol. 2, part 1* (St. Catharines: Vanwell, 2002), 28.

9 Stacey, *Arms, Men, and Governments*, 102-7; Robert Bothwell, "Defense and Industry in Canada, 1935-1970," in *War, Business and World Military-Industrial Complexes*, ed. Benjamin Franklin Cooling (Port Washington, NY: Kennikat Press, 1981), 108.

10 Tim Cook, *Warlords: Borden, Mackenzie King, and Canada's World Wars* (Toronto: Allen Lane, 2012), 207-34.

11 Jonathan Fennel, *Fighting the People's War: The British and Commonwealth Armies and the Second World War* (Cambridge: Cambridge University Press, 2019).

12 For more on Canada's home front, see Jeffrey Keshen, *Saints, Sinners, and Soldiers: Canada's Second World War* (Vancouver: UBC Press, 2004).

13 Robert Bothwell and William Kilbourn, *C.D. Howe: A Biography* (Toronto: McClelland and Stewart, 1979), 128-79; Joy Parr, *Domestic Goods: The Material, Moral, and the Economic in the Postwar Years* (Toronto: University of Toronto Press, 1999), 21-39; Peter S. McInnis, *Harnessing Labour Confrontation: Shaping the Postwar Settlement in Canada, 1943-1950* (Toronto: University of Toronto Press, 2002), 20-36; Broad, *A Small Price to Pay*, 125-38.

14 Jeremy Stuart, "Captains of Industry Crewing the Ship of State: Dollar-a-Year Men and Industrial Mobilization in WWII Canada, 1939-1942" (master's thesis, University of Calgary, 2013), 22-30; Robert Bothwell, "A Curious Lack of Proportion: Canadian Business and the War," in *The Second World War as a National Experience*, ed. Sidney Aster (Ottawa: Canadian Committee for the History of the Second World War, 1981), 24-37.

15 Stuart, "Captains of Industry," 22-38; Bothwell and Kilbourn, *C.D. Howe*, 128-40.

16 Stuart, "Captains of Industry," 37-61.

17 O.J. Firestone, *Encouragement to Industrial Expansion in Canada: Operation of Special Depreciation Provisions, November 10, 1944-March 31, 1947* (Ottawa: Department of Reconstruction and Supply, 1948), 13, 21.

18 Stuart, "Captains of Industry," 42-48.

19 Firestone, *Encouragement to Industrial Expansion*, 21.

20 Stuart, "Captains of Industry," 42-48.

21 Robert Bothwell, "'Who's Paying for Anything These Days?' War Production in Canada, 1939-1945," in *Mobilization for Total War: The Canadian, American, and British Experience*, ed. N.F. Dreisziger (Waterloo: Wilfrid Laurier University Press, 1981), 62. Bothwell is quoting a 1976 interview with Henry Borden about Howe's statements.

22 For more on Mutual Aid, see Robert B. Bryce, *Canada and the Cost of World War II: The International Operations of Canada's Department of Finance, 1939-1947*, edited by Matthew J. Bellamy (Montreal and Kingston: McGill-Queen's University Press, 2005), 146-88.

23 Alex Souchen, *War Junk: Munitions Disposal and Postwar Reconstruction in Canada* (Vancouver: UBC Press, 2020), 5-9.

24 Canada, Department of Reconstruction and Supply, *Disposal and Peacetime Use of Crown Plant Buildings* (Ottawa: HMSO, 1948), foreword, 9–14.

25 Matthew J. Bellamy, *Profiting the Crown: Canada's Polymer Corporation, 1942–1990* (Montreal and Kingston: McGill-Queen's University Press, 2005).

26 Pierrick Labbé, "L'arsenal canadien: Les politiques canadiennes et la fabrication de munitions au Canada durant la Deuxième Guerre mondiale" (PhD diss., University of Ottawa, 2012), 93–150; Bothwell, "Defense and Industry in Canada," 106–10.

27 J. de N. Kennedy, *History of the Department of Munitions and Supply: Canada in the Second World War*, vol. 1, *Production Branches and Crown Companies* (Ottawa: HMSO, 1950), 103–45.

28 Donald Avery, *The Science of War: Canadian Scientists and Allied Military Technology during the Second World War* (Toronto: University of Toronto Press, 1998), 96–121.

29 Kennedy, *History of the Department*, 104–10.

30 Kennedy, *History of the Department*, 109; Avery, *The Science of War*, 96–121.

31 Kennedy, *History of the Department*, 103–45, 290–317.

32 John R. Leslie, *Summary Record and History of Allied War Supplies Corporation: From Incorporation in July 1940 to December 31st, 1943, Vol. 1* (Montreal: Allied War Supplies Corporation, 1945), 26–28.

33 Leslie, *Summary Record*, 27.

34 Kennedy, *History of the Department*, 103.

35 Labbé, "L'arsenal canadien," 167, 187; Serge Marc Durflinger, *Fighting from Home: The Second World War in Verdun, Quebec* (Vancouver: UBC Press, 2006), 127–30.

36 Durflinger, *Fighting from Home*, 127–30; *Canadian Industries Limited Annual Report 1945* (Montreal: CIL, 1945), 12–16.

37 Kennedy, *History of the Department*, 103–45, stats from 142.

38 Kennedy, *History of the Department*, 122–25, 142.

39 *Canadian Industries Limited Annual Report 1945*, 14.

40 Labbé, "L'arsenal canadien," 151–63.

41 Ernest Forbes, "Consolidating Disparity: The Maritimes and the Industrialization of Canada during the Second World War," *Acadiensis* 15, 2 (1986): 3–27.

42 Bothwell, "'Who's Paying for Anything These Days?'" 65; Labbé, "L'arsenal canadien," 181–92.

43 Labbé, "L'arsenal canadien," 190–92.

44 Stacey, *Arms, Men, and Governments*, 104–5; Kennedy, *History of the Department*, 81, 110–11.

45 Summary Record: Project No. 1, Nobel – DIL (DIL Nobel Summary Record), section 3, 2, Allied War Supplies Corporation sous-fonds (AWSC), RG 61-2, vol. 1, Library and Archives Canada (LAC).

46 Barbara Dickson, *Bomb Girls: Trading Aprons for Ammo* (Toronto: Dundurn, 2015), 67.

47 DIL Nobel Summary Record, section 3, 2, LAC.

48 Labbé, "L'arsenal canadien," 168–69; Ken Smith, *Ajax: The War Years, 1939–1945* (Oshawa, ON: self-published, 1989), 11–13.

49 Bellamy, *Profiting the Crown*, 23–87; Sarah Marie Wiebe, *Everyday Exposure: Indigenous Mobilization and Environmental Justice in Canada's Chemical Valley* (Vancouver: UBC Press, 2016).

50 "Nobel Munitions Plant Blast Kills Three: 2 Buildings Destroyed with Roar," *Globe and Mail*, 19 November 1940, 1.

51 "Number of Major Injuries by Months," vol. 3, section 3, 24 and chart, DIL Bouchard Works Plant History, CWM.

52 C.E. Richardson, "Works Accidents – 1886 to 1949: Ammunition Division, Brownsburg, Que.," 1–23; "Disabling Injuries, 1929–1965," 24 March 1965, 1–3, both in Canadian Industries Limited fonds, R15655–0–3-E, vol. 133, file 2, LAC.

53 Jehuda Yinon, *Toxicity and Metabolism of Explosives* (Ann Arbor: CRC Press, 1990), 38–39.

54 For examples, see DIL Nobel Summary Record, section 3, Appendix 3, LAC; Summary Record: Project No. 2, De Salaberry – DIL (DIL de Salaberry Summary Record), section 3, Appendix 2, AWSC, RG 61–2, vol. 1, LAC; Summary Record: Project No. 16, Winnipeg – DIL (DIL Transcona Summary Record), section 3, Appendix 2, AWSC, RG 61–2, vol. 4, LAC.

55 Smith, *Ajax*, 11.

56 *General and Special Rules* (Brownsburg: Defence Industries Limited, 1941), R15655–1013–6-E, vol. 127, file 2, LAC.

57 "Measures for Prevention of T.N.T. Absorption," vol. 2, section 6, Appendix C-1, Defence Industries Limited, Shell Filling Department: Cherrier Works Plant History (DIL Cherrier Works Plant History), 55B 1 2, CWM.

58 Dickson, *Bomb Girls*, 67–76, 187–88.

59 Dickson, *Bomb Girls*, 41–42, 67–76; Lisa Tubb, "Assembling Victory: Defense Industries Limited, Ajax 1941–1945," *Ontario History* 111, 1 (2019): 6; *General and Special Rules*, 15–35, LAC.

60 *General and Special Rules*, 15–35, LAC.

61 "Melting T.N.T.," vol. 1, section C, 36-42, quote from 38, Defence Industries Limited Shell Filling Department: Pickering Works Process Manual: Shell Q.F. H.E. S/L 25 Pr. Mk. 1D, T.N.T. Fuzed 119B (DIL Pickering Works Process Manual Shell 25 Pr.), 55B 2, CWM.

62 Jeong-Hyeon Jo et al., "Treatment of TNT Red Water Using Ice Crystallization," *Propellants, Explosives, Pyrotechnics* 43 (February 2018): 203.

63 "Minutes of the Meeting of the Committee Dealing with the Decontamination of Buildings and Equipment," 4 December 1945, 2, 4, RG 28, vol. 156, file 3-P-13, LAC ("Minutes of the Decontamination Committee," LAC).

64 "Minutes of the Decontamination Committee," 4 December 1945, 2, 4, LAC; "Sketch of Sewage & Process Water Disposal, Cordite & T.N.T. Plant, Nobel Ontario," Public Health Engineering Division, July 1940, Department of National Health fonds, RG 29, vol. 631, file 455–14–5, vol. 1, LAC; Anna Martin, "The Nobel Lands: The Cause of Nearby Cancer and Chronic Illnesses?" Parry Sound Project, 10 May 2017, 15–17, https://gumptioninc.org/wp-content/uploads/2017/05/Parry-Sound-Project-Website-Official-Compressed.pdf.

65 DIL Transcona Summary Record, section 4, 4, LAC.

66 "Historic Sites of Manitoba: Defence Industries Limited Cordite Plant," Manitoba Historical Society, http://www.mhs.mb.ca/docs/sites/corditeplant.shtml; "Cordite Trail," Winnipeg Trails Association, https://www.winnipegtrails.ca/trails-maps/cordite-trail/.

67 Norman E. Cooke, "Report on Preliminary Study of Pollution of West River at Brownsburg Works, Study No. 286," CIL Engineering Department, 11 May 1956, 2.

68 Cooke, "Report on Preliminary Study of Pollution of West River," 2–3, 17.

69 Jamie Benidickson, *The Culture of Flushing: A Social and Legal History of Sewage* (Vancouver: UBC Press, 2007), 270–74; Cooke, "Report on Preliminary Study of Pollution of West River," 2.

70 Souchen, *War Junk*, 79–110.

71 Chief Inspector of Explosives to G.M. Thomson, "Re: U.S. Ordnance Dept. Safety Bulletin #94," 4 June 1945; C.G. Smith to G.M. Thomson, "Decontamination & Desensitization of

Explosive Buildings Tests at Project #45, Miner Rubber Co. Granby," 8 June 1945; C.G. Smith to G. Ogilvie, 18 June 1945, 1–4; C.H. Magee to G.M. Thomson, 31 August 1945, all in General Engineering Company (Canada) fonds, F 2082–1–1–7, box 3, Archives of Ontario (AO).

72   Various progress reports and considerable correspondence between safety officers are available in "Decontamination + Desensitizing, 1945–1946," F 2082–1–1–7, box 3, AO.

73   See procedures and reports in A.L. Ouimet, "Burning Ground Procedures" (DIL: L & T Department, April 1944), Defence Industries Limited Files and Correspondence, 64A, box 18, CWM; "Disposal of Explosive Waste, 1946," R15655–1013–6-E, vol. 151, file 2, LAC.

74   Dickson, *Bomb Girls*, 246–47.

75   Smith, *Ajax*, 110.

76   "Minutes of the Decontamination Committee," 18 September 1945, 3–4, and 26 October 1945, 1, LAC; "Special Meeting on Decontamination," 11 October 1945, 1–3, RG 28, vol. 156, file 3-P-13, LAC.

77   C.G. Smith to G.M. Thomson, "Re: Explosion at the Destroying Ground," 23 July 1945, 1–2, F 2082–1–1–7, box 3, AO.

78   For example, see "Minutes of the Decontamination Committee," 20 December 1945, 4, LAC.

79   "Minutes of the Decontamination Committee," 5 October 1945, 6, LAC; G. Ogilvie to G.K. Sheils, "Re: St. Maurice Proof Range Decontamination," n.d., 1, RG 28, vol. 156, file 3-P-13, LAC.

80   "Minutes of the Decontamination Committee," 26 October 1945, 5, LAC.

81   "Minutes of the Decontamination Committee," 4 December 1945, 2–3, LAC.

82   "Minutes of the Decontamination Committee," 18 February 1946, 5–6, LAC.

83   "Minutes of the Decontamination Committee," 18 February 1946, 5, LAC.

84   "Minutes of the Decontamination Committee," 26 March 1946, 1–4, and 1 June 1946, 1–4, LAC.

85   Martin, "The Nobel Lands," 18–22.

86   Canada, *Disposal and Peacetime Use*, 25.

87   Smith, *Ajax*, 44–59.

88   Canada, *Disposal and Peacetime Use*, 20–21.

89   *Central Mortgage and Housing Corporation Annual Report to the Minister of Reconstruction and Supply for the Year 1948* (Ottawa: Department of Reconstruction and Supply, 1949), 25.

90   For more on "defense dependence" in the United States, see Ann Markusen and Joel Yudken, *Dismantling the Cold War Economy* (New York: Basic Books, 1992); Gordon Gauchat et al., "The Military Metropolis: Defense Dependence in U.S. Metropolitan Areas," *City and Community* 10, 1 (March 2011): 25–48.

91   Firestone, *Encouragement to Industrial Expansion*, 13.

92   H. Duncan Hall and C.C. Wrigley, *Studies of Overseas Supply* (London: HMSO, 1956), 46, 47–52.

93   Bothwell, "Defense and Industry in Canada," 113–19.

2

Military Dispossession
Alberta's Suffield Experimental Station, 1939–47

Brandon Davis

FEW AREAS ACROSS THE GLOBE have escaped the pressures of militarization.[1] Even nations with relatively small military establishments have long devoted significant portions of their territory to the needs of defence and security. With, for example, over 2.2 million hectares formally reserved for military purposes, and considerable amounts of additional territory and airspace utilized for training and strategic defence, Canada dedicates more space to military purposes than all but a handful of countries.[2] The bulk of Canadian defence lands have served the shifting needs of air warfare. Cold Lake, Goose Bay, and a host of smaller air bases collectively represent well over half of all designated defence land in Canada. The demands of air warfare transformed, not only the geographies of the air bases, but also developments in the Canadian North. As new vulnerabilities to air power emerged in the years after the Second World War, top military analysts and authorities began to see the North as a strategic barrier rather than an exposed flank. These perceptions prompted a holistic form of government intervention during the early Cold War, in which both Canadian and American demands drove a variety of military modernization projects in the North, including the construction of the Alaska Highway and the Distant Early Warning Line.[3] In contrast to the American West, these northern environments were treated, not as empty sacrifice areas for destructive military activities, but as strategic spaces for defence training and military modernization. Yet this does not mean that Canada had no military sacrifice zones. In many respects, Alberta's Suffield Experimental Station (SES), New Brunswick's Canadian Forces Base (CFB) Gagetown, and other defence establishments embody some of the signature characteristics of sacrifice zones and are indistinguishable from their more notorious counterparts in the American West.

How a nation popularly celebrated as a "peaceable kingdom" or an "unmilitary people" possesses some of the world's largest and most heavily used militarized landscapes is a question that, surprisingly, has not attracted much attention from scholars.[4] Indeed, as P. Whitney Lackenbauer and Matthew Farish contend, "the relationship between military activity and natural landscapes in Canada has received minimal scholarly attention."[5] Even one of the nation's most noteworthy domestic wartime contributions – the Second World War's highly ambitious British Commonwealth Air Training Plan – has "been largely ignored by historians."[6] Such neglect, however, should not be taken to indicate lack of importance. Arguably, one of Canada's most significant contributions to collective security and common defence has been Ottawa's willingness to put Canadian geography in the service of the military-industrial complex (MIC).

Broadly speaking, the MIC refers to the seemingly permanent mobilization of the government and economy for industrial warfare, and the MIC concept is particularly associated with the mid-twentieth-century buildup of US military forces. It draws attention to the deep political and economic ties forged between the military, federal and state bureaucracies, high-tech corporations, private and public research entities, and many other industrial forces. President Dwight Eisenhower and subsequent critics have warned that, in normalizing conflict and military preparedness as the industrial basis of the nation, the MIC has infused a permanent state of militarization in all elements of American social, economic, and political life. Rather than a marked event or aberration, war has become a underlying condition.

As detailed in the introductory chapter of this collection, academics from a variety of disciplinary backgrounds have skilfully examined the cultural, economic, and political dimensions of America's MIC. One thing perhaps not fully appreciated in this literature is how modern military-industrial power rests on the control of land and other natural resources. The rise of the MIC brought about, not only new formations of economic organization and political power, but also new forms of land segregation and use. As both the scale and lethality of weapons technologies and military tactics rapidly increased during and after the Second World War, so did the need for what was commonly described as "realistic," "operational," or "full-scale" training and testing grounds. In the United States, total military landholdings jumped by over 800 percent from the late 1930s to 1945 (from 3 million to more than 25 million acres). By the mid-1950s, the total exceeded 30 million acres – a figure that has remained relatively constant.[7] In serving as "a cornerstone of DOD's [Department of Defense] operations," these lands have become, as John Beck puts it, both "metaphorically and literally, the arsenal, proving ground, and disposal site for American military-industrial power."[8]

A major impetus driving the rise of the MIC was the potential of weapons of mass destruction. Not only did such weapons technologies destabilize the global political order but they also brought about a multitude of disruptions at local sites. A number of studies from a variety of disciplines have investigated the so-called nuclear-weapons complex, or the consortium of public and private defence, energy, security, industrial, and scientific interests tied to the research and development of nuclear weapons. These studies have done an impressive job of mapping the social and ecological consequences of the "internal nuclear colonization" and "radioactive nation-building" that have shaped the "secret alternative geographies" and "plutonium cities" of the nuclear-weapons complex.[9] Although perhaps less commonly known than its nuclear counterpart, a similar consortium of private and public interests has also been tied to the research and development of chemical and biological weapons (CBW). They too have formed an industrial complex of "scientific cities" and "secret alternative geographies," including prominent sites and research activities in Canada.[10]

Described by historian Donald Avery as the "nerve centre" for Canadian, British, and American CBW field testing and training, southeastern Alberta's Suffield Experimental Station (SES) is one of the world's largest, most secretive, oldest, and heavily utilized CBW proving grounds (Figure 2.1).[11] Due to its significant research contributions and unique land use demands, the SES represents an excellent place to examine both the possible origins of Canada's MIC and some of its social and environmental legacies. More specifically, by scrutinizing the policies and practices governing its initial establishment and continuing operations, this chapter offers a deeper look into how the MIC first took hold in Canada and was given a permanent spatial arrangement.

At the time of its establishment in 1941, the SES represented an unprecedented bounding and transformation of Canadian territory, in terms of both the scale of land involved and the way in which the government handled its acquisition. The urgent demands of war in the 1940s gave a select group of defence and scientific authorities the mandate to rapidly take control of a huge tract and clear away its inhabitants. The dispossessed landowners, who had held property or lease rights to over 230,000 agricultural acres, "were forced," as one displaced resident later recounted, "to give up their land, leave their homes, find somewhere to live, on very short notice." To many of the so-called Suffield evacuees, the government's heavy-handed approach constituted a "grave injustice."[12] All too often, the consequences of controversial military activities are blamed entirely on the exigencies of war. Suffield and other military sites, for example, have commonly been passed off as necessary products of wartime emergencies, "created," as a Suffield evacuee put it, "to assist in saving the world from Hitler's beasts."[13] What is harder to recognize, as this chapter demonstrates, are the various ways in which the exceptional conditions of war have become normalized at places such as Suffield and continue to shape spatial and power relations.

In this chapter, I rely on formerly classified government documents and first-hand accounts of evacuees to look at how a full-scale CBW field experimental station came into being in southeastern Alberta. I then detail how differing visions and portrayals of state-sponsored land reform shaped both history and

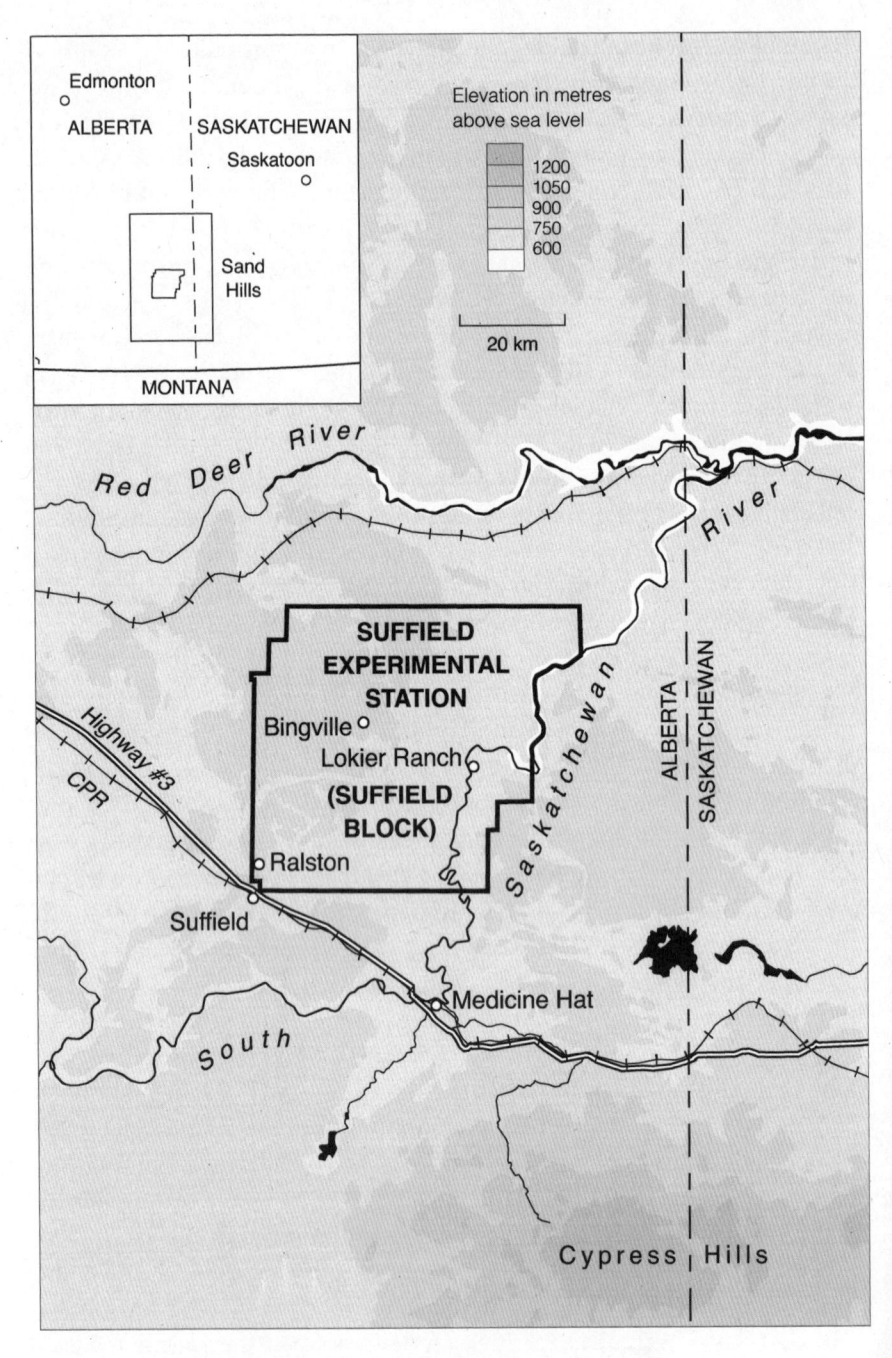

Figure 2.1 Suffield Experimental Station. | Cartographer Eric Leinberger.

landscapes in southeastern Alberta during the first half of the twentieth century. The next sections of the chapter analyze how military dispossession and compensation played out in the Suffield area, and the final parts examine how the demands of permanent war allowed defence interests to resist local opposition and solidify their long-term claims to land. Before delving into this case study on Suffield's establishment, I will provide a short overview of its larger operational history and some of its broader social and environmental legacies.

Suffield's Operational History and Impact

Many of the major advancements in modern warfare capabilities and technologies could not have been achieved without the use of "large areas of suitable land."[14] In the case of the SES, CBW research imperatives also spurred a number of significant developments, including a large multinational investment in land, resources, labour, and expertise. Furthermore, the research demands called for the construction of highly specialized labs, storage facilities, field-testing sites, airfields, and a general hospital. Perhaps most significantly, in the years immediately after the Second World War, military investment in the area culminated in the construction of the city of Ralston, which included ample amenities suitable for SES employees and their families.[15]

Drawing from Canadian military, industry, and universities, Suffield employed almost 600 people during the Second World War, including over 150 specially trained lab and field technicians as well as about 50 professional staff with backgrounds in chemistry, physics, meteorology, mathematics, pharmacology, pathology, bacteriology, physiology, entomology, veterinary science, and mechanical and chemical engineering.[16] Defence authorities believed that some of "the best scientific brains" from Canadian universities and industry were included among these recruits. This already robust workforce was further supplemented by close to a dozen scientists from the British Chemical Defence Experimental Station at Porton Down, England, as well as a "constant stream of notable British and American military scientists" who "became temporary members of the Suffield staff while work was being carried out on projects of special interest to them."[17] With the establishment of Canada's Defence Research Board (DRB) in April 1947, these largely ad hoc wartime arrangements for recruitment of expertise at the SES were formalized. Over the next few decades, Suffield's research activities attracted a large portion of funding from the DRB's extramural granting program, helping to turn this globally oriented CBW field-testing station into a central "campus" for Canada's version of the so-called military-industrial-academic complex.[18]

Beyond development activities, the formation and use of defence lands have also entailed enormous disruptions. This chapter details the rapid and forcible removal of approximately six hundred settlers in southeastern Alberta; yet, as noteworthy as their experiences may have been, they represent just some of the first casualties of Suffield's research and testing activities. During the open-air period of field trials, which lasted until the early 1970s, numerous extremely hazardous and unpredictable chemical, biological, and radioactive warfare agents were released, often in very large quantities, into the environment as part of routine weapons testing. Perhaps the one thing unifying all of Suffield's research and testing was the overriding element of risk. As a 1961 report noted, in "working with the most toxic chemical substances known to mankind," its staff "engaged daily in a far from normal situation," and the occasional injury or death was not entirely unexpected.[19] Despite stringent safety protocols, such dangers were not always contained within Suffield's boundaries. Shortly after it commenced operations, for example, reports surfaced of dead "cattle gassed by phosgene" in areas immediately adjacent to the site.[20] In the spring of 1944, wildlife officials also responded to reports of about two thousand migratory ducks found dead on and around the shore of a lake next to the SES, "with locals noting the odor of gas in the vicinity of the lake [being] very strong."[21]

As the scale of CBW technologies dramatically increased in the 1950s and 1960s, field trials extended "well beyond the boundaries of SES."[22] In the mid-1960s, for example, American CBW scientists found that the areas "over distances of 100 to 200 miles downwind" to the east of Suffield offered ideal "flat open terrain analogous to that of North Central Europe" to conduct biological weapons field trials.[23] Preliminary studies suggested that these ambitious trials would covertly expose "about 500,000 civilians per trial out to a distance of 250 miles from the source," including low levels of expected exposure in Saskatoon, Moose Jaw, and Regina.[24] Notably, these trials used aerosols of *Bacillus gobligi*, a simulant of anthrax, along with fluorescent particles of zinc cadmium sulfide as a tracer material. Both were believed to be innocuous at the time, but years later many people who learned that they were unknowingly exposed during such secret open-air trials believe that these "simulants as well as select agents had caused previously unexplained illnesses."[25]

As disturbing as such incidents and revelations may be, such hazardous military activities were not uncommon during the period. They may not always be easy to access, but similar occurrences of risk, exposure, contamination, and waste disposal are fundamental parts of the histories of other military installations devoted to the testing and development of weapons of mass destruction and comparable activities. Not only did the toxic warfare agents released at these sites potentially pose dangers to nearly every living creature that happened to come into contact with them, but they also contributed to a slow, often imperceptible "environmental violence" against both human and non-human populations.[26]

Investigations into the environmental impact of military activities have made significant contributions to our understanding of contaminated landscapes, wildlife conservation, military environmentalism, and other prevalent issues.[27] In looking at such important contemporary concerns, most of these studies have concentrated on the present or the recent past. Often lacking in this growing body of research is a clear understanding of the origins of militarized environments or how we got to where we are. Instead of focusing on "interpretations and practices in the present of landscapes constituted by past military activities," this chapter approaches the study of a contaminated militarized environment from the opposite end of its development cycle.[28]

Arriving at Suffield

Suffield's initial formation stemmed primarily from the strategic problem of air defence, particularly against chemical weapons. In the early years of the Second World War, opinions seemed "to be quite unanimous that when chemical warfare does break out," aircraft would "undoubtedly play a very large part."[29] Due to "a lack of space," British chemical warfare scientists "had not been able to test potential weapons and methods of neutralizing them, except on a small scale."[30] Experiments with large aircraft using real chemical agents simply could not be undertaken in the British Isles. Consequently, finding a suitable place "for carrying out C.W. [chemical warfare] trials on a scale of the same order as Actual C.W. operations in war" became a matter of "major importance."[31]

According to Britain's chief chemical warfare officer, E.L. Davies, the "chief requirement" for a large-scale field-testing station was a "practically flat" 2,500-square-mile area that was "devoid of population," that boasted "suitable landing grounds for large aircrafts," was near "a convenient railway siding," could "be traversed by army vehicles," and did not "experience any freak meteorological conditions" or contain large rivers or thick forests.[32] Despite the apparent difficulties involved in finding a site that satisfied all these requirements, British weapons scientists remained optimistic. Whereas "it was realised no such area could be found in the British Isles," it was believed that "one of the Dominions, (say Canada), could easily meet the requirements laid down."[33]

The British government's initial inquiry "as to the possibility of suitable ground being made available in Canada for the conduct of larger scale C.W. experiments" received highly favourable responses from leading scientific and defence authorities in Canada. Fortunately for the United Kingdom, not only did Canada possess attractive geographic assets, but it had also been primed, as Avery describes it, to "assume a major role in allied chemical warfare research, development, production, and testing."[34] Early warnings about the threat of biological warfare from Frederick Banting, Canada's first Nobel laureate, and other influential scientists helped to assure that Canada's military and scientific establishments would be receptive to the demands of both chemical and biological warfare. By the time Britain made its request for an experimental area, scientists from Canada's National Research Council (NRC), which provided federal support for military research in Canada prior to the formation of the DRB in 1947, had already established close working relations with British scientists at the Porton Down chemical and biological warfare research centre.

Although officials and scientists from both countries played important roles, one person, above all, made the SES a reality: E.L. Davies, Britain's former chief chemical warfare officer and Suffield's first chief superintendent. Often credited as the "Father of the Establishment and the 'first settler' in Suffield," Davies spearheaded the movement to establish a full-scale field-testing station in Canada; he personally guided "all of the spade work in building up the organization at Suffield" and, in exercising "all functions of command" there, he played a central part in the design and implementation of several hundred CBW field trials during the war.[35] After the war, he also played a pivotal role in pushing for the establishment of the DRB, and he served in its top leadership positions until the early 1960s, when he and his wife retired in their home country of Wales.[36]

Over two decades earlier, in October 1940, Davies arrived in Canada with the message that the "need for a large-scale experimental field was now of the greatest urgency."[37] Soon after, a "paper survey" of possible sites was initiated.[38] Under the rationale that a 2,500-square-mile area could "only be obtained where climatic conditions are abnormal," authorities shifted their focus to the semi-arid west.[39] In both the United States and Canada, the supposed emptiness and underdevelopment of western landscapes made them attractive targets for a variety of federal development schemes. In the case of a major chemical warfare proving ground, the situation was no different. In "spite of the large areas involved," defence surveyors in Ottawa confidently believed that Davies's exacting specifications could "be easily met in Saskatchewan."[40]

With such advice in mind, Davies set out west with representatives from both the NRC and the Department of National Defence (DND) to investigate "certain barren areas in Canada as to suitability as a site for a full scale C.W. Experimental Station."[41] Once in the prairie provinces, they gathered figures and information regarding land characteristics, ownership patterns, and costs. After deciding upon the general location, they instructed local surveyors to select "the most nearly level" areas they could find, and then, from the midpoint of these level areas, lay out larger fifty by fifty square-mile blocks of land for further investigation.[42] As shown in Figure 2.2, this process led to the demarcation of "two very

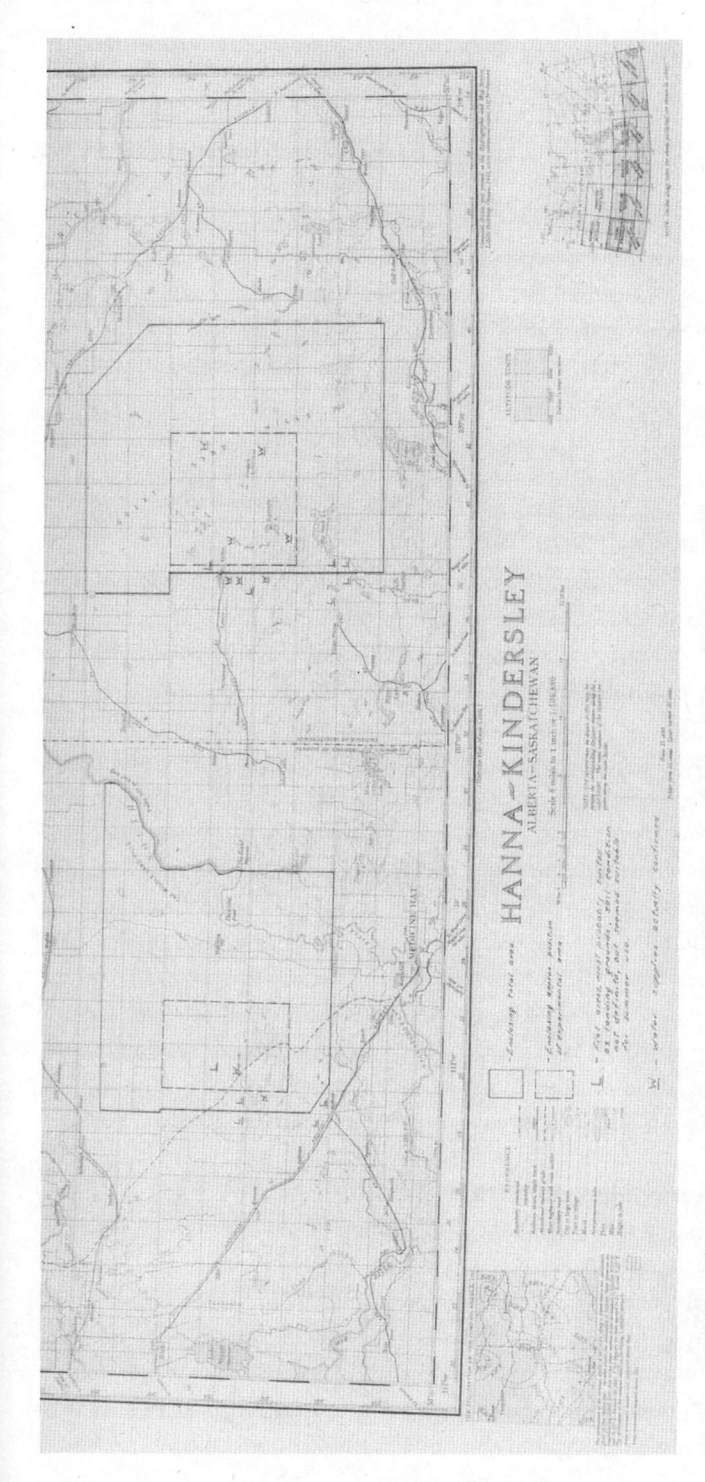

Figure 2.2 The final choices for an experimental station in Canada. | *Hanna-Kindersley, Alberta-Saskatchewan,* 1940, image 2387, LAC reel C-5002, RG 24, Library and Archives Canada.

suitable properties," one in southeastern Alberta and one in southwestern Saskatchewan.[43]

Both sites were "very desirable for full scale C.W. trials" and were indistinguishable "from a technical point of view."[44] With initial estimates suggesting that the purchase of land and the removal of residents in Alberta would cost less than the more densely settled Saskatchewan alternative, the Alberta block became regarded as the only practical option.[45] To expedite the necessary approval from the government, Canadian officials "strongly recommended that authority be granted immediately to proceed with the project in order that essential trials may be carried out in May 1941."[46] While these administrative wheels were set in motion, residents in the Suffield Block remained largely in the dark about the newly hatched plans of the Canadian and British governments.

Mobilizing History along Strict Lines

Official military accounts have consistently asserted that the Suffield development converted over 700,000 unproductive acres to the cause of defence and security, while simultaneously rescuing hundreds of impoverished farm families from their futile attempts at scratching a living on land deemed "worthless from an agricultural point of view."[47] This notion was based on the impression that, at the time of the DND takeover, most residents had already abandoned the area and that the few who remained were in destitute circumstances. Instead of a threat to their livelihoods, "the Canadian government should have been regarded as a great benefactor by many of these people by helping them establish themselves in more prosperous agricultural areas."[48] As one official military publication declared, it was "a welcome decision taken out of their hands."[49] Such oft-repeated claims have appeared, ad nauseam, in nearly every official military account of Suffield, and they stand as the accepted interpretation in news articles, government studies, websites, academic theses, and other works dealing with the history of the SES.[50] As authoritative and influential as these sources may be, they fall well short of capturing southeastern Alberta's complex environmental history.

The military's arrival in southeastern Alberta during the early 1940s followed colonial patterns of displacement and resettlement that had marked the country for well over a century. Among other things, settler visions of arid western landscapes as barren, uninhabited lands that could be had for the taking erased histories and ongoing practices of violence, conquest, dispossession, and occupation.[51] As bison numbers collapsed in the late 1800s, disease spread, and the treaty and Indian reserve system was imposed by the federal government across the country, the Siksikaitsitapi and neighbouring Indigenous groups were forced off their homelands in the shortgrass prairies of southern Alberta and Saskatchewan during the 1870s and 1880s.[52] In the Suffield Block, cattle and sheep grazers moved in and appropriated the recently inhabited Indigenous land until 1909, when the area was opened for homesteading. The presence of a railroad siding in the town of Suffield, as well as the region's supposed potential for irrigation, made the Suffield Block particularly attractive to settlers. From 1909 to 1921, over two thousand farms were established in the block, making it one of the most densely homesteaded areas in southeastern Alberta.[53] Around the town of Suffield, the British-based Canadian Wheatland Company embarked on what one local commentator described as "the most auspicious undertakings ever attempted in Canada," investing approximately $11 million in farming and irrigation works in the area.[54]

The misguided and failed attempts of European settlers to develop small crop-based farming communities on the shortgrass prairies of western Saskatchewan and eastern Alberta during the early twentieth century have been well documented elsewhere, as has the poverty, individual suffering, and environmental ruin left in the wake of these famously misbegotten colonial ventures.[55] Less well recognized are the local adaptations made in the years immediately following this ruin and destitution. Settlers in the densely homesteaded Suffield Block may have suffered some of the earliest and most severe hardships due to a series of localized droughts in the mid-to-late 1910s. But, in the years that followed, some of these same settlers became model examples of how to adapt farming and grazing practices to arid conditions.

In 1921, settlers and provincial authorities began to adopt plans to reduce the region's population and convert small-scale homestead farms "into large scale, self-sufficient ranching-farming" operations, with the bulk of these initial efforts focused on the Suffield area. Whereas most early homesteaders had moved away, some remained.[56] These so-called stickers, according to government assessments at the time, were just the "class of farmer that the area requires." Planners treated these "most desirable settlers" with particular regard, seeking out their knowledge and recommendations and making special efforts to ensure that they had "the first opportunity to use the vacant lands."[57]

The transition from small-crop farms to large-scale mixed farming and grazing began in earnest during the late 1920s after the passage of a law that put the Suffield Block, then known as the Tilley East Area, under the stewardship of a provincially appointed land management board. By 1935, this board – considered the predecessor of the Special Areas Board of Alberta – had, through land exchanges and confiscation, taken control of up to 80 percent of Tilley East. After making a number of reclamation efforts, the board sold and leased back "this land to the few viable rancher-farmers left in Tilley East and create[d] community pastures out of the rest."[58] By 1940, over 150,000 acres had been successfully converted to grazing and mixed-grazing operations. This was still in progress at the time of the military takeover. According to John W. McLachlan, a former Tilley East resident, many settlers "were just getting into livestock and mechanical farming" and "could see a future ahead."[59]

To defence surveyors, Tilley East may have seemed the perfect "poor crop" area to meet their needs, but in their efforts to highlight that it was "very poor agriculturally" and sparsely populated, E.L. Davies and others saw mainly what they wanted to see.[60] In fact, the sparseness was not an indicator of unproductivity, but rather a sign of adaption to local environmental conditions. Most of the settlers, moreover, were not the last remnants of failed settlement polices, but the chief benefactors of a provincially sponsored, twenty-year-long land-use rehabilitation plan. That the formation and administration of Alberta's Special Areas is widely seen as one of the most successful state-sponsored adaptions to arid conditions in North America further suggests that, instead of a life of indigence and failure, most settlers in the Suffield Block probably "had a reasonably assured future" prior to the DND arrival.[61] Thus, Suffield's history follows strict lines, with official boundaries unofficially marking the borders between two distinct and irreconcilable histories of land rehabilitation. The land within the SES boundaries is considered "useless for any normal agricultural purposes."[62] But immediately outside these boundaries, the land has sustained a viable mixed farming and grazing economy for generations.

The Suffield Expropriation

Historically, Canada has been very generous in supporting development interests, granting land acquisition powers to "virtually anyone that in meeting a public need might require land."[63] Such powers have been highly accommodating to the needs of contemporary warfare and national defence, often at the direct expense of Indigenous people's claims to land and other natural resources.[64] Whereas purchase or lease appear to have been the DND's preferred method of acquisition, when such measures were not convenient, defence officials also relied on the government's extensive statutory expropriation powers. Typically understood as a last resort, in the case of Suffield and other mid-century defence land acquisitions, the sovereign power for expropriation was frequently employed as a blunt instrument. In the case of Suffield, the decision to take such a heavy-handed approach was largely a matter of military expediency and seems to have been made with little deliberation. Under pressure from leading UK defence and scientific authorities, the Canadian state – at both the federal and provincial levels – operated with relentless efficiency.

The official notice of the expropriation, which had been filed under the authority of the Expropriation Act, was registered on 31 May 1941. During the first week of June, Royal Canadian Mounted Police officers served notices to local landowners, which stated that they were "hereby required to quit, vacate, and deliver up possession ... on or before the 30th of June, A.D. 1941 ... lands and premises as are occupied by you or are in your possession."[65] Suffield officials and personnel offered to help the evacuees move out, but they also kept a close eye on their activities. Defence planners anticipated "difficulties ... with the local inhabitants" during the initial stages of operation.[66] The option of obtaining "possession by forcible means" was discussed but not recommended.[67] To help deal with potential problems, officials attempted to recruit "a man of tact and experience as well as a sound disciplinarian."[68] They also took care to ensure that the whole area was "properly policed until actually taken over for Experimental purposes."[69] Predictably, unexpected encounters with suspicious police officers became one of the most commonly reported experiences described by the evacuees as they moved out.[70]

These various measures had their desired effect. Within thirty days of receiving their expropriation notices, the evacuees removed most buildings, machinery, fences, and other salvageable materials from the area – many of which ended up just outside the new boundaries of the SES.[71] As would be expected, most found the experience quite unpleasant. Many resented being ordered, not asked, to leave. Nor did they understand the rush to get them out. Shock and disbelief were commonly reported.[72]

Expelling the residents was the DND's first challenge. The government still had to settle compensation claims for the expropriated lands and other properties. Military accounts typically note that the "farmers who had to be evacuated were given fair compensation." The farmers themselves, however, felt that the compensation "was ridiculous" and that it "served one purpose only, that of getting possession of land and removal of fences, buildings and livestock, but contained no moral or social value in the way of re-establishment credit to purchase land and feed for livestock for winter and seed for the following year's operations, and a loss for one year's operations."[73] Given the contentious nature of the transaction, such differences in opinion are not surprising, especially because there was a wide gap between the evacuees' asking price and what they actually received. They had initially asked the government for a minimum of $10 per acre and $6 per acre for crops sown, as well as the full value of other improvements. On average, the DND ended up paying $1 per acre for private lands and 50 cents an acre for leased lands. Payments for improvements, such as wells, were also decidedly undervalued.[74]

The DND compensation may have been well below the landowners' valuations, but the payments provide only one indication of the government's handling of the expropriation. Assessing the broader consequences of military dispossession at Suffield is more challenging than identifying possible discrepancies over compensation. Many evacuees scattered across North America after being pushed out, leaving few traces of their experience.[75] However, the varying accounts of those who remained in the region offer glimpses into how military dispossession shaped the lives of evacuees.[76]

Some residents managed to start a new life after being forced to move. For example, Eliza Lokier lost a prosperous thirteen-thousand-acre ranch. After recovering from the shock, she put her settlement money to the purchase of a home north of Medicine Hat. With the help of relatives, she used lumber salvaged from the ranch to build a barn and a hennery, which allowed her to raise horses and some cows, and to carry on a modest egg business in the later years of her life.[77] For Eliza's husband, Thomas, however, the loss of the ranch was an altogether different matter. He and his family had spent nearly forty years developing their land into "a fine ranch and beauty spot on the prairie." According to his son William, its abrupt loss was "a terrible wrench ... one from which Tom never fully recovered." After vowing never to live in Alberta again, Thomas eventually settled in his own home in Victoria, British Columbia, but could not understand why "a block producing range was chosen in a country with millions of acres of wild land that would never produce at all." Although he did reestablish himself, for him, and probably for other evacuees, no amount of compensation "could pay for the work, thought and love which had gone into the development of the homes they were forced to leave."[78]

Others were less fortunate than the Lokiers. The expropriation left rancher Jack Lust and his family not only resentful but also in dire economic straits. Like the Lokiers, the Lusts ran a ranch in the Suffield Block, although it was much smaller at about a thousand acres. In a February 1942 letter to Prime Minister Mackenzie King, Lust wrote that he had received $1,608.25 in compensation, though he had originally paid $2,725.00 for the ranch years earlier, something the defence real estate advisor had openly acknowledged at the time of the transaction. After being forced off his land in less than thirty days, Lust had to sell his livestock to raise enough money to buy new property and apparently went into debt in the process. By the time he wrote to King, he claimed to have "lost what little I got together in years of hard work." As he explained,

> We are living on next to nothing now the children are out of school now they haven't enough cloath [sic] to go to school in as much as I hate to do it but I can't help it if you don't do something by the end of the month will have to take the family and turn em over to the police.

He wished that King would "realize that I've made a living until this was forced on me by a Government which I been loyal to and supported." He ended on a bitter note – he had "come to the conclusion that if this is the kind of justice and freedom we are fighting for we might as well quit."[79]

The Demands of Wartime Emergencies

Most wartime military endeavours are predicated on sacrifice, and the establishment of the SES was no different in this respect. Instead of lives lost or harmed in battle, people were displaced and livelihoods were disrupted and lost. As many evacuees discovered, standing in the way of military developments was not an easy position, especially during a wartime emergency. In the years after the war, some sought recognition and redress for their losses. "Now that the war is over and the day of adjustment of wrongs committed under the strain of war is at hand," a 1946 resolution noted, "I take this opportunity to draw the attention of our Government and the people of Canada to the grievance of the evacuees of the British Block. We refuse to believe that it was the wishes of the British and Canadian people that any individual should assume loss from any national emergency of such great importance."[80]

From the perspective of the British and Canadian chemical weapons scientists and defence authorities, getting a major testing installation off the ground in a relatively affordable and timely manner must have seemed a considerable achievement. If, at least in part, this timeliness and affordability came at the expense of the people who had once lived on the site, most authorities would have pointed out that war demands sacrifice and concurred that the benefits of the field-testing station made it worthwhile.

For their part, most evacuees appear to have understood that they were required to make sacrifices for the war effort. Even in their protests, they took care not to blame the government outright, emphasizing instead that "owing to the urgency of war preparation, a grave injustice in the matter of compensation was inadvertently committed against the evacuated settlers of what is known as the 'British Block.'" Yet, though many may have understood the nature of the situation and, like Jack Lust, "been loyal to and supported" the government, they also believed that this same government would be responsive to their needs and ultimately protect their interests. Though critical of government actions, Lust's appeal to Prime Minister King and similar petitions also displayed a certain faith in Ottawa's ability to recognize and address alleged wrongdoings.[81]

For Lust and other evacuees, the government's lack of responsiveness was most troubling. Under the management of the Special Areas Board, farmers and ranchers in the Suffield area had grown accustomed to working with local officials, who not only valued their experience and knowledge, but who also made special provisions on their behalf. Under the new wartime regime, however, they were rapidly demoted from the "most desirable" class of settlers to an inconvenient problem that needed a quick fix.[82] Above all, the Suffield development signalled a new type of relationship between the federal government and Canadians, one in which the "urgency of war" superseded normal government priorities and democratic controls, making authorities far less responsive to the public interest.

The Demands of Permanent War

Both the evacuees and the government were well aware that the demands of war could make controversial actions easier to implement. There was little opportunity for public input at the time of Suffield's acquisition, but if given a chance to weigh in, most Canadians would probably have recognized that the urgent need to defend against pressing threats pushed the government to ignore the appeals of residents and take a heavy-handed approach in removing them. It is harder to explain why, after the war ended, Ottawa displayed little willingness to address the possible "wrongs committed under the strain of war" at places such as Suffield.[83] War undoubtedly makes demands and requires sacrifices, yet in Canada, some of these sacrifices have seemingly occurred with minimal recognition, debate, or redress.

As the evacuees probably did not perceive at the time, the imperatives that drove developments such as Suffield would not disappear when peace came in 1945. Although many wartime projects were shut down when hostilities ended, the threats that spurred the creation of the SES merely expanded in the years after the war, as both the scale and lethality of CBW technologies increased. If anything, Canadian authorities were ahead of the curve in recognizing that unorthodox weapons of mass destruction would shape global defence and security in the postwar period. In an August 1945 letter to Alberta premier E.C. Manning, for example, outgoing defence minister Andrew McNaughton insisted that it had become "very clear that our future safety depends at least in some considerable measure on the continued investigation and experiments in these fields [of CBW] so that we may know definitely what may be in prospect should unscrupulous forces seek to break out against world security." McNaughton believed that the SES held a "unique and far-reaching importance," and that its continued operation on "a permanent post war basis" was "one of the essential means by which Canada may contribute effectively to the system of collective security."[84]

In taking a longer view of defence developments, we can see that the circumstances involving Suffield are more complex than a government failing to acknowledge possible wrongdoings committed during a crisis. It may initially have regarded the SES as a temporary militarized landscape "formed during the emergency period of war," but with its mission so closely tied to one of the primary impetuses driving the rise of the MIC, the facility quickly outgrew such characterizations. At Suffield, questions linger, not only about the wartime exigencies, but also about how the ongoing demands of defence and security have shaped spatial and power relations. In other words, a large part of the reason for the unwillingness to address the possible "wrongs committed under the strain of war" is that, at places such as Suffield, "the urgency of war preparation" has become a permanent, underlying condition.[85]

Perhaps if the SES had closed down at the end of the war, or the threat of chemical and biological weapons had subsided, more opportunities could have arisen to debate the rapid and forcible manner in which the area had been commandeered. At Suffield, however, the postwar period was marked, not by reparation, but by entrenchment. Instead of shutting its doors, the SES greatly expanded. At a time when Ottawa was working to transition to peacetime conditions, officials were also devoting considerable sums from the Canadian defence budget to the construction of permanent world-class facilities at Suffield.[86] Over the next few decades, the ongoing need of Canadian, British, and American weapons scientists for a large-scale CBW testing site, along with the stable funding from the DRB extramural program, helped to turn the SES into a global centre of the military-industrial apparatus.

Far from fading away after the war years, disputes over land claims in the Suffield region reached peak levels. As defence interests were making a case for "the urgent need for Suffield as a post-war CW Field Testing Station," the Province of Alberta began to reassert its own claims to the Suffield Block. "Now that hostilities have ceased," Premier Manning wrote to the defence minister in September 1945, "we feel that the area required for the continuation of experimental work might be reduced in size which would make available to the Province portions of this tract of land which are required for local purposes which the Government considers important."[87] A main issue, according to SES officials, was that the Province "looked upon the [Suffield] project as only a temporary wartime measure" and was "reluctant to tie up the area with consequent prevention of other possible developments."[88]

It was clear to many Albertans that the Suffield Block was not the hopelessly unproductive area that defence officials had made it out to be during the war, but defence authorities did not suddenly become any more interested in understanding the local history of the land in the postwar period either. Perhaps the only change was that their haphazard "simplification of local economies and environments" appeared to grow firmer over time.[89] Through such sustaining myths, Suffield became recognized not as a temporary landscape of wartime controversy and militarized exception but as a natural outgrowth of ongoing security imperatives and collective defence efforts – a place widely accepted as part of the natural environment of the nation.[90]

Epilogue

Undoubtedly, far worse injustices occurred during the Second World War than the rapid and forcible eviction of some six hundred settlers in southeastern Alberta. Even in the context of wartime events in Canada, their plight looks relatively mild in comparison to that of over twenty-three thousand Japanese Canadians who were interned and relocated or of the approximately three thousand Canadian soldiers who were exposed to chemical warfare agents at the SES. Far from being uncommon, moreover, dispossession and displacement are a cornerstone of Canadian nation building, tactics that were still employed with relative frequency during the twentieth century.[91] The Suffield acquisition, by comparison, stands out, not because of its extraordinary injustice, but because it was one of the first cases in which the principle of sacrificing both landscapes and livelihoods to the higher needs of security- and defence-related developments was put into practice on a large scale.

The Suffield expropriation may have had few precedents in its day, but its forced displacements, disruptions, and relocations would soon epitomize the way in which a large segment of Canada's contemporary defence lands came into being. Some of the techniques of acquisition and legitimation that were first worked out at Suffield were applied – often by the same defence officials – during the development of other prominent defence- and security-related projects over the next fifteen years. The grievances of the Suffield Block evacuees would soon be shared by members of the expropriated Stoney Point First Nation reserve in Ontario, the displaced farmer-lumberers of Gagetown, New Brunswick, the uprooted trappers at Cold Lake, Alberta, and the nearly one hundred Inuit who were forced to relocate to the High Artic in the mid-1950s during the height of Cold War tensions.[92] Far from remaining a novelty or an aberration, the principle of sacrificing people and places to the higher needs of military-industrial power quickly became a defining characteristic of Canada's mid-twentieth-century buildup of defence lands.

Notes

1   In this chapter, the term "militarization" loosely refers to a diverse set of social processes that extend military objectives, approaches, and values into non-military realms of social life. For further discussion, see Rachel Woodward, "Looking at Military Landscapes: Definitions and Approaches," in *The Evolving Boundaries of Defence: An Assessment of Recent Shifts in Defence Activities,* ed. Renaud Bellaius (Bingley, UK: Emerald Group, 2014), 141–55.

2 National Defence, *Defence Energy and Environment Strategy, 2020–2023* (Ottawa: Department of National Defence, 2020), 1; Treasury Board of Canada, "Directory of Real Federal Property: National Defence," http://www.tbs-sct.gc.ca/dfrp-rbif/home-accueil-eng.aspx. For a broader overview of global defence landholdings, see Rachel Woodward, *Military Geographies* (Malden, MA: Blackwell, 2004), 13–20.

3 P. Whitney Lackenbauer and Matthew Farish, "The Cold War on Canadian Soil: Militarizing a Northern Environment," *Environmental History* 12, 4 (2007): 924; Ken Coates et al., *Arctic Front: Defending Canada in the Far North* (Toronto: Dundurn, 2010); P. Whitney Lackenbauer and Matthew Farish, "High Modernism in the Arctic: Planning Frobisher Bay and Inuvik," *Journal of Historical Geography* 35, 3 (2009): 517–44.

4 This chapter focuses on the real property managed by the Canadian Department of National Defence. For more in-depth discussions over what constitutes a militarized landscape, as well as acknowledgment that such environments can encompass a wide variety of potential sites and uses, see R.H. Edgington, *Range Wars: The Environmental Contest for White Sands Missile Range* (Lincoln: University of Nebraska Press, 2014), 3–5; Chris Pearson, "Researching Militarized Landscapes: A Literature Review on War and the Militarization of the Environment," *Landscape Research* 37, 1 (2012): 115–33; Chris Pearson, Peter Coates, and Tim Cole, eds., *Militarized Landscapes: From Gettysburg to Salisbury Plain* (London: Continuum, 2010); Woodward, "Looking at Military Landscapes," 141–55.

5 Lackenbauer and Farish, "The Cold War on Canadian Soil," 920. Since publishing this statement, Lackenbauer, Farish, and others have examined the topic more closely. Among others, see P. Whitney Lackenbauer, *Battle Grounds: The Canadian Military and Aboriginal Lands* (Vancouver: UBC Press, 2007); Matthew Evenden, *Allied Power: Mobilizing Hydro-electricity during Canada's Second World War* (Toronto: University of Toronto Press, 2015); Alex Souchen, *War Junk: Munitions Disposal and Postwar Reconstruction in Canada* (Vancouver: UBC Press, 2020).

6 Allan Newell, "A Plan for the Future: The Legacies of the British Commonwealth Air Training Plan in Canada's Prairie Provinces" (master's thesis, University of British Columbia, 2007), 3.

7 103 Cong. Rec. 5520 (1957); Brandon Davis, "Defending the Nation, Protecting the Land: Executive Power and the Militarization of American Public Lands," in *Proving Grounds: Military Landscapes, Weapons Testing, and the Environmental Impact of U.S. Bases,* ed. Edwin A. Martini (Seattle: University of Washington Press, 2016), 19–41.

8 John Beck, *Dirty Wars: Landscape, Power, and Waste in Western American Literature* (Lincoln: University of Nebraska Press, 2009), 4; Jack Utter et al., *Military Land Withdrawals: Some Legal History and a Case Study,* College of Agriculture Paper 541 (Tucson: University of Arizona, 1985), 48.

9 Valerie L. Kuletz, *The Tainted Desert: Environmental and Social Ruin in the American West* (New York: Routledge, 1998), 5–9; Joseph Masco, *Nuclear Borderlands: The Manhattan Projects in Post-Cold War New Mexico* (Princeton: Princeton University Press, 2006), 337; Kate Brown, *Plutopia: Nuclear Families, Atomic Cities, and the Great Soviet and American Plutonium Disasters* (New York: Oxford University Press, 2013), 3.

10 Studies on the CBW complex include Donald Avery, *Pathogens for War: Biological Weapons, Canadian Life Scientists, and North American Biodefence* (Toronto: University of Toronto Press, 2013); Brian Balmer, *Britain and Biological Warfare: Expert Advice and Science Policy, 1930–65* (New York: Palgrave, 2001); Jeanne Guillemin, *Biological Weapons: From the Invention of State-Sponsored Programs to Contemporary Bioterrorism* (New York: Columbia University Press, 2005); Edmund Russell, *War and Nature: Fighting Humans and Insects with Chemicals from World War I to Silent Spring* (Cambridge:

Cambridge University Press, 2001); Jonathan B. Tucker, *War of Nerves: Chemical Warfare from World War I to Al-Qaeda* (New York: Pantheon, 2006); Mark Wheelis, Lajos Rózsa, Malcolm Dando, eds., *Deadly Cultures: Biological Weapons since 1945* (Cambridge: Harvard University Press, 2006).

11 Donald Avery, *The Science of War: Canadian Scientists and Allied Military Technology during the Second World War* (Toronto: University of Toronto Press, 1998), 124.

12 William Lokier, "Mr. and Mrs. W.R. (Bill) Lokier," 1907–77, 5, Bill and Gertrude Lokier History, William and Gertrude Lokier fonds, M2007.2.4, Esplanade Archives, Medicine Hat, Alberta (Esplanade); John W. McLachlan, "A Letter to the Prime Minister of Canada and Members of Parliament," 1946 reprinted in Grace Roth, ed., *Prairie Crucible: Roads of History, 1891–1941–1991* (Medicine Hat, AB: Prairie Sod History Book Society, 1991), 104–5, Esplanade.

13 "History of British Block," 1993, Dan and Marion Jensen fonds, M2009.20.2 and M2009.20.3, Esplanade.

14 Order-in-Council P.C. 1/6687, 26 August 1941, 112.352009 (D51), Directorate of History and Heritage, National Defence Headquarters, Ottawa (DHH). Donald Avery's work offers especially strong overviews of Canada's contributions to the research and development of CBW. See his *Pathogens for War* and *The Science of War*.

15 N.J.W. Smith to Q.M.G., 4 August 1945, 4354–2, C-5002, Library and Archives Canada, Ottawa (LAC); G.M. Bowes to Deputy Minister (C), 6 September 1944, 4354–2, C-5002, LAC; Department of National Defence (DND) and Suffield Experimental Station, *Suffield Experimental Station, 1941–1961* (Ralston, AB: Suffield Experimental Station, 1961), 18–37, https://bac-lac.on.worldcat.org/oclc/506120578; D.J. Goodspeed, *A History of the Defence Research Board of Canada* (Ottawa: Queen's Printer, 1958), 146.

16 "Progress Report for the Experimental Station, Suffield, Alberta," 4/1-9/30 1947, 91/364, DHH; DND and Suffield Experimental Station, *Suffield Experimental Station, 1941–1961*, 35; Goodspeed, *A History of the Defence Research Board*, 146–47; Experimental Station Suffield, "Information Brief," n.d., 4354–26–1–1, C-5013, LAC; Experimental Station Suffield, "Proposed Press Release," n.d., Records of the Chemical Warfare Service, RG 175, Station Series 1942–5, 680.2 Canada, box 179, National Archives at College Park, Maryland (NACP).

17 Experimental Station Suffield, "Proposed Press Release," n.d., NACP.

18 Matthew S. Wiseman, "Canadian Scientists and Military Research in the Cold War, 1947–60," *Canadian Historical Review* 100, 3 (September 2019): 439–63; Stuart W. Leslie, *The Cold War and American Science: The Military-Industrial-Academic Complex at MIT and Stanford* (New York: Columbia University Press, 1993).

19 DND and Suffield Experimental Station, *Suffield Experimental Station, 1941–1961*, 10, 43; V.L. Dixon, "Compensation for Injury or Death Resulting from the Carrying out of Official Duties," RG 24, DRBS 356–4–31/0, LAC; "Regulations and Order Injury or Death-General," RG 24, DRES 356–1, vol. 1, LAC.

20 O. Maass, "Court of Inquiry: Injury to Cattle," 15 November 1943, 4354–26–8, C-5015, LAC.

21 Jim Mcghee to E.S. Huestic, 16 April 1944, 4354–26–8–5, C-5015, LAC.

22 DRB, "Canadian Participation in Project Deseret WEST SIDE II," 22 April 1965, RG 24, DRBS 1800–60/141–1, LAC.

23 H.J. Fish, "Details of Deseret Test Centre Programme WEST SIDE II and Arguments for Carrying It Out at SES," 5 February 1965, RG 24, DRBS 1800–60/141–1, LAC.

24 "Brief of WEST SIDE II Proposals," 18 February 1965, RG 24, DRBS 1800–60/141–1, LAC.

25 Leonard A. Cole, "Open-Air Biowarfare Testing and the Evolution of Values," *Health Security* 14, 5 (2016): 318; pages 315–22 of this article give an informative summary of past testing activities and current studies on possible health impacts.

26 Rob Nixon, *Slow Violence and the Environmentalism of the Poor* (Cambridge, MA: Harvard University Press, 2011); Joseph Masco, "Mutant Ecologies: Radioactive Life in Post–Cold War New Mexico," *Cultural Anthropology* 19, 4 (2004): 517–50; Linda Nash, *Inescapable Ecologies: A History of Environment, Disease, and Knowledge* (Berkeley: University of California Press, 2006).

27 For overviews of studies on militarized environments, see Pearson, "Researching Militarized Landscapes"; Rachel Woodward, "Military Landscapes Agendas and Approaches for Future Research," *Progress in Human Geography* 38, 1 (2013): 40–61.

28 Woodward, "Military Landscapes Agendas," 45.

29 I.M. Rabinowitch to J.C. Murchie, 1 March 1940, RG 77, 32–1–12, vol. 2, box 69, 87–88–104, LAC.

30 Experimental Station Suffield, "Information Brief," LAC.

31 "Notes on Specifications of an Experimental C.W. Base in Canada," 7 November 1940, 4354–2, C-5002, LAC; Order-in-Council P.C. 1/6687, DHH; T.A. Crerar, "A Project to Establish a Chemical Warfare Experimental Station in Canada," n.d., 4354–2, C-5002, LAC.

32 "Notes on Specifications of an Experimental C.W. Base," 7 November 1940, LAC; "Canadian Chemical Warfare Experimental Station, Suffield, Alberta," n.d., 745.043 (D1), DHH.

33 C. Ross, "Brief Specification of Experimental Area," n.d., RG 77, 4-C9–19, vol. 1, box 6, LAC.

34 Crerar, "A Project to Establish," n.d., LAC; Avery, *The Science of War*, 149.

35 DND and Suffield Experimental Station, *Suffield Experimental Station, 1941–1961*, Foreword; E.A. Flood to W.W. Goforth, 28 May 1942, 745.043 (D1), DHH; J. Morris, "16th Meeting of the C.W. Inter-Service Board," 25 August 1942, RG 77, 4-C9–41, box 10, LAC.

36 DND and Suffield Experimental Station, *Suffield Experimental Station, 1941–1961*, Foreword, 1–2; Jonathan Turner, "The Defence Research Board of Canada, 1947 to 1977" (PhD diss., University of Toronto, 2012), 29.

37 Crerar, "A Project to Establish," n.d., LAC.

38 DND and Suffield Experimental Station, *Suffield Experimental Station, 1941–1961*, 1.

39 O. Maass to C.P. Morrison, 16 October 1940, RG 77, 4-C9–19, vol. 1, Box 6, LAC.

40 John E. Lyon, "D.M.A," 16 August 1940, 4354-2, C-5002, LAC.

41 E.A. Flood to C.P. Morrison, 9 December 1940, RG 77, 4-C9–19, vol. 1, box 6, LAC.

42 E.A. Flood and E.L. Davies, "Notes on Visit Paid to Maple Creek and Medicine Hat," 9 November 1940, RG 77, 4-C9–19, vol. 1, box 6, LAC; D.A. Smith to J.R. Hill, 9 November 1940, RG 77, 4-C9–19, vol. 1, box 6, LAC.

43 Crerar, "A Project to Establish," n.d., LAC.

44 Flood to Morrison, 9 December 1940, LAC.

45 DND and Suffield Experimental Station, *Suffield Experimental Station, 1941–1961*, 1; E.L. Davies to DDG/CD(R), 4 December 1940, RG 77, 4-C9–19, vol. 1, box 6, LAC; "Canadian Chemical Warfare Experimental Station, Suffield, Alberta," n.d., DHH.

46 Crerar, "A Project to Establish," n.d., LAC.

47 A. Ross to J.A.G., 7 February 1945, 4354–2, C-5002, LAC.

48 DND and Suffield Experimental Station, *Suffield Experimental Station, 1941–1961*, 16.

49 BATUS and others, *Dinosaurs to Defence: A Story of the Suffield Block* (London: Purnell, 1986), 105.

50   For a sampling of works that highlight this official version of Suffield's history, see Wilfrid Eggleston, *Scientists at War* (Toronto: Oxford University Press, 1950); Goodspeed, *A History of the Defence Research Board*; C.H. Baker and DRES, "A Brief History of DRES, 1941 to 1981," 1981, Ralston Public Library, Ralston, Alberta; "Defence Research Establishment Suffield, 50th Anniversary Open House, 1941 to 1991," 6 September 1991, M93.22.7, Esplanade; Editor, "Defense Research Station 40 Years Old," *Brooks Bulletin*, 8 July 1981; BATUS and others, *Dinosaurs to Defence*; D.J. Lowry, *Drill Rigs, Tanks, Pronghorns: The Suffield Military Reserve* (Edmonton: Alberta Department of Environment, 1981), 20–22.

51   Ned Blackhawk, *Violence over the Land: Indians and Empires in the Early American West* (Cambridge: Harvard University Press, 2006); Kuletz, *The Tainted Desert*; Traci Brynne Voyles, *Wastelanding: Legacies of Uranium Mining in Navajo Country* (Minneapolis: University of Minnesota Press, 2015).

52   James Daschuk, *Clearing the Plains: Disease, Politics of Starvation, and the Loss of Aboriginal Life* (Regina: University of Regina Press, 2013), 96–126; Betty Bastien and Jürgen W. Kremer, *Blackfoot Ways of Knowing: The Worldview of the Siksikaitsitapi* (Calgary: University of Calgary Press, 2004), 14–35.

53   D.C. Jones, *Empire of Dust: Settling and Abandoning the Prairie Dry Belt* (Calgary: University of Calgary Press, 2002); Alex Johnston and Harold G. Vriend, "Historical Overview," in "Range and Wildlife Committee, Canadian Forces Suffield: Effects of Livestock Grazing on Mixed Prairie Range and Wildlife within PFRA Pastures, Suffield Military Reserve" (13 January 1977), A4-A5, Alberta Government Library Great West Life, Edmonton; Wallace Tewinkel, "Wallace Tewinkel's Story of Life in the British Block"; "Bill Lokier History Book Project for British Block," 1969–70, William and Gertrude Lokier fonds, M2007.2.6, Esplanade.

54   L.P. Ericksen, "Sketch on Canadian Wheatland Company and Suffield Alberta, 1969," 6, M3734, Glenbow Western Research Centre, University of Calgary, Calgary.

55   Jones, *Empire of Dust*. For how neighbouring First Nation farming efforts compared and contrasted to those of homesteaders, see Sara Carter, *Lost Harvests: Prairie Indian Reserve Farmers and Government Policy* (Montreal and Kingston: McGill-Queen's University Press, 2019).

56   G.P. Marchildon, "Institutional Adaptation to Drought and the Special Areas of Alberta, 1909–1939," *Prairie Forum* 32, 2 (2007): 1–33; Jones, *Empire of Dust*, 219–23; Johnston and Vriend, "Historical Overview," A4-A5.

57   Tilley East Area Commission, "Report on Land Sections - Tilley East Report," M85.23.1, Esplanade.

58   Marchildon, "Institutional Adaptation," 7, 13.

59   McLachlan, "A Letter to the Prime Minister," 104–5.

60   Davies to DDG/CD(R), 4 December 1940, LAC.

61   Johnston and Vriend, "Historical Overview," A4-A5; G.P. Marchildon, ed., *A Dry Oasis: Institutional Adaptation to Climate on the Canadian Prairies* (Regina: CPRC Press, 2009).

62   Experimental Station Suffield, "Information Brief," LAC.

63   Law Reform Commission of Canada, *Report on Expropriation* (Scarborough, ON: Information Canada, 1976), 5. At both the provincial and federal levels, governments have granted the power to take property to thousands of expropriating authorities. For the acquisition of military lands, defence officials could rely on the War Measures Act, National Defence Act, Expropriation Act, and Atomic Energy Control Act, among other statutes. For further details, see Law Reform Commission of Canada, *Report on Expropriation*; Eric C.E. Todd, *The Law of Expropriation and Compensation*, 2nd ed. (Scarborough, ON: Carswell, 1992).

64 For a thorough account of how expropriation and similar statutory powers were employed to establish Canadian military lands on First Nation territory, see Lackenbauer,
   Battle Grounds.
65 McLachlan, "A Letter to the Prime Minister," 104–5; "Re: British Block Alberta," 8
   November 1944, 4354–2, C-5002, LAC; "Notice of Expropriation," May 1941, Barnes-
   Tinney Family fonds, M85.25.4 1–3 F.4, Esplanade.
66 C.P. Morrison to M.G.O., 19 May 1941, 4354–2, C-5002, LAC.
67 Minister of Defence to Governor-in-Council, 11 June 1941, 4354–2, C-5002, LAC.
68 Morrison to M.G.O., 19 May 1941, LAC.
69 Goodwin Gibson to Quartermaster General, 23 July 1941, 4354–2, C-5002, LAC.
70 For evacuee accounts of interactions with police, see Bill Musgrove, "After Expropriation," reprinted in Roth, *Prairie Crucible*, 101; Tewinkel, "Wallace Tewinkel's Story."
71 Gibson to Quartermaster General, 23 July 1941, LAC; Tewinkel, "Wallace Tewinkel's
   Story."
72 Tewinkel, "Wallace Tewinkel's Story"; McLachlan "A Letter to the Prime Minister"; Don
   Thomas, "British Block Wiped out Many Farm Homesteads," *Calgary Herald*, 20 October
   1970.
73 Goodspeed, *A History of the Defence Research Board*, 145–46; McLachlan, "A Letter to
   the Prime Minister."
74 For figures, see DND and Suffield Experimental Station, *Suffield Experimental Station,
   1941–1961*, 1–2; C.D. Howe to the Minister, 27 June 1941, 4354-9-14, C-5004, LAC;
   H.A. Young to Deputy Minister, 9 January 1946, 4354-2, C-5002, LAC; Lokier, "Mr. and
   Mrs. W.R. (Bill) Lokier," Esplanade.
75 Thomas, "British Block Wiped Out"; Tewinkel, "Wallace Tewinkel's Story."
76 Nearly thirty years after the DND acquisition, Ruth Daw and William Lokier, who, as
   teenagers, had watched their families lose their homes in the Suffield Block, decided to
   make a book on the area's history. They contacted the families of former evacuees and
   tried to "lay hands on facts and figures that would disprove" the "official reasons given by
   the government ... for the eviction," which they knew were not true. Ruth M. Daw to Mr.
   Lokier, 6 December 1969, "Bill Lokier History Book Project for British Block," 1969–70,
   William and Gertrude Lokier fonds, M2007.2.6, Esplanade. Their findings and personal
   accounts, currently housed in the Esplanade Archives in Medicine Hat, were invaluable
   to this study.
77 Lokier, "Mr. and Mrs. W.R. (Bill) Lokier," Esplanade; C.V. Faulknor, "Pioneer Rancher,"
   September 1954, Thomas and Eliza Lokier fonds, M2007.1.2, Esplanade; "Mr. and Mrs.
   Thomas Lokier Riverbend Ranch," 1905-41, Thomas and Eliza Lokier fonds, M2007.1.1,
   Esplanade.
78 Lokier, "Mr. and Mrs. W.R. (Bill) Lokier," Esplanade; Faulknor, "Pioneer Rancher,"
   Esplanade.
79 Jack Lust to Mr. Mackenzie King, 7 February 1942; Real Estate Advisor to Harry Allen, 3
   March 1942, both in 4354-9-14, C-5004/5, LAC.
80 McLachlan, "A Letter to the Prime Minister," 104.
81 McLachlan, "A Letter to the Prime Minister," 104–5; Lust to King, 7 February 1942, LAC.
82 Tilley East Area Commission, "Report on Land Sections - Tilley East Report," Esplanade.
83 McLachlan, "A Letter to the Prime Minister."
4 A.G.L. McNaughton to E.C. Manning, 20 August 1945, 4354-2, C-5002, LAC; C.J.
   Dewar, "Minutes Thirty-Seventh Meeting Canadian CW Inter-Division Board," 10 September 1945, RG 77, 4-C9–19, vol. 1, box 6, LAC; A.G.L. McNaughton to E.C. Manning,
   3 August 1945, 4354-2, C-5002, LAC.

85 "Proposed Postwar Experimental Station Suffield," n.d., RG 77, 4-C9–41, box 10, LAC; McLachlan, "A Letter to the Prime Minister."

86 Goodspeed, *A History of the Defence Research Board,* 148–50.

87 O. Maass, "Draft of Organization for Suffield," 8 August 1945, 4354–2, C-5002, LAC; E.C. Manning to Douglas C. Abbott, 17 September 1945, 4354–2, C-5002, LAC.

88 W. Catto, "Accommodations and Fire Prevention," 26 June 1945, 4354–2, C-5002, LAC.

89 Beck, *Dirty Wars,* 30; Chris Pearson, *Mobilizing Nature: The Environmental History of War and Militarization in Modern France* (Manchester: Manchester University Press, 2012) 12.

90 Shiloh Krupar, *Hot Spotter's Report: Military Fables of Toxic Waste* (Minneapolis: University of Minnesota Press, 2013), 271.

91 Tina Loo, *Moved by the State: Forced Relocation and Making a Good Life in Postwar Canada* (Vancouver: UBC Press, 2019).

92 Lackenbauer, *Battle Grounds,* 115–76; Joy Parr, *Sensing Changes: Technologies, Environments, and the Everyday, 1953–2003* (Vancouver: UBC Press, 2010), 4–5, 25–51; Alan R. Marcus, *Relocating Eden: The Image and Politics of Inuit Exile in the Canadian Arctic* (Lebanon, NH: Dartmouth College, University Press of New England, 1995).

Part 2
Ethics and Experts

3

The Human Sciences at Downsview
Military Research in Cold War Toronto

Matthew S. Wiseman and Matthew Farish

> *In the twentieth century, scientists and physicians seeking to solve problems of advanced and sophisticated armed forces began to build a detailed picture of the human body as a target. They assessed the best ways to destroy it and the best ways to keep it functioning so that it could continue to destroy other bodies.*
> – SUSAN LINDEE[1]

ON A COLD WINTER DAY in February 1954, the journalist Ron Kenyon received a guided tour of a military facility in the north end of Toronto. He encountered scientific equipment and apparatuses designed to test the limits of human endurance and watched as employees demonstrated the capabilities of what he later described as "modern torture gadgets."[2] Kenyon was attending the formal opening of the Defence Research Medical Laboratories (DRML), built and maintained by the Department of National Defence (DND) at Royal Canadian Air Force (RCAF) Station Toronto in the neighbourhood of Downsview.[3] Scientists and engineers at the DRML were charged with studying the "operational" problems of healthy, physically fit military personnel under various testing conditions: "the functioning of man in a military environment."[4] The DRML's features included temperature-controlled rooms, a decompression chamber, a human centrifuge, and other instruments designed for chemical, physical, and psychological experiments on animal and human subjects.[5]

In this chapter, we place the DRML at the centre of a history of military investment, infrastructure, and experimental research in mid-century Toronto. Kenyon's tour occurred during a period of intense military-sponsored scientific inquiry in the city and a "Golden Age" in Canada-based defence research.[6] From the opening of the University of Toronto's (U of T) Institute of Aerophysics in a "renovated former RCAF hangar" provided by the Defence Research Board (DRB) at Downsview to the expansion of the RCAF's wartime Institute of Aviation Medicine (IAM), Toronto housed some of the country's most significant scientific research facilities during the early years of the Cold War.[7] Charles Best, Wilbur Franks, Donald Solandt, J. Tuzo Wilson, and other prominent U of T scientists who had played significant roles in wartime science resisted demobilization in their professional work. Instead, they built on their wartime efforts in various ways, securing government support, joining military committees, and continuing military-sponsored research, some of it classified. Many were close to the DRB, which encouraged projects in Toronto and facilitated cooperation among academic, government, and private institutions.[8] Omond Solandt, the influential first head of the DRB (until 1956), was a multiple graduate of U of T and had been recommended to the military by Charles Best, his former supervisor.[9] Solandt, who received an honorary doctorate from U of T in 1954, formally returned to the university as chancellor from 1965 to 1971 – a period that overlapped with his tenure at de Havilland, an aircraft firm with long-standing ties to Downsview.

Recent studies, including some of our own, have examined the DRB's crucial role in postwar telecommunications, along with its significant influence on North American Arctic and sub-Arctic research in the human, environmental, and physical sciences. During the early Cold War, across northern lands and waters, scientific and strategic imperatives imposed from the South were largely compatible, comingling to alter imaginative and material geographies of "the Arctic" from the scale of global geopolitics to that of the individual soldiering body.[10] But this literature only indirectly confronts the shape and scope of what historian Stuart W. Leslie called the "military-industrial-academic complex": the deep and influential associations forged during and immediately after the Second World War across these three sectors.[11]

For all its resonance, the idea of the "complex" is a broad and rather flexible one. In this chapter, we *locate* ties between the Canadian military and academia by focusing on two institutions in one city and on a scholarly realm that drew these actors together in Toronto: the human sciences.[12] The DRB's research efforts in such subjects as human factors and environmental medicine, two subsets of the human sciences, were scattered across various sites in Canada, but by the time of Ron Kenyon's tour, they were centred on the DRML.[13] And during the 1950s, the DRML, in turn, drew on and was closely tied to the faculty and resources of the city's only university.[14] The two sites were connected by circuits of people and ideas that transgressed perceived and physical boundaries between military and civilian, classified and public realms.

This chapter is also a modest intervention into a set of discussions, largely conducted in science and technology studies and the history of science, about the relationships between bodies, machines, and institutions during the Cold War. Multiple overlapping fields of interdisciplinary inquiry concerned with these relationships, from cybernetics and human engineering to operations and systems research, were birthed or dramatically expanded during the 1950s and 1960s. Military medical research, with its focus on the capacities of the human body and the potential to expand or at least test those capacities through various biological or technical means, is well suited to these conversations. Very little of the existing scholarship on these subjects addresses Canada-based histories.[15] But we also suggest, following literature on the geographies of science, that the context for this particular work – a defence research laboratory set in the suburbs of a major city and tied to a large public university just fifteen kilometres away – was consequential.[16] This place-specificity is crucial to the study of the military-industrial complex (MIC) in Canada.[17] As historians have demonstrated, leading US academics and university administrators embraced "big science" during the early decades of the Cold War, including research-centred economic development policies that fundamentally altered both the character of university science and the landscapes that supported academic research.[18] With the formation of the DRB in 1947, it seemed sensible if not inevitable to the board's leaders that military-focused medical research be drawn together in a single location, at a "collection of laboratories" in one of Canada's largest urban centres.[19]

Downsview before the DRML

The initial conditions for the history told in this chapter were formed by the dispossession of the Mississaugas of the Credit First Nation and the chain of events known as the Toronto Purchase in the late eighteenth and early nineteenth centuries.[20] In their wake, the Downsview area became the site of substantial settler agriculture, including the land (dubbed Downs View) from which the community's name was drawn. Crucially, a railway was built through its heart, running north from a depot near the site of Toronto's Union Station and then from iterations of the station itself.

In the 1910s and 1920s, with the First World War and the arrival of popular aviation, flat land around Toronto was converted into several airfields. One of these, on farmland south of Sheppard Avenue, was occupied in 1929 by the new Canadian branch of de Havilland Aircraft. Adjacent to the railway, the company began assembling planes at a twenty-thousand-square-foot plant.[21] De Havilland expanded these operations rapidly over the next decade, adding more manu-facturing buildings and growing to employ some 2,400 workers. By the onset of war in 1939, the Downsview plant was primed to support the manufacturing needs of the RCAF and the British Commonwealth Air Training Plan. However, the "demands of wartime production" exceeded de Havilland's capabilities, encouraging it to acquire additional land and to construct more facilities. After the war, de Havilland resumed commercial operations (focusing on aircraft for northern Canada), and in the 1950s, it responded to the military's expansion at Downsview by relocating operations just to the south, where it continued to sit until 2022 (alongside Bombardier Aviation), on the eastern border of what is now Downsview Park.[22]

Downsview's existing infrastructure was obviously significant for the move by DND officials to expropriate land around the de Havilland plant in 1937 and to establish RCAF Station Toronto.[23] As planning historian Richard White documents, Toronto was transformed by a "vast increase in industrial production" prompted by Canada's entry into the Second World War.[24] As the population boomed, this expansion continued in the immediate postwar period, shaping the industrial, military, and suburban landscapes of the city's north end.[25] In 1952, the Canadian defence department cemented its hold at Downsview, acquiring additional land and buildings owned by de Havilland. Over the next four years, the RCAF embarked on something of a construction spree.[26]

Aviation Medicine in Toronto

In both Canada and the United States, one of the most dramatic military transformations of the 1940s was the expansion and increased prominence of the two national air forces.[27] Unsurprisingly, this was closely tied to and had significant implications for aircraft industries. But, although aircraft that flew faster, higher, and were more manoeuvrable changed discussions of air power, they also placed the bodies of pilots and crew under tremendous stresses, challenging the ability of aviators to perform inside these advanced machines. Research on this predicament was a classic example of mid-century "cyborg science," drawing together experts from universities and the military.[28]

By the late 1930s, the Canadian government was supporting a range of research on what Morley Whillans later called "environmental factors and equipment as these affected the fit man, and ... studies of his performance in assigned tasks." A great deal of this coalesced in the field known as aviation medicine, and much of this work occurred in Toronto, fixing projects and assets in place before the nominal onset of the Cold War.[29] Some of these stories, dense with acronyms, are familiar. In 1936, the Nobel Prize–winning medical scientist Frederick Banting, then head of the U of T Banting and Best Department of Medical Research (named as such in 1930, when it was moved to the new Banting Institute on College Street), had been invited to a position on Canada's National Research Council (NRC), where he spearheaded the effort to create an Associate Committee on Medical Research (ACMR).[30] Importantly, the NRC funded and facilitated military research projects in Canada prior to the creation of the DRB in April 1947. When the ACMR was established in 1938, Banting, who was its first chair, travelled across Canada to survey the state of the field. Following his tour, the committee's plans were altered by the onset of war in 1939, which also led to an enormous increase in the NRC budget. The ACMR focus effectively became military medicine, along with the study of the civilian population during wartime. Three additional NRC committees were created, each with a tie to one of the Canadian armed services.[31]

One of the three additional associate committees created during the war was titled the Associate Committee on Aviation Medical Research (ACAMR), which Banting also initially chaired. Prompted by a member of the Royal Canadian Army Medical Corps, he and other researchers at U of T had already begun to craft programs in aviation medicine.[32] Rooted in the Banting and Best Department, site of "the first decompression chamber for human studies in Canada," and extending later to physics and psychology at U of T, along with other universities and facilities, this committee acted as the key bridge between academic and air force inquiries on "the physiological problems which face flyers."[33] Meanwhile, in 1940, Banting and his U of T colleague G. Edward Hall created the No. 1 Clinical Investigation Unit (CIU).[34] It was located at the Eglinton Hunt Club property on Avenue Road in central Toronto, recently purchased by Banting on behalf of the federal government, where classified work could be conducted "without observation" behind the screen of an evaluation office for aircrew recruits.[35] After Banting died in an airplane crash in 1941, en route to London on a military mission, the CIU continued to operate under Hall's direction for the remainder of the war.[36] Banting was succeeded as chair of the ACAMR by Duncan Graham, who chaired the U of T Department of Medicine (for twenty-eight years, until 1947).[37] And Charles Best took over leadership of the Banting and Best Department (until 1967).

Famously, Banting invited his U of T colleague Wilbur Franks, a cancer researcher, to join the CIU: Franks then designed a water-filled rubber flying suit that could withstand the G-forces of high-altitude, high-speed flight (later suits were filled with compressed air).[38] Initially tested rather riskily in aircraft, by 1941 the suit was tied to a pioneering human centrifuge (also called an accelerator). The centrifuge, funded by an NRC grant, was powered by a Toronto streetcar motor, and "installed" at the CIU "under the direction" of U of T's Department of Electrical Engineering.[39] The CIU also hosted two decompression chambers for understanding the "capabilities" of humans and equipment in relation to temperature and altitudinal extremes.[40]

In 1945, at the end of the war, the CIU was renamed the RCAF Institute of Aviation Medicine (IAM), consolidating work on "aviation medical research, medical selection, medical indoctrination, medical statistics, and an active program of development." By then, the Avenue Road grounds also housed Air Force Auxiliary Squadrons, as well as a small "chamber" that simulated "tropical conditions."[41] This research shared a close affinity with that conducted at the US Army's Climatic Research Laboratory in Lawrence, Massachusetts.[42] As a later report noted, the IAM remained partly distinct from the DRML during the 1950s and 1960s – even as both were renamed – but "the activities of the two ... were in many respects parallel," and "frequently collaborative or complementary," including the location of some IAM work at Downsview. But the formally tri-service (army, navy, and air force) DRML "became a physical reality with the acquisition of part of the facilities of the IAM."[43]

As a huge influx of veterans arrived on campus after 1945, U of T was also taking steps to preserve the research ties developed during the war, establishing an Advisory Committee on Scientific Research that would keep the university president (Sidney Smith, installed in 1945) and board of governors informed and sustain "co-operation with Federal and Provincial research organizations."[44] Even as Smith upheld the "the lonely scholar" with "inexplicable interest in a seemingly trivial question," he contrasted this with "applied research" that "universities should not refuse to perform." In his official history of the university, Martin Friedland notes the emergence of the DRB and its influence on U of T's computer science programs. Friedland suggests that the Institute of Aerophysics – which, as Omond Solandt conveyed to Smith, *required* DRB support – best "illustrates the continuing involvement of the University in defence work during the cold war." Although the institute was located at Downsview from 1950 to 1959, Friedland does not mention the many additional U of T connections with the base during that decade, even as the DRML was a clear outgrowth of wartime university work and employed many U of T graduates.[45]

In 1946, as a step toward a distinct Medical Research Council, the ACMR was replaced by a more substantial Division of Medical Research, with a research budget directed entirely to extramural programs. It was at this juncture that the emerging DRB began to oversee military medical research. A decade after Banting conducted his first national survey, a second one in 1948 included among its leaders the DRB's Morley Whillans, who soon became the first DRML superintendent.[46]

Extending Military Sponsorship: Enter the DRB

The DRB headquarters in Ottawa was home to a Scientific Staff, separated into various divisions that linked the board with researchers – at existing government establishments or elsewhere – who conducted relevant inquiries in fields such as armaments or clothing and equipment. Advisory committees composed of military, academic, and industry members were associated with subsections of each division. For example, the Arctic Research Advisory Committee included U of T faculty members J. Tuzo Wilson and Donald Solandt (Omond's brother) in the late 1940s and early 1950s.[47] Out of this committee, a Panel on Arctic Medical Research was spun; the Solandt brothers attended its first meeting, in December 1948, where Morley Whillans acted as secretary.[48]

E.A. Bott, head of the U of T Department of Psychology and a member of the wartime ACAMR, was one of the early academics employed by the DRB as a consultant in the field of "aviation psychology." In 1948, when the DRB offered him the consultancy position, Bott wrote to Sidney Smith, seeking his approval for the proposed arrangement. He noted that "there are tangible advantages for universities which have members of staff with consultative connections of this sort ... quite apart from any prestige value there might be with the public," since individuals employed by the DND would be favourably positioned to secure additional funding for laboratory work and graduate student stipends. This added assistance was "particularly timely" for Canadian universities, Bott argued, since federal funding, especially for graduate work, was modest. As a result, consultancies offered "a direct and mutually agreeable means of helping our Federal Departments technically and at the same time of helping our science and our graduate students."[49] Charles Best, Omond Solandt's mentor and a singularly important academic figure in the early years of the DRB, was also a recipient of board funding: $70,000 in March 1951 for a "radiation unit" at U of T, for example.[50]

Omond Solandt moved quickly to blur the boundaries – or to re-establish wartime ties – between military and academic research, emphasizing that DRB employees could publish in unclassified venues and launching an annual DRB symposium (first held in 1948) featuring "senior faculty members of various Canadian universities." These universities were graduating the students, some funded by DRB scholarships, who would go on to work for the board. Moreover, "from the beginning" the board made use of academic facilities and sponsored university research. This included the creation of "small research units in selected universities," clusters set up to conduct inquiries of interest to the DND "but which had not previously been covered by graduate teaching."[51]

One of Solandt's most significant early moves was to establish, with the aid of Charles Best, the DRB's Medical Research Advisory Committee (MRAC), whose initial members included Best and Franks (from the IAM), along with representatives from five universities and multiple government departments. Led by Ray F. Farquharson, a veteran who had recently become the chair of medicine at U of T (along with physician-in-chief at Toronto General Hospital), the MRAC first met in June 1948.[52] Its first recommendation was that the DRB should focus on "the capabilities and limitations of the fit man, his efficiency in the military role, the environmental factors and hazards affecting him, and the assessment of his task with a view to improving his performance in it."[53] This concern for *adaptation* formed the core of the DRB's medical research program. Work on "diagnosis and treatment" would remain with universities, albeit occasionally funded by the DRB, under its extramural research program, which we address later in this chapter.[54]

The Move to Downsview

The challenge of organizing disparate fields and scholars eventually prompted the creation of a broad Defence Medical Research Co-ordinating Committee in 1951, concurrent with the creation of the DRML. The ACAMR was folded into this new group, led by Best.[55] The proliferation and shifting alignment (and naming) of committees is less important than the attempt by senior authorities in the DRB to control and support a wide range of both internal and external research on interdisciplinary subjects related to military bodies. The official history of the DRB describes work in this field occurring at the Defence Research Northern Laboratory in Fort Churchill, Manitoba, within the DRB's Operational Research cluster, inside specific services, and at numerous Canadian universities. But the synthesis sought within the DRB was embodied by the creation, in 1950, of the Defence Research Medical Laboratories.[56]

Morley Whillans, a pharmacology professor from Dalhousie University who had spent time at the Banting Institute during the late 1930s and was involved in the CIU studies during the war, was named head of the DRB Biological Division in 1948. He replaced psychologist Nelson Whitman Morton, formerly of McGill University, who moved on to the DRB's new Operational Research Group.[57] Whillans, who had worked under the wartime ACAMR, also assumed the role of secretary of the MRAC, a responsibility that took him on his survey of medical research institutions in Canada ten years after Banting's equivalent. He also visited defence medicine facilities in the United States. The result was the creation of the DRML out of his division. Whillans moved from Ottawa to Toronto in 1950; as the IAM was pulled away from the air force to the DRB, he acquired several pieces of the institute for his new venture, along with some IAM staff.[58]

In the initial months, when there was "an urgent need for proper accommodation," the DRML employees worked on Avenue Road, above a delicatessen on Bathurst Street, and elsewhere in Toronto, sometimes renting laboratory space. In 1951, forty-three staff moved to a Downsview RCAF hut, "Canada's first human factors laboratory." By late 1953, these dispersed facilities were consolidated in the much larger Downsview DRML structure, designed by the prominent modernist architect Gordon Adamson and built by the massive Piggot Construction firm next to the wind tunnel building of the Institute of Aerophysics.[59] Before that point, the vast majority of the DRB's medical research was external, enabled and carried out primarily through extramural support to leading academic scientists, with some 40 percent of annual medical research grants directed toward studying "life in Arctic regions," including experiments on cold tolerance and acclimatization.[60]

For the next two decades, the DRML hosted most of the DRB's human scientific work. Whillans described the collection of facilities as "each profiting by a single administrative service, by the sharing of large expensive items of equipment and most important of all, each deriving benefit from the partnership of other scientific disciplines in other sections."[61] Research projects dealt with such subjects as clothing for diverse "climatic conditions," motion sickness, aircraft instruments and controls, and the development of methods for the selection and recruitment of personnel.[62] As illustrated in Figure 3.1, the research and development of new and specialized military kit and materiel for the armed forces was a fundamental responsibility of the Toronto-based laboratories. Engineers, chemists, and physiologists, among other experts, worked in lockstep with military personnel to study and improve upon existing military equipment and techniques. Work at the DRML produced new ration and survival packs, helmets and oxygen masks, and other military gear that functioned under various severe and diverse climatic conditions. This was clearly interdisciplinary, cross-pollinating research, calling for contributions from many types of scholars, but at the heart of the inquiries was that single character: "man."[63]

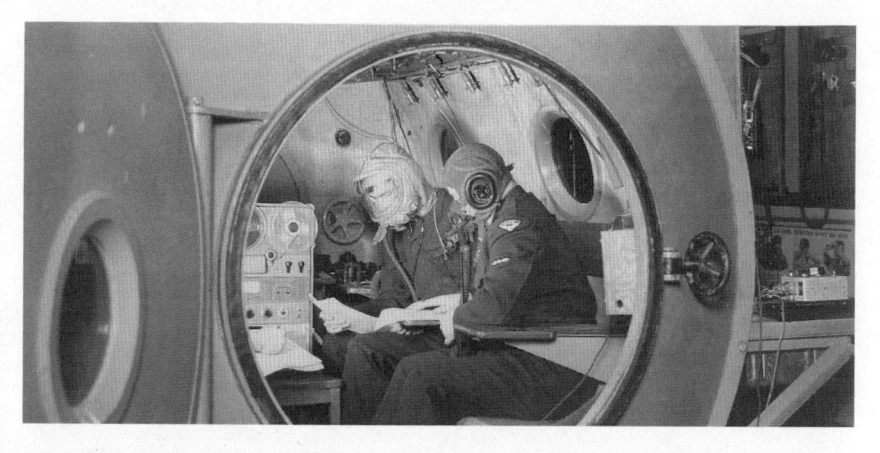

Figure 3.1 A nine-person chamber being used to test full pressure suit equipment in the late 1950s. This chamber, before retirement, was used extensively as a windblast facility to qualify helmets and oxygen masks for pilot ejection. | *DCIEM, The First Fifty Years, 1939–1989* (North York: Defence and Civil Institute of Environmental Medicine, 1989), 22. Courtesy of Defence Research and Development Canada.

Experimentation at the DRML

Governor General Vincent Massey officially opened the newly constructed DRML at Downsview in February 1954. The ceremony and tour were attended by Sir William Penny, lead organizer of the British atomic weapons testing program, as well as Ron Keynon and other journalists. During the event, Whillans described the DRML as "unique" and "an example in co-operation by the three fighting services."[64] Kenyon reported that the laboratory rooms intended for climatic research included devices that simulated the conditions of winter storms, rough seas, rain, and high winds. One room included a sunken floor that could be filled with water and used for experiments that required a pool. Kenyon witnessed "volunteer" soldiers plodding through chest-high saltwater while wearing full packs, subjected to rain and wind simulations during a series of tests designed to study the stresses of amphibious landings.[65] By the mid-1950s, media coverage of experimental research at the DRML had become reasonably common. Amid the heightened secrecy of the early Cold War period, DRB public relations staff occasionally invited journalists to tour the state-of-the-art DRML facilities and report on Ottawa's financial and intellectual investments in defence research.[66] In the DND, news accounts and photographs of such cutting-edge research were seen as reassuring Canadian taxpayers that they were receiving value for their money, but such stories doubled as a means to protect and promote continued investment in military-sponsored science.

During this period, the financial ties between the DND and university researchers were profound. Senior DRB officials sat on newly created committees, overseeing the distribution of funding allocated for research under the national defence budget. Funding for extramural initiatives paid for short- and long-term projects conducted by faculty and graduate students. In the summer of 1954 alone, 23 professors and 140 students joined the DRB on a temporary basis, carrying out either independent work or joint research projects with the hundreds of scientists, engineers, and technicians who comprised the full-time DRB staff at the DRML and other state-owned research facilities.[67] For annual recruitment drives, military representatives travelled the country to visit campuses, distributing posters and employment brochures. As one 1956 internal publication made clear, the "DRB's main source of engineers and scientists originates from the professional and graduate schools of Canadian universities."[68] Moreover, as the example of the U of T Institute of Aerophysics suggests, encouraging and assisting research in this manner helped universities to develop research capabilities beyond their financial resources.[69] Meanwhile, contracts paid for work that could be accomplished more effectively outside DRB establishments because of existing skills and facilities in academic or industrial research settings. And experimental trials in northern Canada and other outdoor locales supplemented laboratory work conducted inside DRB facilities and enabled researchers to further test equipment and techniques.

In Toronto, on-site experiments involving human subjects predated the construction and official opening of the Downsview laboratories. In August 1952, after observing a series of research experiments at the DRML space on Avenue Road, the journalist Len Marquis described a "mediaeval-looking plastic cage" whose purpose was to measure a person's tolerance of the G-forces imposed by high-speed aerobatics.[70] The research subject sat securely in a large twenty-foot motion-sickness swing, as instruments attached to his head recorded his sensitivity to simulated airsickness. In a related experiment, scientists used an inter-arterial needle to determine the effect of motion sickness on blood pressure (see Figure 3.2). Although this research was primarily intended to develop RCAF recruitment and personnel selection standards, scientists and engineers at the DRML argued that it could also be used to test sailors and naval recruits for hypersensitivity to seasickness.[71]

In the weeks leading up to the February 1954 official opening at Downsview, six RCAF members participated in a three-week study to test a new ration pack developed by DRML chemists.[72] They lived in an isolated dormitory, surviving on nothing more than water and a daily ration of nine experimental

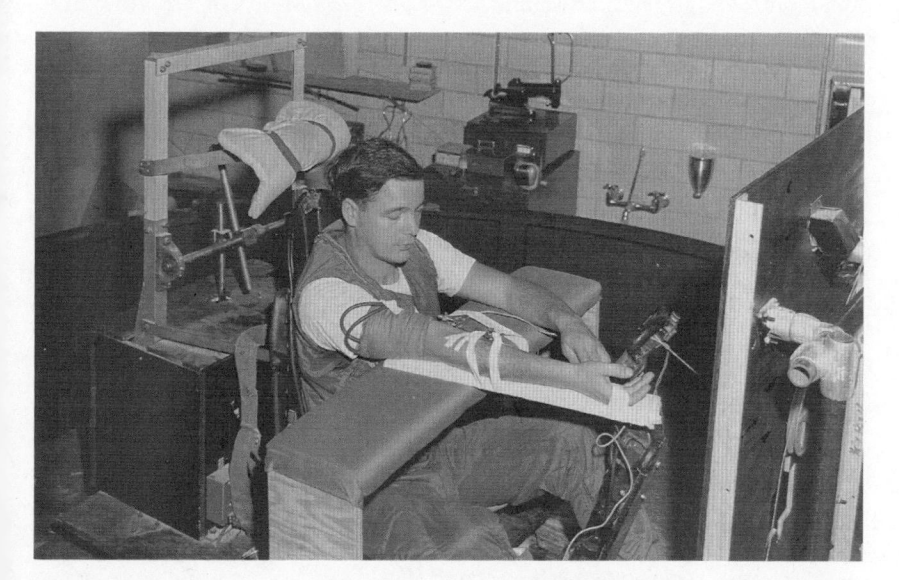

Figure 3.2 Wing Commander Charles Bryan tests an inter-arterial needle to measure blood pressure changes with motion sickness. | *DCIEM, The First Fifty Years,* 26. Courtesy of Defence Research and Development Canada.

"gumdrops" per person. Dressed only in a pair of trouser shorts, each man had his own cot. A microphone hidden in the ceiling recorded his remarks as he experienced boredom, hunger, fatigue, stress, and other miseries. During the twenty-one days, the room temperature never rose above 14 degrees Celsius, and none of the men used the shower, because technicians had cut off the hot water. "That can be a chilly climate when you're in your underwear," DRML scientist Guy Marier told the press.[73] In fact, the men became so cold that they spent much of the time hugging their knees to retain body heat. The ration provided nine hundred calories daily, or about one-quarter of the expected minimum intake. Each man lost at least fifteen pounds during the study but emerged from the isolation room apparently in good health. The reward for enduring the experiment was a period of extra leave and an unspecified payment known as "danger money."[74]

The DRML underwent a structural reorganization in early 1957 to better accommodate the DRB research program, with the human sciences receiving the bulk of attention.[75] As the DRML head of experimental psychology, R.B. Bromiley, had explained in October 1956, "Today, our culture works on the system that the machine is more accurate than the man. The answer is to do something about the man."[76] Under this guiding principle, the reorganized and expanded DRML included a newly constructed "Climatic Suite" consisting of three laboratory rooms, each capable of achieving intense temperature fluctuations, controlled air flows, and simulated weather conditions. In terms of studying "man in relation to his environment," the DRB's internal newsletter noted in April 1957, "this type of research need no longer be seasonable."[77] By this time, the DRML's Environmental Physiology Group was focusing its studies on the Canadian Army.[78]

To mark the DRB's tenth anniversary on 1 April 1957, DRML superintendent E.A. Sellers was interviewed by Percy Saltzman on *Tabloid*, a popular Toronto television program produced by the Canadian Broadcasting Corporation. During the interview, Sellers discussed the unclassified DRML research into unexplained aircraft crashes and pilot safety.[79] That same month, sixteen admirals and generals from the North Atlantic Treaty Organization's (NATO) Military Committee, representing thirteen countries, arrived at Downsview Airport to inspect de Havilland's facilities and visit the DRML, where staff proudly served them a unique lunch prepared entirely from newly created dehydrated foods.[80] Although the DRB's focus on military medical research derived in part from the specific needs and experiences of the Canadian armed services both during and after the Second World War, its founding representatives promoted Canadian defence research among the North Atlantic partners and, after April 1949, NATO allies. In other words, the DRML research program helped to support both the Canadian military and Ottawa's wider alliance commitments to military preparedness and collective security during the early Cold War.

The unification of the Canadian Armed Forces in 1968 and the budget cuts to national defence and procurement had a drastic impact on DRB activities, but environmental stress research with military "volunteers" continued at Downsview into the 1970s. "It's 30 Below in Metro," blared the front page of the *Toronto Sun* on 3 December 1973.[81] The paper's cover story and centre-spread featured images of Exercise Kool Stool, in which soldiers underwent an endurance experiment designed to simulate a long march in the Arctic. Wearing twenty-five pounds of cold-weather military clothing and carrying fifty-pound packs, they marched on treadmills inside an air-conditioned "climatic chamber."[82] Scientists observed and monitored the soldiers during their seven days in the cold room, ultimately comparing the recorded results to data from an actual soldier's march carried out on Qikiqtaaluk (Baffin Island).[83] The researchers and their sponsors clearly held on to the belief that the armed services required and could generate beneficial human scientific knowledge for military activity in "extreme" environments.

Conclusion

On 20 November 1967, William White, a recruiting agent for Dow Chemical of Canada, found himself barricaded in the Placement Services building at U of T by a crowd of protestors. Approximately 150 students and professors had gathered to protest Dow's presence on campus, due to the company's controversial role as the sole supplier of napalm for the US military.[84] For several tense hours, White remained trapped inside the building while students and faculty marched outside, chanting anti-war slogans such as "Dow shalt not kill" and "napalm burns bodies," and demanding the banning of war-complicit companies from campus.[85] The protest eventually dissipated, but the incident was a flashpoint for anti-war activism at U of T, setting off a series of clashes in the coming months between activists and their opponents on campus.

The demonstrators took issue with White for his role as a Dow recruiting agent, but their protests were grounded in the demand that university administration bar from campus any firm that fuelled the "war machine."[86] Groups such as the Students' Administrative Council (later the University of Toronto Student Union) and the Committee to End the War in Vietnam organized rallies and debates on the subject, while the student newspaper *The Varsity* ran editorials decrying the influence of the military at U of T. Before long, the debate spilled onto the pages of the *Globe and Mail* and the *Toronto Daily Star* (now the *Toronto Star*), where intellectuals and government officials argued over the merits or dangers of military-funded research.[87] Campus-based groups were joined by other anti-war organizations active in Toronto, including the Campaign for Nuclear Disarmament, the Communist Party of Canada, and the Voice of Women. Eventually, the issue even reached the provincial legislature at Queen's Park, thanks to a few progressive members. Perhaps for the first time, defence research was the subject of public debate in Toronto, and on the U of T campus it folded into the larger sphere of student activism and crises in university governance.

Yet most of the research projects discussed in this chapter went virtually unnoticed in these disputes. This included U of T's close ties to the DRML and the role of faculty as consultants and advisors to the DRB. Ironically, on the very day that White was confined in the Placement Services building, U of T chancellor Omond Solandt was attending a DRB symposium in Ottawa, where he delivered a speech titled "The Place of Defence Research in the Scientific Community." As the founding chair of the DRB told his audience, "One has only to look at the experience of the Korean War and the war in VietNam [*sic*] to see how this important field of applying science to the apparently simple problems of ground-air warfare has been neglected." Aided by the DRB, he continued, the Canadian armed services "could become world leaders in this important field."[88] U of T's ceremonial head, undoubtedly shaped by his deep personal and professional ties to the DND research branch, clearly viewed military research differently than did a growing chorus at his university. In fact, during Solandt's tenure as chancellor between 1965 and 1971, his military career and ties to defence research were increasingly decried in *Varsity* stories.[89]

Solandt was certainly not alone, however. The construction, financing, and operation of a permanent military research facility in Toronto were the result of several interconnected factors, from abundant government financial support to the commitment of like-minded individuals who shared a common belief in the application of science to military problems.[90] During the 1950s and 1960s, members of the DRML routinely discussed research findings at military gatherings and lectured directly to the armed services, while institutional collaboration was central to the sustainment of the Toronto facilities. Scientists and engineers employed at the DRML cooperated with colleagues at the IAM, regularly participated in research and teaching activities at U of T, joined the executive councils of numerous professional bodies, and, farther afield, staffed sites such as the Human Engineering Institute at McGill University.[91] Even as Toronto became a site of significant anti-war mobilization in the 1960s – a subject for another, fuller discussion – the combined efforts of U of T faculty, supported by university administrators and the DRB, had for over two decades cultivated military-funded science in the north end of the large city. The DRML and its antecedents had firmly embedded Toronto, U of T, and many leading scientists and engineers in the world of military research.

Notes

1 Susan Lindee, *Rational Fog: Science and Technology in Modern War* (Cambridge: Harvard University Press, 2020), 132 (emphasis in original).

2 Ron Kenyon, "Modern 'Torture' Gadgets Test Human Endurance," *Toronto Telegram*, 12 February 1954, RG 24, vol. 10341, file August 28/[19]53 to August 14/[19]54, Library and Archives Canada (LAC).

3 RCAF Toronto became RCAF Downsview in October 1958. With the unification of the Canadian Armed Forces in 1968, the site was renamed Canadian Forces Base (CFB) Toronto. Shortly before that, the DRML was renamed Defence Research Establishment Toronto. See "Downsview Park: Past, Present and Future," https://downsviewpark.ca/our-story; Bruce Forsyth, "Toronto's Cold War Sentinel," May 2007, Canadian Military History, https://militarybruce.com/torontos-cold-war-sentinel/.

4 L.H. Turl, "The Defence Research Establishment Toronto (Formerly the Defence Research Medical Laboratories)," *Medical Services Journal, Canada* 23, 8 (1967): 1032; E.A. Sellers, "Defence Research Medical Laboratories," *Medical Services Journal, Canada* 14, 2 (1958): 119. Similar language is quoted in Bill Rawling, *The Myriad Challenges of Peace: Canadian Forces Medical Practitioners since the Second World War* (Ottawa: Department of National Defence, Directorate of History, 2004), 198. Both Turl and Sellers were crucial to the DRML's early history. In 1951, the Toronto-born Leslie Turl, who held a PhD in physics from the University of Toronto (U of T), was recruited by Morley Whillans, the first formal DRML superintendent (1952–54). In subsequent years, Turl led several DRML divisions and by 1967 was assistant to the director general. Edward A. Sellers, a navy veteran and student of Charles Best, was a long-time professor (of physiology and pharmacology) and administrator at U of T. He followed Whillans to become DRML superintendent from 1955 to 1958. See *DCIEM, The First Fifty Years, 1939–1989* (North York: Defence and Civil Institute of Environmental Medicine, 1989).

5 On the DRML research program, see *Annual Report of the Defence Research Medical Laboratories, 1958* (Ottawa: DRB, 1959), 1, RG 24 C-1-c, vol. 32168, file 2380–50–46–4, LAC. Although we do not discuss research on animals, they were fundamental to several of the "stress" experiments performed at the DRML. See, for example, James Senter, "Research Eases Work for Aerial Navigator," *Globe and Mail*, 10 October 1956, 10.

6 "The Golden Age of Canadian Defence Research" is the title of Chapter 3 in Jonathan Turner's essential "The Defence Research Board of Canada, 1947 to 1977" (PhD diss., University of Toronto, 2012). For a published synthesis, see Jonathan Turner, "Politics and Defence Research in the Cold War," *Scientia Canadiensis* 35, 1–2 (2012): 39–63.

7 Ben Etkin, "Our Story: Beginnings," n.d., University of Toronto Institute for Aerospace Studies, https://www.utias.utoronto.ca/our-story/; Martin L. Friedland, *The University of Toronto: A History* (Toronto: University of Toronto Press, 2002), 375–79. Championed by the restless, prominent U of T physicist Gordon N. Patterson, the Institute of Aerophysics was launched in 1949. The following year, the DRB provided $250,000 to convert the Downsview building and $100,000 for the institute's operation in the first three years. After construction, including the addition of a supersonic wind tunnel, the building was operational in September 1950. Julius Lukasiewicz, "Canada's Encounter with High-Speed Aeronautics," *Technology and Culture* 27, 2 (1986): 235; Turner, "The Defence Research Board," 110–12; Omond Solandt, "Address at the Opening of the Institute for Aerophysics, University of Toronto, September 26, 1950," Omond McKillop Solandt fonds, acc. B1993–0041, box 33, folder 2, University of Toronto Archives and Records Management Services (UTARMS). In 1963, the institute was renamed the University of Toronto Institute for Aerospace Studies, and since then it has been located a ten-minute drive north of Downsview.

8 The DRB was renamed the Defence Research and Development Branch in 1974 and Defence Research and Development Canada (DRDC) in 2000, a name it retains today.

9 Donald J. Goodspeed, *A History of the Defence Research Board of Canada* (Ottawa: Queen's Printer, 1958), 42; Jason Sean Ridler, *Maestro of Science: Omond McKillop Solandt and Government Science in War and Hostile Peace, 1939–1956* (Toronto: University of Toronto Press, 2015), 118. For another connection between the DRB and U of T, see Scott M. Campbell, "The Premise of Computer Science: Establishing Modern Computing at the University of Toronto (1945–1964)" (PhD diss., University of Toronto, 2006), 38–40; Michael R. Williams, "UTEC and Ferut: The University of Toronto's Computation Centre," *IEEE Annals of the History of Computing* 16, 2 (1994): 4–12; John N. Vardalas, *The Computer Revolution in Canada: Building National Technological Competence* (Cambridge: MIT Press, 2001).

10 Stephen Bocking, "A Disciplined Geography: Aviation, Science, and the Cold War in Northern Canada, 1945–1960," *Technology and Culture* 50, 2 (2009): 265–90; Matthew Farish, "Frontier Engineering: From the Globe to the Body in the Cold War Arctic," *Canadian Geographer* 50, 2 (2006): 177–96; Matthew Farish, "Making 'Man in the Arctic': Academic and Military Entanglements, 1944–49," in *Cold Science: Environmental Knowledge in the North American Arctic during the Cold War*, ed. Stephen Bocking and Daniel Heidt (New York: Routledge, 2019), 85–106; Edward Jones-Imhotep, *The Unreliable Nation: Hostile Nature and Technological Failure in the Cold War* (Cambridge: MIT Press, 2017); Matthew S. Wiseman, "Unlocking the 'Eskimo Secret': Defence Science in the Cold War Canadian Arctic, 1947–1954," *Journal of the Canadian Historical Association* 26, 1 (2015): 191–223; Matthew S. Wiseman, "The Development of Cold War Soldiery: Acclimatisation Research and Military Indoctrination in the Canadian Arctic, 1947–1953," *Canadian Military History* 24, 2 (2015): 127–55.

11 Stuart W. Leslie, *The Cold War and American Science: The Military-Industrial-Academic Complex at MIT and Stanford* (New York: Columbia University Press, 1993).

12 For a useful synthesis of debates around the military-industrial complex in Canada, see Vardalas, *The Computer Revolution*, 8–11. We do not significantly discuss the DRB's ties to industrial firms, but the board's Toronto-based facilities did have occasional dealings with private industry. See *Annual Report of the Defence Research Medical Laboratories, 1958*, 12–13, LAC.

13 M.G. Whillans, "The Defence Research Medical Laboratories: Their Character and Opportunities," *Canadian Medical Association Journal* 68 (1953): 267. This article was based on an address given by Whillans in June 1952. Medical research made up a comparatively minor part of the DRB research program. In 1951, for example, around 10 percent of the DRB's scientific staff was engaged in medical research – a sizeable portion but not as much as in special weapons or armaments research. See Turner, "The Defence Research Board," 139. But the extent of the DRB medical research program is also difficult to trace, in part because it was less centralized than other fields. Unlike more dangerous or politically sensitive work – such as efforts related to chemical and biological warfare, which mainly took place at the secluded Suffield Experimental Station in Alberta – medical research supported by the DRB was not necessarily or entirely of a classified nature. Consequently, a substantial portion of the DRB medical research program was conducted extramurally, through grants and bursaries awarded to researchers in major Canadian universities. See Turner, "The Defence Research Board," 96–113. On Suffield, see Archie Pennie, *Suffield Experimental Station, 1941–1961* (Ralston: Defence Research Board, 1961); Susan L. Smith, *Toxic Exposures: Mustard Gas and the Health Consequences of World War II in the United States* (New Brunswick, NJ: Rutgers University Press, 2017), 32–41; Brandon C. Davis, "Grounds for Permanent War: Land Appropriation,

Exceptional Powers, and the Mid-Century Militarization of Western North American Environments" (PhD diss., University of British Columbia, 2017), Chapter 3.

14 Ryerson University (now Toronto Metropolitan University) originated as the Ryerson Institute of Technology in 1948, and York University was launched in 1959. Ryerson received university status in 1993. See "A Brief History of Ryerson University (1948–2007)," Toronto Metropolitan University Archives and Special Collections, https://library.torontomu.ca/asc/archives/ryerson-history/brief-history/.

15 Some exceptions are Farish, "Making 'Man in the Arctic'"; Wiseman, "Unlocking the 'Eskimo Secret'"; Wiseman, "The Development of Cold War Soldiery."

16 We are specifically inspired by Richard C. Powell, "Science, Sovereignty and Nation: Canada and the Legacy of the International Geophysical Year, 1957–1958," *Journal of Historical Geography* 34 (2008): 618–38; Scott Kirsch, "Laboratory/Observatory," in *The SAGE Handbook of Geographical Knowledge*, ed. John Agnew and David N. Livingstone (London: Sage, 2011), 76–88.

17 See also Matthew Farish and Patrick Vitale, "Locating the American Military-Industrial Complex: An Introduction," *Antipode* 43, 3 (2011): 777–82; Alasdair Pinkerton, Stephen Young, and Klaus Dodds, "Postcards from Heaven: Critical Geographies of the Cold War Military-Industrial-Academic Complex," *Antipode* 43, 3 (2011): 820–44.

18 See, for example, Peter Galison and Bruce Hevly, eds., *Big Science: The Growth of Large-Scale Research* (Stanford: Stanford University Press, 1992); Margaret Pugh O'Mara, *Cities of Knowledge: Cold War Science and the Search for the Next Silicon Valley* (Princeton, NJ: Princeton University Press, 2005), 6.

19 Whillans, "The Defence Research Medical Laboratories," 266.

20 This dispossession, of course, did not and does not obviate the presence of many thousands of Indigenous people in Tkaronto. See Denise Bolduc et al., eds., *Indigenous Toronto: Stories That Carry This Place* (Toronto: Coach House Books, 2021), particularly Margaret Sault, "A Story about the Toronto Purchase," n.p.; Victoria Freeman, "'Toronto Has No History!' Indigeneity, Settler Colonialism, and Historical Memory in Canada's Largest City," *Urban History Review* 38, 2 (2010): 21–35. In *none* of the historical materials that we consulted for this chapter is there any reference to Indigenous Toronto.

21 After a period of uncertainty, parts of this facility were repurposed by Centennial College into a new Downsview Campus, opened in 2019, which houses the college's Centre for Aerospace and Aviation. In 2023, work continues on a larger Downsview Aerospace Innovation and Research "hub," a consortium of Centennial College, all three Toronto universities (York, Toronto Metropolitan, and the University of Toronto, including the Institute for Aerospace Studies), Queen's and McMaster Universities, and several industry partners.

22 On the history of de Havilland at Downsview, see "Downsview Park" (the source of the quote); Forsyth, "Toronto's Cold War Sentinel."

23 Following the war, in 1946–47, the RCAF moved 400 Squadron (Auxiliary) to the Downsview site and built an Air Material Base on the expropriated properties. See "Downsview Park"; Forsyth, "Toronto's Cold War Sentinel."

24 Richard White, *Planning Toronto: The Planners, the Plans, Their Legacies, 1940–80* (Vancouver: UBC Press, 2016), 12.

25 Just as the DRML was being established in the 1950s, what John Sewell calls "Canada's First Corporate Suburb," Don Mills, was under development due east. John Sewell, *The Shape of the City: Toronto Struggles with Modern Planning* (Toronto: University of Toronto Press, 1993), Chapter 3. See also Richard Harris, *Creeping Conformity: How Canada Became Suburban, 1900–1960* (Toronto: University of Toronto Press, 2004), 129–54.

26 See "Downsview Park"; Forsyth, "Toronto's Cold War Sentinel." For other military uses of RCAF Station Toronto during the 1950s, see Bruce Forsyth, "Ontario: Canadian Forces Base

Toronto," Canadian Military History, https://militarybruce.com/abandoned-canadian
-military-bases/closed-bases-with-military-presence/ontario/. For reasons of space, this
chapter does not address the base's formal closure in April 1996 and the conversion of
the "Downsview Lands" into a park.

27 On Canada, see Richard Goette, *Sovereignty and Command in Canada-US Continental
Air Defence, 1940–57* (Vancouver: UBC Press, 2018). On the United States, see Michael
S. Sherry, *The Rise of American Air Power: The Creation of Armageddon* (New Haven:
Yale University Press, 1987).

28 Andrew Pickering, "Cyborg History and the World War II Regime," *Perspectives on Science* 3, 1 (1995): 1–48; Philip Mirowski, *Machine Dreams: Economics Becomes a Cyborg
Science* (Cambridge: Cambridge University Press, 2001). Of course, aviation medicine
was not new in the Second World War and was closely tied to terrestrial high-altitude
physiological research, as well. See, for example, Lindee, *Rational Fog,* 134–36. Green
Peyton, *Fifty Years of Aerospace Medicine* (Brooks Air Force Base, TX: Aerospace Medical Division, Air Force Systems Command, 1968), 93, 104, notes that Harry George
Armstrong, a hugely significant figure in US aviation medicine, responsible for what
became the Aero Medical Laboratory at Wright Field, Ohio, spent a year at U of T in
1940–41, where he earned a degree.

29 Whillans, "The Defence Research Medical Laboratories," 265. On the general emergence
and history of aviation medicine, see "Air Force Medical Research," in *Official History
of the Canadian Medical Services, 1939–1945,* vol. 2, *Clinical Subjects,* ed. W.R. Feasby
(Ottawa: Queen's Printer, 1953), 365–73.

30 On the Banting and Best Department, see Michael Bliss, *Banting: A Biography* (Toronto:
University of Toronto Press, 1984), 182. The Best Institute opened next door to the Banting
Institute in 1954. Banting and Best's relationship is discussed thoroughly in Bliss, *Banting.*

31 These were the Associate Committee on Aviation Medical Research (discussed below),
the Associate Committee on Naval Medical Research (chaired by Charles Best), and the
Associate Committee on Army Medical Research. Alison Li, "Expansion and Consolidation: The Associate Committee and the Division of Medical Research of the NRC,
1938–1959," *Scientia Canadensis* 15, 2 (1991): 91–97; Terrie M. Romano, "The Associate Committees on Medical Research of the National Research Council and the Second
World War," *Scientia Canadensis* 15, 2 (1991): 74; Turl, "The Defence Research Establishment Toronto," 1034.

32 Banting's long military background – he enrolled in the Royal Canadian Army Medical
Corps during the First World War – meant that he was an additionally obvious target for
outreach, specifically from Major A.A. James of the corps, on aviation medicine in the
late 1930s. C.B. Stewart, "Canadian Research in Aviation Medicine," *Public Affairs* 10,
2 (1947): 98. The ACAMR was technically preceded by a Federal Committee on Aviation Medicine, set up in June 1939. See the finding aid "Banting (Frederick Grant, Sir)
Papers," 7, University of Toronto Archives, https://discoverarchives.library.utoronto.ca/
downloads/frederick-banting-papers.pdf. ACAMR subcommittees supported "projects
... on the physiological effects of acceleration, decompression sickness, oxygen equipment, motion sickness, personnel selection, visual problems and protective clothing
design." Turl, "The Defence Research Establishment Toronto," 1035. See also Goodspeed,
A History of the Defence Research Board, 225; Romano, "The Associate Committees," 78.

33 Turl, "The Defence Research Establishment Toronto," 1035; Goodspeed, *A History of
the Defence Research Board,* 224. See also Romano, "The Associate Committees," 78.
For more on related wartime work at U of T, see Friedland, *The University of Toronto,*
Chapter 27; Christopher J. Rutty, "Chapter 6: World War II & Biotech Innovations," n.d.,
https://connaught.research.utoronto.ca/about/history/article6.

34 Bliss, *Banting,* 277, refers to this as the No. 1 Initial Training School (its parallel, second role). A second CIU was set up at the RCAF Station in Regina. Lydia Dotto, "Canada's Aviation Medicine Pioneers," n.d., 19, https://www.asc-csa.gc.ca/pdf/osm_aviation.pdf. In 1945, fresh from wartime work, Edward Hall became dean of medicine at the University of Western Ontario. Two years later, he was named the university's president and held the title from 1947 to 1967, a hugely significant period in the institution's history. While president, Hall led the committee that advocated for a Canadian Forces Medical Council (established in 1953), which he chaired and whose members included J.A. MacFarlane, the U of T dean of medicine. Hall was succeeded as dean at Western by J.B. Collip, Banting and Best's collaborator in the discovery of insulin. A member of ACMR since 1938, Collip became its chair after Banting's death. In 1946, he was named the head of the NRC's new Division of Medical Research and paired with Charles Best in the DRB's Medical Research Advisory Committee and Defence Medical Research Co-ordinating Committee, all mentioned below. On Collip, see Alison I-Syin Li, *J.B. Collip and the Development of Medical Research in Canada* (Montreal and Kingston: McGill-Queen's University Press, 2003).

35 Dennis R. Jenkins, *Dressing for Altitude: U.S. Aviation Pressure Suits – Wiley Post to Space Shuttle* (Washington: National Aeronautics and Space Administration, 2012), 86; *DCIEM, The First Fifty Years,* n.p. The latter source describes this purchase as backed by a $25,000 grant from the NRC. Used in later decades as a military staff school, the property at 1107 Avenue Road, just north of Eglinton Avenue, remained in the possession of the Canadian Forces until its closure in 1994. It was then converted into Marshall McLuhan Catholic Secondary School. In 2000, the City of Toronto designated it a location "of architectural and historical value or interest." See City of Toronto By-Law No. 323–2000, enacted by City Council 8 June 2000; and Kathryn Anderson's appended history, "Schedule 'A': Heritage Property Report," August 1998, 2–8, https://www.toronto.ca/legdocs/bylaws/2000/law0323.pdf.

36 Banting's wartime activities and death are addressed in Bliss, *Banting,* 277.

37 See Graham's obituary in *the Canadian Medical Association Journal* 110, 6 (16 March 1974): 686; and the reference to Ray Farquharson, Graham's successor as Eaton Chair of Medicine, in note 53 below. DRDC's 2011 annual report drew a direct line between the ACAMR and DRDC Toronto. See *DRDC, Ten Years of Scientific Excellence for Canada's Defence and Security: Annual Report for the Year Ending 31 March 2011* (Ottawa: Defence Research and Development Canada, 2012), 4, https://publications.gc.ca/collections/collection_2012/rddc-drdc/D1-19-2011-eng.pdf.

38 Franks first tested his (eventually) eponymous suit in May 1940, at Camp Borden, a hundred kilometres north of Toronto. Dotto, "Canada's Aviation Medicine Pioneers," 3, among other sources. See also George Smith, "The Franks Flying Suit in Canadian Aviation Medicine History, 1939–1945," *Canadian Military History* 8, 2 (1999): 35–41, which does not address the Toronto-based institutional history.

39 Turl, "The Defence Research Establishment Toronto," 1035–36; Dotto, "Canada's Aviation Medicine Pioneers," 5; DCIEM, *The First Fifty Years,* n.p.

40 Turl, "The Defence Research Establishment Toronto," 1035.

41 Whillans, "The Defence Research Medical Laboratories," 266; Turl, "The Defence Research Establishment Toronto," 1036. For a list of IAM personnel in late 1949, see DCIEM, *The First Fifty Years,* n.p.

42 This connection is noted by Turl, "The Defence Research Establishment Toronto," 1036. For more on the Climatic Research Laboratory, see Matthew Farish, "Creating Cold War Climates: The Laboratories of American Globalism," in *Environmental Histories of the Cold War,* ed. J.R. McNeill and Corinna R. Unger (Cambridge: Cambridge University Press, 2010), 51–83.

43   Defence and Civil Institute of Environmental Medicine, *Annual Report, 1971–72* (Toronto: Defence and Civil Institute of Environmental Medicine, 1972), 3; Jane Chamberlain, Pamela Sendrovich, and L.H. Turl, *A Bibliography of Papers and Reports Published by the Defence Research Establishment Toronto (Formerly the Defence Research Medical Laboratories), 1950–1971* (Downsview: Defence and Civil Institute of Environmental Medicine, 1974), iii. In 1968, the IAM was renamed the Canadian Forces Institute of Environmental Medicine. It formally merged with Defence Research Establishment Toronto (previously the DRML) in 1971, to become the Defence and Civil Institute of Environmental Medicine (DCIEM) at Downsview. See *Defence Research Board: The First Twenty-Five Years* (Ottawa: Department of National Defence, 1972), 30; DCIEM, *The First Fifty Years*. Although public information about the current work of what is now called DRDC Toronto is modest, a fact sheet offers some details. "Climatic Facility: DRDC Toronto Fact Sheet," 2010, Defence Research and Development Canada, https://web.archive.org/web/20110706181701/http://www.toronto.drdc-rddc.gc.ca/about-apropos/fact/f05-eng.asp.

44   "Minutes of the University of Toronto Board of Governors," 22 March 1945, quoted in Campbell, "The Premise of Computer Science," 12. On veterans and enrolment, see Friedland, *The University of Toronto*, 363. Smith's term as U of T president (1945–59) was nearly identical to that of Omond Solandt at the DRB. Under a scheme put forward by U of T president Henry Cody in 1944, Smith, president of the University of Manitoba, would become principal of University College and Cody's assistant, and would then take over as university president the following year. A prominent Conservative, Smith left U of T to join John Diefenbaker's government, dying two years later. Friedland, *The University of Toronto*, 364–67.

45   Friedland, *The University of Toronto*, 375–76 (Smith is quoted on page 376). Yet another figure whom we do not discuss here is James Kenneth (Ken) Wallace Ferguson, who after wartime efforts in the RCAF became chair of pharmacology at U of T (in 1945) and then director of the noted Connaught Laboratories (from 1955 to 1972). In 1952, he was listed as the chair of a DRB panel on aviation medicine. Joseph Doupe, "Defence Medical Research," *Canadian Medical Association Journal* 67 (December 1952): 555.

46   Li, "Expansion and Consolidation," 97–98.

47   Goodspeed, *A History of the Defence Research Board*, 75–78. See also Farish, "Making 'Man in the Arctic,'" 92–96; Turner, "The Defence Research Board," 328. A 1948 Toronto conference "on the effects of cold on man" and subsequent advocacy by the Arctic Research Advisory Committee led eventually to a major survey. Alan C. Burton and Otto G. Edholm, *Man in a Cold Environment: Physiological and Pathological Effects of Exposure to Low Temperatures* (London: Edward Arnold, 1955), xi. Burton, another celebrated figure in Canadian medicine, conducted research for the Canadian military on environmental physiology and clothing during the war and then joined the University of Western Ontario's medical school as a biophysicist. See Matthew S. Wiseman, "The Weather Factory: Alan C. Burton and Military Research at the University of Western Ontario, 1945–70," *Scientia Canadensis* 45, 1 (2023): 1–22.

48   Farish, "Making 'Man in the Arctic,'" 95, 105n87; Rawling, *The Myriad Challenges of Peace*, 208.

49   E.A. Bott to Sidney Smith, 18 February 1948, Office of the President fonds, A1968–0007, box 34, file 1, UTARMS. The Canadian Psychological Association was in conversation with the NRC from the association's formation in 1938. In 1946, it converted its wartime NRC-funded Test Research Committee to a Research Planning Committee, chaired by Bott, who had been an air vice marshal in the Royal Air Force and was arguably the most prominent psychologist in Canada (and, like Charles Best, a long-standing U of T department chair). Along with Nelson Whitman Morton and McGill University's

Donald Hebb, who received DRB funding in the 1950s for his later notorious research on sensory deprivation, Bott was one of the initial eight members of the NRC's Associate Committee on Applied Psychology, established in 1948 with the DRB's Morton as chair. See O.E. Ault, "National Research Council Associate Committee on Applied Psychology," *Canadian Journal of Psychology* 2, 4 (1948): 187–88; N.W. Morton, "Psychology and the Defence Research Board," *Canadian Journal of Psychology* 8, 2 (1954): 49–50. Morton specifically mentions the "competence" of the Whillans-led DRML, where "psychologists, sociologists, and kindred scientists, both in and out of uniform, have contributed, along with physiologists, biochemists, nutritionists, and others, to the solution of problems of the human factors in defence" (50).

50   Turner, "The Defence Research Board," 110. At a meeting of the DRB's Standing Committee on External Research, which occurred on 9 March 1951 at National Defence Headquarters in Ottawa, U of T's Edward Sellers, Best's former student and later director of the DRML, received $50,000 from the DRB for research into "cold and radiation." See Turner, "The Defence Research Board," 109–10. The Board of Governors fonds, A1973–0025, boxes 53–58, UTARMS, contains detailed lists of the dozens and dozens of DRB grants directed to U of T researchers during this period.

51   Goodspeed, *A History of the Defence Research Board*, 73–74, 98–99 (the quotes are from pages 74 and 99). On page 74, Goodspeed suggests that "very little interchange has in fact taken place" between the DRB and universities, but this seems (partially) accurate only in the strictest sense of actual personnel movement.

52   Farquharson chaired medicine at U of T until 1960, when he became head of the new independent Medical Research Council of Canada. The council was the outgrowth of the NRC's Division of Medical Research (discussed above), which Farquharson led from 1957, when he took over from J.B. Collip. See Farquharson's obituary in the *British Medical Journal* 1, 5450 (19 June 1965): 1616. On the formation of the MRAC, see Turl, "The Defence Research Establishment Toronto," 1037; Goodspeed, *A History of the Defence Research Board*, 227; Turner, "The Defence Research Board," 96–97.

53   Turl, "The Defence Research Establishment Toronto," 1038.

54   Turl, "The Defence Research Establishment Toronto," 1038; see also Goodspeed, *A History of the Defence Research Board*, 227. On the DRB's extramural grants-in-aid research program, see Matthew S. Wiseman, "Canadian Scientists and Military Research in the Cold War, 1947–60," *Canadian Historical Review* 100, 3 (September 2019): 439–63.

55   Goodspeed, *A History of the Defence Research Board*, 228; Doupe, "Defence Medical Research," 554–55. Doupe, a University of Manitoba physiologist, was executive secretary of the new co-ordinating committee.

56   Goodspeed, *A History of the Defence Research Board*, 228n9, 230, 233–34.

57   On Whillans and the CIU, see Chamberlain, Sendrovich, and Turl, *A Bibliography of Papers*, iii; DCIEM, *The First Fifty Years*, n.p. On Morton's career and work with the DRB, see Edmond Cloutier, *The Defence Research Board and the Defence Scientific Service* (Ottawa: Queen's Printer, 1953), 31.

58   Chamberlain, Sendrovich, and Turl, *A Bibliography of Papers*, iii; Goodspeed, *A History of the Defence Research Board*, 233–34.

59   *Annual Report of the Chairman, Defence Research Board* (Ottawa: Defence Research Board, September 1951), 14, 4; DCIEM, *The First Fifty Years*, n.p.; Goodspeed, *A History of the Defence Research Board*, 235. See also Turl, "The Defence Research Establishment Toronto," 1038–39; Whillans, "The Defence Research Medical Laboratories," 267. The DRML's 1951 *Annual Report*, 6, estimated the cost of the new laboratory at $1.5 million. Goodspeed, *A History of the Defence Research Board*, 235, suggests that the cost was $2 million.

60 *Annual Report on the Progress of Defence Medical Research, 1949* (Ottawa: Defence Research Board, 1949), 1, RG 319, box 856, National Archives and Records Administration, College Park, Maryland.

61 Whillans, "The Defence Research Medical Laboratories," 266.

62 Cloutier, *The Defence Research Board*, 12.

63 For a related discussion, see Farish, "Making 'Man in the Arctic.'"

64 William Stevenson, "Survive on 9 Gumdrops a Day," *Toronto Daily Star,* 12 February 1954, 31, RG 24, vol. 10341, file August 28/[19]53 to August 14/[19]54, LAC. For a photo of Whillans speaking with Penny, see DCIEM, *The First Fifty Years,* n.p.

65 Kenyon, "Modern 'Torture' Gadgets." More discussion on "voluntarism" at the DRML and related facilities is crucial for establishing the context of the experiments and participant experience. Although researchers claimed to care for the wellbeing of test subjects in their reports, the history of human experimentation in Canada is a relatively new field that requires attention and analysis.

66 See Goodspeed, *A History of the Defence Research Board,* 90; "Charles A. Pope Publicity Chief for Defence Board," *Ottawa Journal,* 14 February 1952, RG 24, vol. 10341, file August 28/[19]53 to August 14/[19]54, LAC.

67 "Summer Students," *Defence Research Board Newsletter* 1, 1 (Ottawa: DRB, January 1955), n.p., Hartland Molson Library, Military History Research Centre, Canadian War Museum (CWM), Ottawa.

68 "Feature," *Defence Research Board Newsletter* 2, 4 (Ottawa: DRB, April 1956), n.p., CWM. For context, the DRB's total staff at the time consisted of approximately 2,800 people who worked at DRB HQ in Ottawa, in one of the organization's eleven research centres, or in either of the two liaison offices in London and Washington. See "CDRB's Message to the Staff," in *Defence Research Board Newsletter* 2, 3 (Ottawa: DRB, March 1956), n.p., CWM.

69 "Feature," *Defence Research Board Newsletter* 1, 3 (Ottawa: DRB, March 1955), n.p., CWM. Graduate research at the DRML resulted in advanced degrees for two staff members in 1955. Craig M. Mooney, chief of the Personnel Research Section, received a PhD in psychology from McGill University, and John C. Ogilvie, a vision researcher in the Applied Experimental Psychology Section, received a PhD in psychology from U of T. "DRML Scientists Win Doctorates," *Defence Research Board Newsletter* 1, 10 (Ottawa: DRB, October 1955), n.p., CWM.

70 Len Marquis, "Price of Defence: Constant Experiment," *Saturday Night,* 30 August 1952, 15, RG 24, vol. 10341, file Clippings: March 1947 to November 1952, LAC.

71 "Must Keep Head Still to Help Avoid Nausea," *Globe and Mail,* 25 February 1952, RG 24, vol. 10341, file Clippings: March 1947 to November 1952, LAC.

72 The exact date of the experiment is unknown, but sources indicate that it occurred before the DRML officially opened. See Stevenson, "Survive on 9 Gumdrops a Day," 31, LAC.

73 Stevenson, "Survive on 9 Gumdrops a Day," 31, LAC.

74 Stevenson, "Survive on 9 Gumdrops a Day," 31, LAC. For an equivalent US-set discussion, see Jordan Ernest Bimm, "Anticipating the Astronaut: Subject Formation in Early American Space Medicine, 1949–1959" (PhD diss., York University, 2018), especially Chapter 1.

75 See "DRML Reorganization Completed," *Defence Research Board Newsletter* 3, 3 (Ottawa: DRB, March 1957), n.p., CWM.

76 Senter, "Research Eases Work for Aerial Navigator."

77 "DRML to Create Its Own Weather Conditions," *Defence Research Board Newsletter* 3, 4 (Ottawa: DRB, April 1957), n.p., CWM.

78 See "Environmental Physiology," in *Annual Report of the Defence Research Medical Laboratories, 1958,* 8–9, LAC.

79 "DRB Staff Members and Dependents Star on Television," *Defence Research Board News-letter* 3, 4 (Ottawa: DRB, April 1957), n.p., CWM. The same program also featured Major E.E.S. Wright from the Royal Canadian Army Medical Corps, who discussed food and the challenge of feeding soldiers. In addition, Alma Brazeau, spouse of the DRML sociologist E.J. Brazeau, demonstrated clay modelling and pottery research in connection with the Toronto opening of the 1957 Exhibition of Canadian Ceramics.

80 "NATO Military Committee Visit Toronto," *Defence Research Board Newsletter* 3, 4 (Ottawa: DRB, April 1957), n.p., CWM. Freeze-dried meats prepared by the DRML Food Section also received the approval of the Department of Northern Affairs and National Resources after officers stationed in northern Canada found the samples "entirely suitable" for supplying remote outposts. "Northern Affairs Officers Approve Freeze-Dried Meats," *Defence Research Board Newsletter* 3, 10 (Ottawa: DRB, October 1957), n.p., CWM. A later symposium on the subject at the DRML drew together researchers and food industry representatives. See *Proceedings of the DRML Freeze-Drying Symposium, Held Friday, 28 October 1960* (Ottawa: DRB, 1960).

81 "Ice Cold in Downsview," *Toronto Sun*, 3 December 1973, 1, 18, 31.

82 For an illustration of Exercise Kool Stool and the climatic chamber experiments, see *DCIEM, The First Fifty Years*, n.p.

83 "Ice Cold in Downsview."

84 On the history of Dow Chemical and napalm production in the Cold War, see Edwin A. Martini, "World on Fire: The Politics of Napalm in the Global Cold War," *Cold War History* 16, 4 (2016): 463–81.

85 For news coverage, see John Burns, "Students, Professors Besiege Dow Recruiter," *Globe and Mail*, 21 November 1967, 1; Andrew Szende, "U of T Protestors Drive Dow Recruiter off Campus," *Toronto Daily Star*, 21 November 1967, 17.

86 John Burns, "Score Two for Students," *Globe and Mail*, 13 January 1968, A3; Andrew Szende, "Students to Try Banning War Firm Recruiters," *Toronto Daily Star*, 23 November 1967, 39.

87 "U of T Council Vote: Students Oppose Arms Recruiters," *Globe and Mail*, 23 November 1967, 5; John Burns, "Dow Demonstration: Civil Action Possible over U of T Protest," *Globe and Mail*, 1 December 1967, 5; "U of T Undecided on Letting Dow Recruiters Return," *Toronto Daily Star*, 8 December 1967, A36, B33; "Committee's Decision: University Will Allow Dow Recruiter Back In," *Globe and Mail*, 11 December 1967, 5; "Urges Open Stand: Lewis Wants Officials to Support Protests," *Globe and Mail*, 15 December 1967, 5.

88 For the speech referenced here, see O.M. Solandt, "The Place of Defence Research in the Scientific Community," Address to the Nineteenth Symposium of the DRB, 20 November 1967, 10, Omond McKillop Solandt fonds, B1993–0041, box /002, file 6, UTARMS.

89 For example, "On Pollution, War Research, and the Community of Scholars," *The Varsity*, 3 March 1969, 4.

90 It is worth noting that the DRML research program was also designed to contribute to civil defence and to produce "civilian dividends."

91 DRB funds paid for the institute at McGill, which opened in September 1957, and DRML psychologist Chester H. Baker was named its first director. See "News-Feature: First Human Engineering Institute to Be Established," *Defence Research Board Newsletter* 3, 2 (Ottawa: DRB, February 1957), n.p., CWM. Other notables tied to the DRML include Norman Mackworth, director of applied psychology for Britain's Medical Research Council, and Patrick Foley, who joined the U of T Industrial Engineering Department in 1966, after moving his family to Canada and joining the DRML Human Factors Group in 1954. See University of Toronto, Faculty of Applied Science and Engineering, "Memorial Tribute to Patrick J. Foley," 6 October 2011, https://www.engineering.utoronto.ca/wp-content/blogs.dir/28/files/2015/02/Memorial-Tribute-to-Patrick-Foley.pdf.

4

In Pursuit of Security
Canada's Defence Research Board
and Sensory Deprivation Research, 1950s–1970s

Meghan Fitzpatrick

CANADA IS OFTEN PERCEIVED as a minor actor in the Cold War, alongside more influential partners such as the United States and Britain. But this is far from the truth. As other chapters in this volume demonstrate, Canada was deeply affected by the clash of superpowers that dominated world affairs in the second half of the twentieth century. The same forces that shaped the course of geopolitics globally shaped this country and its defence and security apparatus. Historians and scholars of the Cold War widely consider the Korean War (1950–53) to be the opening salvo of this ideological contest. It represented the first direct confrontation between the West and communism and a critical challenge to the collective security promised by new international organizations, such as the United Nations (UN). Around twenty-six thousand Canadian troops joined a coalition to repel the North Korean invasion of its southern neighbour, one of the largest Canadian deployments in the twentieth century and one that also necessitated a rapid rearmament of the nation's armed forces and defence establishment.[1] But Korea's lasting legacy is not one merely of men and materiel.

Beginning in the summer of 1950, the Korean War was a ferocious conflict that produced over 4 million casualties.[2] A lack of infrastructure and rugged terrain made life difficult for civilians and soldiers alike in a conflict that remained highly mobile during its first twelve months, before becoming a grinding war of attrition. From 1950 to 1953, over 13,500 UN troops were captured by the enemy and spent hostilities as prisoners of war (POWs).[3] Immersed in the paranoid atmosphere of the early Cold War, rumours of brainwashing in the camps surfaced, and a series of false confessions by American servicemen to allegations of germ warfare seemed only to confirm the stories.[4] Without reliable intelligence, senior decision-makers feared that the Communists had developed startling new ways to manipulate the mind. This sparked a drive to understand the limits of psychological endurance, in which scientists and government officials in Canada's Defence Research Board (DRB) played a major part.

Over the following decades, the DRB's senior leaders financed groundbreaking studies on brainwashing, sensory deprivation, and isolation. The dramatic findings left a lasting impact on the field of psychology and our understanding of how human personality is influenced by social and physical environments. This chapter examines how DRB-funded academics contributed to this research and how the results of early studies shaped conduct after capture training for decades to come in Canada, the United States, and the United Kingdom. In addition, it reflects on the ethical challenges of producing research that was also used to develop offensive interrogation tactics. Finally, it considers how researchers and government officials came together to form a community bound by collegial ties that fuelled a uniquely Canadian military-industrial complex, linking soldiers and scientists in a mutually beneficial research ecosystem.

Behind Enemy Lines: Korea and Prisoners of War (1950–53)

The Korean War erupted on 25 June 1950. Despite signs of impending military movement, Communist North Korea's invasion of the Republic of South Korea came as a surprise to the West. Nevertheless, the UN responded quickly by assembling a coalition of seventeen countries, led by the US military. Poorly prepared for what it would face, the coalition was initially compelled to retreat to Korea's south coast. Under the command of American general Douglas MacArthur, it regained the initiative by launching an amphibious assault at Inchon that had pushed the North Koreans back over the border by October 1950. However, the war was far from over. Fearing that the Americans would extend hostilities into neighbouring Manchuria, Communist China deployed its ground forces in November.[5] This helped to ensure that the war continued for over two more years.[6] The majority of POWs captured during the war were apprehended in these early months, when fighting remained mobile and unpredictable.[7] Their experiences in North Korean– and Chinese-run prison camps would prove significant, for both the men and their home countries. Indeed, their time behind enemy lines shaped Canada's military research agenda for years to come.

When apprehended, UN troops were forced to march for days away from the front lines, with little food and water. Throughout their time in captivity, they suffered deplorable conditions, with almost no access to medical care.[8] Many died before the war ended in 1953, including nearly 40 percent of American servicemen in enemy hands.[9] Dotted throughout North Korea, the prison camps where they perished were located in "barren stretches of countryside, hundreds of miles from the coast or front-line fighting."[10] And those who might have considered making a run for it faced a formidable challenge: unforgiving terrain and a hostile population made the chance of escape practically impossible.[11]

For those who survived in these conditions, life behind enemy lines was an extended exercise in psychological endurance. The North Koreans were known for brutality. As one British intelligence report later commented, "North Korean interrogations were ludicrous and infantile, and caused suffering for no reasonable motive."[12] There were many instances of physical torture where prisoners were beaten and mutilated. For their part, Chinese authorities considered all Western POWs to be war criminals, subject to trial and execution.[13] Prisoners could avoid this punishment only if they attended hours of lectures on communist teachings. These "re-education" classes were intended to convince internees that the cause for which they had been fighting was unjust and that they were merely the pawns of Western capitalism.[14] It was in a POW's interest to appear willing to participate.[15] Those who refused were classified as "reactionaries" and punished with brutal methods ranging from sleep deprivation to solitary confinement, stress positions and exposure to sub-zero temperatures.[16] Postwar studies by British and American armed forces revealed that the majority of prisoners cooperated to a degree as a means of survival. Fewer than 10 percent actively resisted and suffered the consequences.[17]

During the war, almost no intelligence was available about re-education or life inside the camps. After all, no POW ever made it back to UN lines, and it was difficult to smuggle out information via military operatives or the Red Cross.[18] In the absence of reliable details, speculation abounded that the North Koreans and Chinese had developed new, mysteriously effective interrogation methods that could "supplant an individual's consciousness with fabricated beliefs, memories, and even traits."[19] These rumours seemed to be confirmed when twenty-three US airmen falsely confessed to allegations of germ warfare, beginning in 1952. The airmen, who were being held as POWs at the time, were used by the North Koreans to "prove" that the United States had participated in bacteriological warfare. In response, allegations of brainwashing were made to suggest that the POWs had been manipulated into a false confession.[20] The revelations generated ever more salacious stories in the media about truth drugs and the possibility of "brainwashing," which quickly became the stuff of science fiction.[21]

The Defence Research Board and the Human Sciences

Founded in April 1947, the DRB was established to provide Canada's armed services with the best in modern research and development.[22] Its first chairman, Dr. Omond Solandt, was a Canadian physiologist who had pursued a distinguished career overseas as a scientific administrator in Britain. During the Second World War, he had risen to become director of the British Army's Operational Research Group. Lured back home to take the reins of Canada's fledgling research agency, Solandt had lofty ambitions for this new arm of national defence. He envisioned the DRB as a link between the military and academia, and as a means to mobilize scientific manpower in the event of a national emergency and to transmit the "benefits of defence science to the

Canadian economy" and vice versa.[23] Under Solandt, the DRB also provided scientists the opportunity to influence government policy at its highest levels. From the beginning, Solandt was appointed as a member of the military's Chiefs of Staff Committee, with the authority of a lieutenant general.[24] By giving him such a role, Ottawa sent a powerful message about the part that science was expected to play in advancing the country's interests.

Addressing military and scientific colleagues at the DRB's annual research symposium in 1967, Solandt argued that the board acted as an ambassador for the military and provided access to foreign research that would otherwise have remained inaccessible.[25] In his autobiography, former minister of national defence Brooke Claxton agreed, noting that the "DRB won for us a place in the councils and work and secrets of our allies."[26] He even went so far as to conclude, "Canadian defence research probably had closer relations both with the British and the United States than these countries had with each other."[27] To be sure, the senior DRB leaders cultivated a program designed to strengthen and complement the work of allies. This included the development of a range of specialties, such as psychology and behavioural research.[28]

The 1940s had been a period of dramatic transformation for the human sciences. As historians Katherine Hubbard and Peter Hegarty point out, war acted as a pivotal catalyst.[29] From 1939 to 1945, psychologists and behavioural scientists became closely tied to the military and provided expertise in everything from clinical care and the enforcement of discipline to the maintenance of morale and the screening of recruits.[30] And in the following decades, these fields continued to grow.[31] Between 1940 and 1970, for instance, the membership of the American Psychiatric Association and the American Psychological Association expanded by 760 percent and 1,100 percent, respectively.[32] The Cold War was an ideal incubator for collaboration between scientists, the state, and the armed forces. As American historian Ellen Herman asserts, "military imperatives provided psychological experts with a hospitable working environment, a policy-making clientele, and a long list of reasons to bring their insights to bear on public issues."[33] Postwar Canada provided a similar climate for researchers. In a 1997 article for the *Canadian Historical Review*, Mona Gleason concludes that the "horrors of [war] encouraged human relations experts like psychologists to teach citizens the world over to manage and negotiate problems more successfully in the 'modern age.'"[34] Indeed, Canada was soon a leader in the field, with pioneering programs at the University of Toronto and McGill.[35] The Cold War offered exciting possibilities as science broke through the restraints of the past.

Addressing the University of British Columbia (UBC) in 1947, Solandt explained the DRB's mission to audience members. Though eager to highlight the economic benefits, he acknowledged that the "ultimate aim of all military research is the production of new weapons or of improved methods for the use of existing weapons."[36] Despite technological developments such as the atomic bomb, individual soldiers, sailors, and airmen remained the most vital of weapons systems. And the mind was the key to it all. Historian Alfred McCoy describes the level of postwar American investment in psychological research as a "veritable Manhattan project of the mind with costs ... that reached, at peak, a billion dollars a year."[37] Canadian efforts were more modest, but the investment was no less strategic.

Authorized in May 1947, the DRB's Psychological Research Panel was one of numerous committees established under the control of the board's Biological Research Division.[38] This group was eventually renamed as the Human Resources Research Advisory Committee (HRRAC) to encompass related disciplines such as sociology.[39] These specialized bodies reviewed priorities, developed programs, and recommended which projects merited financing.[40] Members included representatives from all three branches of the Canadian forces and university-based academics.[41]

Generally, DRB funds supported and enabled psychological research in three ways: internally, by extramural grants, or by contract. The latter two options often presented the most economic choice.[42] The annual extramural grant competition was designed to give "continuing and adequate support to selected research workers with particular competence and interest in defence fields."[43] Whereas the board's senior leaders were chiefly interested in studies with a military application, the grant system gave academics some freedom to explore basic research. In contrast, contracts were awarded for projects with predetermined parameters.[44] Funding for both programs increased substantially throughout this period. During the DRB's first year of operations, grants and contracts with Canadian research institutions totalled around $200,000.[45] Several years later, they employed over a hundred professors and three hundred graduate students, and by the late 1950s, the budget exceeded $2 million annually.[46] These programs and funding opportunities illustrate the deepening ties between the academy and the state. The Cold War political climate encouraged close co-operation, a trend that was not unique to Canada.[47] For instance, the British Department of Scientific and Industrial Research awarded only eighty-one research studentships prior to the Second World War. A decade later, it doled out nearly four hundred, and the "amount spent on research grants to faculty members increased from £11,000 to £268,679" during the same period.[48]

Throughout the 1940s and 1950s, the HRRAC slowly expanded its activities, principally through the personal contacts of committee members themselves. Archival evidence suggests that there was no formal process for selecting those academics who served on the HRRAC during the 1950s. Instead, correspondence shows that these men often had close ties to the Canadian military. Many had served in uniform, and it appears they were initially appointed as reliable individuals whose research aligned closely with the needs and interests of the military. And the same was true of the academics who received grants during this period. Most came from the same universities as HRRAC members or had ties to the defence establishment. Dr. Edwin Belyea of UBC is one such example. He completed a PhD in the early 1940s, looking at military personnel selection. Following this, he served as a lieutenant commander in the Royal Canadian Naval Volunteer Reserve between 1942 and 1946. Upon returning to civilian life, he joined UBC as an assistant professor, where he began receiving DRB grants.[49] Another regular funding recipient, Dr. George Ferguson of McGill University, had a similar background. From 1941 to 1945, he worked in personnel selection in the military, returning to academia after the war, but he continued to maintain ties to Ottawa by working on a contract basis with the DRB during the summer months.[50] Although the grant application process slowly became formalized by the 1970s, men like Belyea and Ferguson were important in the initial expansion of a research network that relied heavily on personal connections. This was especially pivotal during the Korean War years.

The McGill Studies (1951–55)

The DRB and HRRAC involvement in brainwashing research can be traced to the early years when the Korean War first galvanized Canada's small defence scientific community and spurred on investment in military rearmament. Research seemed to offer the solution to numerous challenges, including those involving North Korean and Chinese prison camps. This prompted HRRAC members to arrange a confidential meeting at Montreal's Ritz Hotel on 1 June 1951.[51] That morning, Canadian representatives for the DRB – Professor Donald Hebb of McGill, Dr. Travis Dancey of the Queen Mary Veterans' Hospital, and Dr. James Tyhurst of the celebrated Allan Memorial Institute for Psychiatry at McGill – met with their British and American counterparts, including Sir Henry Tizard, the British War Office scientific advisor, and Commander R.J. Williams and Dr. Caryl Haskins from the Central Intelligence Agency (CIA).[52] At the meeting, they discussed whether the "communists had discovered some new way of controlling the mind," as was suggested by the international press reports.[53] As a group, they agreed it was "essential to find out everything that could be learned about these [alleged] methods, so that ... troops could be told in advance of communist techniques and, to the extent possible, trained to withstand brainwashing."[54] Hebb suggested a possible avenue for research and outlined what became a ground-breaking experiment. He disagreed with speculation that the prisoners were being drugged, arguing instead that prolonged periods of deprivation could reduce a subject's resistance to interrogation and facilitate acceptance of new beliefs.[55]

By the early 1950s, Hebb was already one of Canada's foremost psychologists. Praised as a revolutionary in his field, he won numerous accolades for his work. Throughout his career, he served as president of the Canadian and American Psychological Associations, was granted sixteen honorary degrees, and was nominated for the Nobel Prize.[56] Rising from humble beginnings as a schoolteacher in Nova Scotia, he was and remains a giant of the psychological profession.[57] Moreover, he was connected to the majority of the leading researchers at the time. Without a doubt, McGill was home to the most prominent psychology department in the country, and as a beloved instructor, Hebb played a central role in shaping the careers of colleagues and students.[58] In addition, he was a key member of the HRRAC in the summer of 1951 and one of the numerous academics whose work it actively supported. Indeed, shortly after the meeting concluded, the HRRAC issued Hebb and his faculty collaborators Dr. Woodburn Heron and Dr. William Bexton a contract to investigate the questions posed in that hotel room. There is little documentation to suggest that a formal competition took place to select Hebb for this initiative. Given the political sensitivity of the topic, it is far more likely that HRRAC members saw him as a safe pair of hands to conduct the required work.[59]

Contract X-38 (1951–55) was intended to "cast light on the peculiar confessions elicited by the Communists" and to "discover the mental effects of cutting a person off from the normal world without any discomfort or threat or influence other than that of extreme monotony."[60] As Hebb's collaborators Heron and Bexton facetiously explained, "college students are apt to object to brain operation, so we have had to be satisfied with a less extreme isolation from the environment."[61] The first iteration of the study involved twenty-two male students between the ages of twenty-one and thirty-five, who were paid $20 to $24 a day for participating. Recruited through McGill's job placement service, they were asked to lie on a comfortable bed in a quiet cubicle for twenty-four hours a day, with breaks for eating and the toilet only.[62] During the experiment, they "wore goggles which prevented pattern vision, and cardboard cuffs, extending beyond the fingertips, which permitted free joint movement but little tactual [sic] perception."[63] Meanwhile, they wore headphones playing white noise or "inane ditties like the ... chorus of 'Home on the Range,' repeated several times, and stock market figures, passages from a religious primer for children, numbers and nonsense syllables."[64] Over the next five years, small changes were made to the research design, but the general experimental conditions remained the same.[65]

The results of Contract X-38 were jarring. At the DRB annual symposium in December 1952,[66] Hebb, Heron, and Bexton unveiled their findings to the assembled crowd. They revealed that the mean time spent in the cubicle was only about 43.5 hours and that eleven of the twenty-two subjects had refused to stay for longer than the twenty-four-hour minimum for which they had volunteered.[67] Describing the experience as "torture," the students were eager for any stimulation and willing to listen to anything, no matter how nonsensical.[68] Following the experiment, testing demonstrated slower reaction times, difficulty solving problems (arithmetic, anagrams), and a temporary loss of motivation. Participants also reported feelings of "otherness" and "bodily strangeness."[69] One man even confessed to feeling as if "his head was detached from his body," and another reported that his mind felt like a floating ball of cotton wool.[70] Others experienced vivid visual and auditory hallucinations, with a dream-like three-dimensional quality. One volunteer even saw a "troop of squirrels marching in single file across a snow covered field, wearing snowshoes and carrying little bags over their shoulders."[71] Intriguingly, the students also appeared to be far more open to changing their minds about subjects on which they had previously expressed a strong opinion (belief in ghosts and the paranormal).[72] Several decades later, an investigation into Canadian government funding for these experiments noted that

the conclusions reached ... may be simply stated. A changing sensory environment is absolutely essential. Without it, the brain ceases to function in an adequate way, and abnormalities of behaviour develop; for example, the subject quickly begins to hallucinate. By "softening up" a prisoner through the use of sensory isolation techniques, a captor is indeed able to bring about a state of mind in which the prisoner is receptive to the implantation of ideas contrary to previously held beliefs.[73]

In other words, simple deprivation and isolation could have a drastic impact on the adult human mind.

Rumours that the North Koreans and Chinese drugged their POWs continued to circulate for years. However, the McGill experiments demonstrated that such measures were not needed to manipulate or "brainwash" a subject. Following their repatriation, the prisoners themselves confirmed that the enemy had not used any "special or novel scientific 'gimmick'" to influence behaviour.[74] During a debriefing, Lieutenant D.A. Lankford of the British Royal Naval Volunteer Reserve described his own POW experience. He explained that he was questioned for nearly seventy-two hours, after which he could no longer stay awake.[75] Lankford speculated that his interrogators allowed him to rest for a few minutes before waking him up and pretending that he had slept for hours. This continued for an unknown period.

The medical report on Lankford's testimony concluded that there was no evidence drugs were administered and that "the use of complete sleep deprivation as a means of conditioning a prisoner for suggestion indicates an advanced psychological insight on the part of the Chinese interrogators."[76] The report also argued that "no interrogator untrained in psychology would see the implications of this technique ... [and] it is possible that [it] has been developed as a result of deliberate research."[77] Although Lankford's case was extreme, his experiences of sleep and sensory deprivation were common among fellow detainees.[78] Both techniques were used repeatedly to make prisoners pliable and open to the manipulation necessary to transform them into convenient tools of political propaganda.

The McGill experiments were initially classified because of the political sensitivity involved with brainwashing research. However, Hebb, Heron, and Bexton were soon keen to release their results to the scientific community. In fact, Hebb wrote to the director of the DRB Operational Research Group, Dr. Nelson Morton, several times to ask permission to declassify the work.[79] On one occasion, he even included a drawing of himself "on bended knee beside his signature" and begged "muzzle not the ox that treadeth out the corn – Humbly yours, Don."[80] Morton finally agreed that the results could be published in the *Canadian Journal of Psychology* in 1954, on the condition that a cover story be used to explain the project.[81] This would claim that the goal of the experiment was not to understand brainwashing but to address the mundane realities of jobs that required prolonged attention to monotonous tasks, such as air traffic control.[82] Despite the steps taken to keep the project quiet, the truth eventually came to light when US officials, who had seen the results, mistakenly shared the information with the media.[83]

On the evening of 5 May 1956, the headline of a Montreal newspaper screamed, "McGill Students Brainwashed!"[84] As the correspondent informed readers, "the experiment proved that [people] could be reduced into slobs not knowing right from wrong, could be made to lie, cheat and say anything that was suggested to them."[85] Minister of National Defence Ralph Campney quickly tried to distance himself from the project by claiming that he knew nothing about it until it was written up in the press.[86] Meanwhile, the DRB's chief scientist, Dr. G.S. Field, attempted to explain why the experiments had been conducted in the first place. He argued, "while we abhor brainwashing and all its implications we feel that we must face up to its likely use in a future possible war and strive to find some method of combating such measures by an enemy."[87] In spite of this explanation, public debate on the issue brought an end to both the project and

Hebb's involvement in the research.[88] Nevertheless, he remained an influential member of the HRRAC, and the findings of his work proved simply too intriguing to ignore.

An Expanding Field

The field of sensory and perceptual deprivation continued to grow steadily over the next twenty years. In fact, there were well over a thousand peer-reviewed publications on the subject by 1972.[89] The McGill studies prompted psychologists at universities across North America to launch similar programs at several institutions, including Duke, Princeton, Harvard, and the Universities of Miami and Michigan. Scholars as far afield as West Germany and Japan actively pursued comparable work.[90] Outside of academia, government agencies such as the US National Institute of Mental Health and private companies such as Boeing established their own laboratories.[91] At the height of the Cold War, Hebb's findings had implications for everything from security to mental health and the future of manned space travel.[92] In Canada, the HRRAC continued to lead the field by investing in research that could help explain what had happened in North Korea. By far, the most prominent of those researchers was Dr. John Zubek of the University of Manitoba.

Born in Czechoslovakia in 1925, Zubek immigrated to Canada as a child and grew up in Grand Forks, British Columbia. With a master's degree from the University of Toronto and a PhD from Johns Hopkins, he spent his early career as an assistant professor at McGill.[93] For reasons that remain unclear, he later denied having worked on Hebb's experiment during his time there. But his personal papers contradict this claim. In a handwritten note attached to one of his speeches, he outlined the government's interest in brainwashing and how he and other faculty members had participated in the project. This early experience was formative and would shape the remainder of his career.[94]

At the tender age of twenty-eight, Zubek was appointed head of the University of Manitoba's psychology department and rose to become a leading figure in sensory, perceptual deprivation, and isolation research.[95] Over the next decades, he received a steady stream of awards, including well over $200,000 from such agencies as diverse as the Canadian National Research Council, the US Public Health Service, and the US National Institute of Mental Health.[96] Throughout his career, the HRRAC remained his most reliable financier, and it was DRB money that allowed him to set up a purpose-built laboratory, hire assistants, and pay volunteers to participate in his studies. With these funds, he built an impressive "translucent Plexiglas dome housed in a sound-proofed chamber" equipped with closed-circuit television, microphones, and an escape button for participants (Figure 4.1).[97] The facility was "completely self-contained and could

Figure 4.1 Photographed in October 1959, John Zubek of the University of Manitoba and a member of his research staff, Wilma Sansom, stand beside an isolation dome designed for a series of experiments to examine the effects of sensory deprivation. | *Winnipeg Free Press*, 2 February 1983, 65.

accommodate constant darkness and silence or constant light and white noise."[98] Overall, the HRRAC invested close to $300,000 in the day-to-day operations of the lab throughout the 1960s.[99]

One of Zubek's early applications for funding shows that, like Hebb, he wished to understand the impact of deprivation on the mind and was chiefly interested in answering three key questions:

1. What are the effects of various adverse environmental conditions, operating in restricted quarters, on intellectual and perceptual functioning?
2. What methods or procedures might be employed to counteract or minimize any impairments that might occur under the previously mentioned conditions?
3. What type of personality structure might be most conducive to adequate psychological functioning under various adverse environmental conditions?[100]

In contrast to his colleagues in Montreal, Zubek introduced heightened experimental parameters to illustrate the impact of such conditions. As journalist Cecil Rosner highlighted in a 2010 article for *Canada's History,* Zubek "plunged some people into darkness and silence for up to two weeks; he immobilized others in a coffin-like box" and "asked students to lie quietly ... while he subjected them to constant light and white noise."[101] Periodically, Zubek even insisted on participating himself. On 3 October 1959, a correspondent for the *Winnipeg Free Press* jokingly told readers that the professor had been living in a "giant goldfish bowl" for the past ten days.[102] A similar piece from the *Winnipeg Tribune* mused that the thirty-four-year-old was surviving on a diet of coffee, sandwiches, and the occasional piece of pie while enduring the same conditions of darkness and deprivation as the rest of his subjects.[103]

Despite these extreme conditions, the results of the Manitoba experiments proved surprisingly less dramatic than those coming out of McGill. The participants did not experience hallucinations to the same degree; nor did they experience the same levels of intense sensory and perceptual impairment.[104] Nonetheless, there were notable similarities between the two experimental programs. Both Hebb and Zubek's teams discovered that "prolonged isolation [could] impair a wide variety of intellectual functions ranging from simple arithmetical ability to complex reasoning processes. Various sensory and perceptual processes were also affected, e.g. colour vision, perception of patterns, pain sensitivity, and visual and auditory alertness."[105] Moreover, they concluded that participants experienced a stark loss of motivation and that "changes persist for some time after the experimental period."[106] Consequently, they could "only speculate as to the possible physiological and psychological state of prisoners of war and others who, in the past, have been incarcerated for months or even years."[107]

Donald Hebb and John Zubek, and by extension the HRRAC, were all essential to the development of sensory and perceptual deprivation research in Canada and internationally. As historian Mical Raz observed in 2013, "within seven years of Hebb's team's first publication, 230 articles on sensory deprivation appeared in the leading scientific journals, most citing Hebb's work."[108] Many directly referenced McGill for its impact on psychology. Reviewing grant applications for the HRRAC in 1971, Peter Suedfeld of Rutgers University heaped similar praise on Zubek when he noted, "his work has attracted great interest and respect, both for its original hypotheses and the insightful way in which these ... are tested and their implications followed up."[109] He was undoubtedly "one of the world's leading researchers."[110] In a 1975 book on the field, American psychologist Austin Riesen argued that the "history of sensory deprivation would lack the studies that launched its forward thrust in the mid-twentieth century" without the work first done in Montreal and Winnipeg.[111] The experiments had unexpectedly raised vital questions about how environment affects the human learning process and undergirds both personality and mental stability. As Heron, Bexton, and Hebb first maintained, "the maintenance of normal, intelligent, adaptive behaviour requires a continually varied sensory input.

The brain is not like a calculating machine operated by an electric motor, which is able to respond at once to its specific cues after lying idle indefinitely."[112]

Research in Action: Enhanced Training and Interrogation Practices

The Korean War had revealed the strange, sometimes startling reality of the modern battlefield. For the members of the UN coalition, it had also demonstrated that troops were not prepared to face the rigours of captivity in Communist hands or the indoctrination and interrogation methods they employed. The scientific drive to understand the psychological mechanisms involved in "brainwashing" was initially intended as a defensive measure to grasp how the adversary could manipulate detainees. As one British report reasoned at the time, "forewarned is forearmed."[113] The HRRAC-financed experiments were designed to carefully deconstruct the psychology behind false confessions and indoctrination. Canadian authorities shared the findings of these studies widely among allies, including the United States and Britain. Over the following years, this decision shaped the development of military training practices on both sides of the Atlantic, including the introduction of more realistic conduct after capture (CAC) and resistance to interrogation (RTI) training.

Throughout the first half of the twentieth century, intelligence operatives had been the primary recipients of CAC and RTI training. During both world wars, incorporating such instruction into the basic training for all personnel was seen as inappropriate. This is because it was widely considered "bad for morale since it presupposes the possibility of capture."[114] However, Korea forced officials to reassess the notion. A 1961 British Army memo pointed out, "POW treatment in any future war is bound to follow a similar pattern. In fact, it could be ... far severer."[115] After all, the Soviet Union and China were unlikely to obey the Geneva Convention or refrain from intensive interrogation. Therefore, it was critical to equip servicemen with the ability to "resist and defeat the subtleties of interrogation, persuasion and intimidation by giving them practical experience."[116]

With this in mind, Canada, the United States, and Britain all introduced enhanced training regimes during this period. CAC and RTI training was incorporated in the final phase of escape and evasion exercises. The British Royal Air Force ran between sixty and seventy such exercises each year, beginning in the mid-1950s, for instance. Moreover, Europe and North Africa were frequent destinations for multinational field exercises that included other NATO members, such as Canada and the United States. Pitting one group of troops against the other, they could include anywhere from a few dozen men to hundreds. Dropped into unfamiliar territory, units were expected either to evade or pursue their fellow soldiers. If captured, participants were subjected to questioning by interrogators, whose tactics were closely modelled after Communist methods and informed by sensory deprivation research.[117] A British Joint Services report made clear, "our ... training is based on a psychological approach, assessing and exploiting a man's character and his reaction to circumstances of his arrest/capture and imprisonment."[118] Permissible tactics could include anything from hooding to white noise, sleep deprivation, stress positions, ridicule, and other non-physical abuse, as well as prolonged exposure to the elements.[119] The studies completed at McGill, Manitoba, and other institutions had repeatedly shown that these techniques rapidly wore POWs down and increased suggestibility. Military officials went to great lengths to further heighten the experience by creating a hyperrealistic training environment. For instance, the US military built an entire prison that was meant to resemble a North Korean camp when it opened a survival school at Stead Air Force Base outside Reno, Nevada, in 1953.[120]

This hyperrealism had its merits from a training and preparedness perspective, but it proved extremely controversial when the public discovered what was happening. In the United States, a seventeen-day military survival program was dismissed in 1955 as a "school for sadists" that inappropriately blurred the line between tough training and "outright cruelty."[121] The *Saturday Review* insisted, "brutality is like a bullet: you don't shoot a man to prepare him for war. And when you degrade a man and humiliate and damage him the end result is measured in the damage it does to him, not in the supposed 'training' he receives."[122] The clamour surrounding CAC and RTI training forced the Pentagon to limit it to those who volunteered to participate. Moreover, Congress insisted on the introduction of new principles to govern the conduct of exercises. The British and Canadian forces were similarly pushed to adopt stricter rules and regulations. During the 1960s, limits were introduced as to how long servicemen could be continuously questioned or kept awake. More importantly, a doctor had to be present and could remove anyone from the exercise at risk of physical or mental harm. Military officials also scaled back the number of personnel who were required to participate, limiting them to men who had a good chance of being taken captive, such as aircrew and special forces.[123] Nonetheless, Korea and the research that came out of that conflict ensured realistic survival schools remained an essential feature of the Cold War military training apparatus.

In addition to these defensive initiatives, sensory and perceptual deprivation research is widely acknowledged to have informed the development of offensive military interrogation. Methods such as sleep deprivation and hooding could be used as a "teaching tool" but could easily be weaponized. This became readily apparent following the release of the Compton and Parker Reports in Britain during the early 1970s. Launched as parliamentary inquiries, they were intended to investigate the legality of interrogation practices used on detainees in

Northern Ireland. The final reports detailed the security forces' use of so-called depth interrogation techniques that included wall standing, sleep deprivation, prolonged deprivation of food and drink, and constant noise.[124] Committee members examined the genesis of these practices and traced their introduction back to Korea and early research on brainwashing. When the Parker Report was released in March 1972, the minority report produced by Lord Gardiner further pointed out that there was a "considerable bibliography of experiments in this field, particularly in Canada."[125]

This history left no illusions as to the origins of interrogation techniques; nor is there much doubt that the research started at McGill had a long-lasting impact. Several years later, in 1976, the European Commission of Human Rights concluded the use of techniques like sensory deprivation, in combination with sleep deprivation, wall standing, hooding, stress positions, and prolonged noise or "enhanced interrogation" techniques, constituted torture.[126] The case, originally brought by the Republic of Ireland, was then referred to the European Court of Human Rights. Contradicting the commission, the court ruled that the techniques were "inhuman and degrading" but did not rise to the level of "torture."[127] This left the door open for military forces around the world to continue employing these controversial techniques, which were originally intended to protect their own personnel. In the past twenty years alone, revelations about the abuse of detainees by US forces at Abu Ghraib prison and the death of Iraqi civilians such as Baha Mousa in British custody have compelled the international community to once again confront the ugliness of modern war. Perhaps even more significantly, these incidents have prompted yet another reconsideration of the role that scientific experimentation and experts play in informing the practice of interrogation.[128]

Ethical Challenges

The original experimental research discussed in this chapter took place at a time when ethical standards for scientific experimentation had yet to achieve the level of rigour that is now expected. Codified rules for human experimentation, such as the Nuremberg Code, first emerged following the Second World War. And though various scientific bodies accepted this guidance, regulations frequently lacked legal force. In 1986, lawyer and former Conservative Party MP George Cooper was tasked with investigating whether the Canadian government had knowingly funded psychiatric experiments at Montreal's Allan Memorial Institute that were covertly funded by the CIA as part of its behavioural research program. Cooper concluded that officials were not aware of these ties and had no "moral or legal responsibility for the activities" that took place at the institute.[129] But summing up his thoughts, Cooper reflected on the permissive research environment of the 1950s and the 1960s that allowed such experiments to proceed. In his report, he noted that funding agencies in the immediate postwar period relied heavily on the integrity and expertise of researchers.[130] He pointed out that ethical questions were placed "squarely in the hands of the responsible investigator" and that federal funding committees simply assumed "ethical people did ethical things."[131] The informal manner in which the HRRAC awarded funding at this time also suggests that members often assumed the best of colleagues with whom they shared close ties and did not feel it necessary to enforce rigorous ethical review.

There is no evidence to suggest that any of the HRRAC-financed experiments were intended *knowingly* to expose participants to danger or to inflict short- or long-term psychological damage. Moreover, it is clear the researchers were often aware of the ethical challenges involved in their work. In several instances, DRB management even expressed opposition to pushing the limits for the sake of scientific curiosity. For example, Chief Superintendent Morley Whillans of the Defence Research Medical Laboratories – the Toronto DRB facility discussed in Chapter 3 – aired his anxieties about conducting experiments where subjects believed they were involved in life-or-death situations. In a letter written in 1965, he argued, "The moral implication of putting men in such a situation and then generating a crisis so that some deserted their post is, in our opinion, unforgivable ... It is certain that years later some of these men will still feel shame at their behaviour and all for what?"[132]

In spite of these misgivings, it is also clear that Canadian authorities were aware of British and American experiments involving subjects who were routinely exposed to "psychological stress by introducing a situation, which apparently poses a real threat to life and limb, but is in fact under the control of the experimenter."[133] For example, HRRAC observers attended an exercise run by an American agency on behalf of the US military in 1955. The project was intended to measure fighting ability by reproducing the stress of combat. During each experiment, participants were stationed at an outpost and "confronted with an apparent danger (either smoke stemming from a supposed forest fire or blasts from artillery shells exploding nearby) and no means of rescue."[134] To secure help, they had to repair a broken radio, armed only with the available instructions. Meanwhile, "hidden wires connected with the experimenter's station transmit and record signals of [the] subject's performance." In a report on the exercise, a HRRAC observer acknowledged that it had been sharply criticized by the American Psychological Association for failing to secure informed consent from participants.[135] Nonetheless, the same observer appeared to have no qualms about sharing the research findings with colleagues.

Throughout this period, members of the HRRAC may not have directly funded research that was intended to cause harm, but it is evident that they knowingly contributed to a climate where researchers willingly pushed the envelope in the name of science and security. As historian Joy Rohde notes in her 2013 book on the American military-industrial complex, academics during the early Cold War actively joined forces with the defence establishment. It was a mutually beneficial relationship. Moreover, researchers commonly believed that they were contributing to national security against a skilled, unprincipled, and often covert enemy.[136] But such work could have unintended and serious ramifications. Reviewing the McGill study, historian Alfred McCoy discovered that four of the original volunteers complained at the time of having experienced terrifying hallucinations, akin to the effects of mescaline.[137] Furthermore, one suffered a complete breakdown following the experiment and had not recovered several years later.[138] What is more, one of Hebb's former students, Dr. Maitland Baldwin, went on to work for the US National Institute of Mental Health. In an experiment modelled after the McGill studies, he confined one US Army volunteer to a sensory deprivation box for nearly forty hours, by which time the man began to cry and kick violently.[139] Previously classified documents indicate that Baldwin was encouraged to expose his subjects to extreme forms of deprivation. On one occasion, he even informed CIA officials that he would be willing to complete "terminal" experiments, if the agency were willing to provide him with "expendable human subjects."[140]

Conclusion

There is no denying that the research completed by Hebb, Zubek, and their colleagues on sensory and perceptual deprivation has left a complicated, divisive legacy behind. Born from a Cold War environment of paranoia, the initial experiments were intended to help explain whether brainwashing were possible and to counter the impact of interrogation. The findings that emerged from institutions such as McGill and the University of Manitoba fundamentally challenged contemporary conceptions of human consciousness and how sensory environment affects personality. This represented a turning point for psychology as a young, growing discipline. However, these results also revealed how vulnerable we all are to influence and manipulation, under the right conditions. That reality sparked prolonged military investment in a host of measures intended to bolster the psychological resilience of those in uniform. For better or worse, this included enhanced training in CAC and RTI. Those initiatives arguably straddled a fuzzy line between necessary realism and subjecting trainees to possible trauma. Even more contentious, the scientific research indisputably informed the development of offensive interrogation techniques that have been categorized as torture on numerous occasions.

These research findings were the product of a defence scientific community that has received little recognition from scholars to date. During the Cold War, America's military-industrial complex was well financed and vast in scale. In contrast, the Canadian government's investments in this field were relatively modest. Having said that, this chapter has demonstrated that the investments were often highly strategic and that they made an outsized impact globally. This work was also facilitated by the close personal ties among military officials, defence bureaucrats, and scientists across the country. What is more, those links were not viewed as contentious in an era where scientific experts and the state were still considered natural and "indispensable partners," operating in a competitive and dangerous world.[141] This contributed to the development of a uniquely Canadian defence scientific landscape that began to shift and change only with the political tumult of the 1970s and the rise of anti-war and anti-military sentiment tied to the Vietnam War.

Today, we live in an environment where there has never been more opportunity for both state and non-state actors to manipulate and influence populations around the world. The fear of brainwashing has not disappeared but has been transformed and amplified in an online world filled with mis- and disinformation. Governments and militaries globally continue to rely on scientific inquiry as a means to protect the civilian population and military personnel. But as this chapter has made readily evident, there is a fine balance to be achieved in pursuing this knowledge. The not-so-distant past forces us to realize that what is intended as defensive can quickly become offensive and begs us to pause and think of what we are willing to do in pursuit of security.

Notes

1 Anthony Farrar-Hockley, *The British Part in the Korean War*, vol. 2, *An Honourable Discharge* (London: HMSO, 1995), ix; Richard Trembeth, *A Different Sort of War: Australians in Korea, 1950–53* (Melbourne: Australian Scholarly Publishing, 2005), 1; "Commonwealth Forces' Record in Korea: 'A Successful Experiment,'" *Times of London*, 21 July 1953; Herbert Fairlie Wood, *Strange Battleground: The Operations in Korea and Their Effects on the Defence Policy of Canada* (Ottawa: Queen's Printer, 1966), 257.

2 Richard Whelan, *Drawing the Line: The Korean War, 1950–1953* (London: Faber and Faber, 1990), 373.

3 Walter Hermes, *Truce Tent and Fighting Front, US Army in the Korean War* (Washington: Office of the Chief of Military History, 1966).

4 "Communist Treatment of British Prisoners of War in Korea, Paper by AI9," Air Ministry, n.d., WO 32/20490, National Archives, Kew (TNA); Robert Gentner, "Understanding the POW Experience: Stress Research and the Implementation of the 1955 US Armed Forces Code of Conduct," *Journal of the History of the Behavioral Sciences* 51, 2 (Spring 2015): 143.

5 Chinese troops deployed to Korea were known as the Chinese People's Volunteer Army. Although all were members of the army, they were called "volunteers" to avoid a formal declaration of war between China and the United States.

6 Meghan Fitzpatrick, *Invisible Scars: Mental Trauma and the Korean War* (Vancouver: UBC Press, 2017), 23–24; Tim Carew, *The Commonwealth at War* (London: Cassell, 1967), 13, 27, 71; Jeffrey Grey, *The Commonwealth Armies and the Korean War: An Alliance Study* (Manchester: Manchester University Press, 1988), 172; Cyril Barclay, *The First Commonwealth Division: The Story of British Commonwealth Land Forces in Korea, 1950–1953* (Aldershot: Gale and Polden, 1954), 12, 34.

7 US Senate, *Communist Treatment of Prisoners of War: A Historical Survey* (Washington: US Government Printing Office, 1972); Hermes, *Truce Tent and Fighting Front;* "Notes on Behaviour of British and Allied Prisoners of War," c. 1957, WO 32/20493, TNA.

8 Ministry of Defence, "Treatment of British Prisoners of War in Korea," 1955, ADM 1/25760, TNA; Jonathan Vance, *Objects of Concern: Canadian Prisoners of War through the Twentieth Century* (Vancouver: UBC Press, 1994), 217–34.

9 Robert Klein, Michael Wells, and Janet Somers, US Office of Assistant Secretary for Policy, Planning and Preparedness, "Former American Prisoners of War," 2005, 3.

10 App to AC 8/2/362B, "Report by Lt. Seeger, Royal Marines on Combat Survival Course No. 2," 4 July 1961, ADM 201/126, TNA.

11 App to AC 8/2/362B, "Report by Lt. Seeger," TNA.

12 "Communist Treatment of British Prisoners of War in Korea, Paper by AI9," TNA; "Chairman's Amendments to Report (PWP/P(55)8) for Discussion at Meeting of Panel," 16 May 1955, WO 32/20493, TNA.

13 "Communist Treatment of British Prisoners of War in Korea, Paper by AI9," TNA; Julius Segal, *Factors Related to the Collaboration and Resistance Behavior of US Army PWs in Korea* (Washington, DC: Human Resources Research Office, George Washington University, 1956), 19.

14 "Communist Treatment of British Prisoners of War in Korea, Paper by AI9."

15 "Communist Treatment of British Prisoners of War in Korea, Paper by AI9."

16 "Communist Treatment of British Prisoners of War in Korea, Paper by AI9."

17 "Communist Treatment of British Prisoners of War in Korea, Paper by AI9."

18 POW Coordinating Committee, "Treatment of UN Prisoners in Korea, Memo by Chairman," 29 December 1950, DEFE 7/1992, TNA.

19 Timothy Melley, "Brainwashed! Conspiracy Theory and Ideology in the Postwar United States," *New German Critique* 35, 1 (Spring 2008): 145.

20 "Communist Treatment of British POWs in Korea, Paper by AI9," TNA; Gentner, "Understanding the POW Experience," 143.

21 James Price, "Brainwashing – A Cross Cultural Chinese Puzzle," *World Affairs* 131, 1 (April, May, June 1968): 17; Edward Hunter, "Brain-Washing in 'New' China," *New Leader*, 7 October 1950, 6–7.

22 Bill Rawling, *The Myriad Challenges of Peace: Canadian Forces Medical Practitioners since the Second World War* (Ottawa: Department of National Defence, Directorate of History, 2004), 198; Jason Ridler, "Dr. Omond Solandt and Canada's Approach to Defence Research Diplomacy 1946–1956," *Diplomacy and Statecraft* 21, 3 (2010): 398.

23 Omond Solandt, "Policy and Plans for Defence Research in Canada, a Preliminary Review," 1946, RG 24, acc. 83–84/167, box 539, file 1700–147/63, vol. 3, Library and Archives Canada (LAC).

24 Jason Sean Ridler, *Maestro of Science: Omond McKillop Solandt and Government Science in War and Hostile Peace, 1939–1956* (Toronto: University of Toronto Press, 2015), 126.

25 Omond Solandt, *Place of Defence Research in the Scientific Community: Address to Symposium of the DRB* (Ottawa: DRB, 1967), 2.

26 Quoted in Ridler, "Dr. Omond Solandt," 400.

27 Ridler, "Dr. Omond Solandt," 400.
28 D.J. Goodspeed, *A History of the Defence Research Board of Canada* (Ottawa: Queen's Printer, 1958), 45–49.
29 Katherine Hubbard and Peter Hegarty, "Blots and All: A History of the Rorschach Ink Blot Test in Britain," *Journal of the History of the Behavioral Sciences* 52, 2 (2016): 151.
30 Simon Wessely, "War and Psychiatry" (lecture at the Global History Seminar, London Centre of University of Notre Dame, 27 March 2013).
31 Andrew Scull, "The Mental Health Sector and the Social Sciences in Post-World War II USA Part 2: The Impact of Federal Research Funding and the Drugs Revolution," *History of Psychiatry* 22, 3 (2011): 268.
32 Ellen Herman, "Psychology as Politics: How Psychological Experts Transformed Public Life in the United States, 1940–1970" (PhD diss., Brandeis University, 1993), 9.
33 Herman, "Psychology as Politics," 8.
34 Mona Gleason, "Psychology and the Construction of the 'Normal' Family in Postwar Canada, 1945–1960," *Canadian Historical Review* 78, 3 (1997): 445.
35 R.A. Cleghorn, "Eye Witness," n.d., MG4204, 1997–0051, C. 1, 1/3, 1205A, McGill University Archives (MUA).
36 Omond Solandt, "Address at Twenty-First Congregation of UBC," 29 October 1947, RG 24, vol. 2425, LAC.
37 Alfred McCoy, "Science in Dachau's Shadow: Hebb, Beecher, and the Development of CIA Psychological Torture and Modern Medical Ethics," *Journal of the History of the Behavioral Sciences* 43, 4 (2007): 402.
38 DRB, "Semi-Annual Report of the Chairman, 1—30 April 1947," September 1947, RG 19, vol. 520, file 124–62, LAC.
39 T.W. Cook, Human Resources Research Advisory Committee, to Dr. Falardeau, Department of Sociology, Laval University, 31 August 1951, RG 24, vol. 4121, DRBS 3–150–43, pt. 1, LAC; Omond Solandt to Dr. Blackburn, Queen's University, 2 December 1953, RG 24, vol. 4121, DRBS 3–150–43, pt. 3, LAC.
40 Goodspeed, *A History of the Defence Research Board*, 76–78.
41 Goodspeed, *A History of the Defence Research Board*, 76–78.
42 DRB, "Semi-Annual Report of Chairman, 1 April 1948—30 September 1948," 10 December 1948, RG 19, vol. 520, file 124–62, LAC.
43 DRB, "Programme of Scientific Work for Fiscal Year 54/55," March 1953, RG 24, vol. 2425, Speeches and Reports etc., vol. 2, LAC.
44 Donald Hebb, Chairman, HRRAC, "Annual Report," 11 December 1953, RG 24, vol. 4121, DRBS 3–150–43, pt. 3, LAC; Donald Hebb, Chairman, HRRAC, "Annual Report of Chairman," c. 1952, RG 24, DRBS 3–150–43, vol. 2, LAC; "First Meeting of HRRAC," 25 February 1951, RG 24, DRBS 3–150–43, pt. 1, LAC.
45 DRB, "Semi-Annual Report of the Chairman, 1 October 1947—31 March 1948," 5 June 1948, RG 19, vol. 520, file 124–62, LAC.
46 DRB, "Annual Report of Chairman," October 1952, RG 24, vol. 2425, LAC.
47 P. Thompson, *Graduate Education in the Sciences in Canadian Universities* (Toronto: University of Toronto Press and Presses de l'Université Laval, 1963), 16–17, 73–74, 93–95; James Ledbetter, *Unwarranted Influence: Dwight D. Eisenhower and the Military-Industrial Complex* (New Haven: Yale University Press, 2011), 5, 7, 37.
48 Jonathan Turner, "The Defence Research Board of Canada, 1947 to 1977" (PhD diss., University of Toronto, 2012), 120–21.
49 Biography of E. Belyea, n.d., RG 24, vol. 5250, HQ File No. HQ-S19–73–4, vol. 2, LAC.
50 Biography of G. Ferguson, n.d., RG 24, vol. 5250, HQ file No. HQ-S19–73–4, vol. 2, LAC.

51 George Cooper, *Opinion of George Cooper, Q.C., regarding Government Funding of the Allan Memorial Institute in the 1950s and 1960s* (Ottawa: Minister of Supply and Services, 1986), 30–33.

52 Anne Collins, *In the Sleep Room: The Story of the CIA Brainwashing Experiments* (Toronto: Lester and Orpen Dennys, 1988), 48.

53 Cooper, *Opinion of George Cooper*, 30.

54 Cooper, *Opinion of George Cooper*, 30.

55 Cooper, *Opinion of George Cooper*.

56 Christopher Beltran, "Donald Olding Hebb: An Intellectual Biography" (PhD diss., Carlos Albizu University, 2000), 102, 105–6; Peter Milner and Brenda Milner, "Donald Hebb, 22 July 1904–20 August 1985," *Biographical Memoirs of Fellows of the Royal Society* 42 (1996): 193.

57 Habibollah Ghassemzadeh, Michael Posner, and Mary Rothbart, "Contributions of Hebb and Vygotsky to an Integrated Science of the Mind," *Journal of the History of the Neurosciences: Basic and Clinical Perspectives* 22, 3 (2013): 296.

58 Beltran, "Donald Olding Hebb," 89; Stuart Gilman, "Mind, Miracle and Machine: An Interview with Chancellor D.O. Hebb," *McGill Reporter* 2, 23 (20 March 1970): 1–5, 0000-2364.01 78, 1341C, MUA.

59 D.O. Hebb to A.H. Black, McMaster University, 22 January 1970, 0000--2364.01 101.1 1341C, MUA; Milner and Milner, "Donald Hebb," 192–204.

60 D.O. Hebb and W. Heron, "Effects of Radical Isolation upon Intellectual Function and the Manipulation of Attitudes," October 1955, 2, DRDC, DRB Report No. HR 63.

61 W. Heron, W.H. Bexton, and D.O. Hebb, "Cognitive Effects of a Decreased Variability in the Sensory Environment," DRDC, DRB Contract X-38.

62 D.O. Hebb, W. Heron, and W.H. Bexton, "Military Medicine I: Effect of Isolation upon Attitude, Motivation, and Thought" (paper presented at DRB Symposium, Ottawa, 8–10 December 1952); Cecil Rosner, "Isolation," *Canada's History*, August-September 2010, 28–37.

63 Heron, Bexton, and Hebb, "Cognitive Effects of a Decreased Variability," 2.

64 Hebb, Heron, and Bexton, "Military Medicine I."

65 W. Heron and B.K. Doane, "EEG Changes during Prolonged Isolation," March 1956, DRDC, DRB Contract X-38, Project D77–94–85–9; Collected Papers 1959–1962, Psychology Department, 0000-2039.02.4, MUA; T.H. Scott et al., "Cognitive Effects of Perceptual Isolation," *Canadian Journal of Psychology* 13 (1959): 200–9; B.K. Doane et al., "Changes in Perceptual Function after Isolation," *Canadian Journal of Psychology* 13 (1959): 210–19; B.K. Doane, "Changes in Visual Function with Perceptual Isolation" (PhD diss., McGill University, 1955), 0000-2364.01 132, 1341O, MUA.

66 In 1948, the DRB began to hold an annual symposium allowing its scientists to share their work in a conference setting with defence scientific organizations internationally. This eventually expanded to include academics. Turner, "The Defence Research Board," 127.

67 Hebb, Heron, and Bexton, "Military Medicine I."

68 Hebb, Heron, and Bexton, "Military Medicine I."

69 Beltran, *Donald Olding Hebb*, 98.

70 Beltran, *Donald Olding Hebb*, 98.

71 Frank Croft, "Look What Utter Boredom Can Do," *Maclean's*, 15 May 1954, 19, 0000-2364.01 78, 1341C, MUA.

72 Beltran, *Donald Olding Hebb*, 98.

73 Cooper, *Opinion of George Cooper*, 35.

74 Albert Biderman, "Image of 'Brainwashing,'" *Public Opinion Quarterly* 26, 4 (1962): 550.

75 Mr. Cunningham, Senior Psychologist, Air Ministry, AI9, "Interrogation Report on Lt. Lankford, AI9(a)/150/87/4," 15 January 1954, WO 208/4021, TNA.
76 Cunningham, "Interrogation Report," TNA.
77 Cunningham, "Interrogation Report," TNA.
78 "Communist Treatment of British POWs in Korea, Paper by AI9," TNA.
79 Collins, *In the Sleep Room,* 50.
80 Collins, *In the Sleep Room,* 50; Mical Raz, "Alone Again: John Zubek and the Troubled History of Deprivation Research," *Journal of the History of the Behavioral Sciences* 49, 4 (2013): 381.
81 Raz, "Alone Again," 381.
82 Heron, Bexton, and Hebb, "Cognitive Effects of a Decreased Variability."
83 McCoy, "Science in Dachau's Shadow," 406.
84 "McGill Students Brainwashed!" *Midnight,* 5 May 1956, 0000–2364.01 78, 1341C, MUA.
85 "McGill Students Brainwashed!" MUA.
86 Arthur Blakely, "Ottawa Day by Day: Life in a Crucible I," n.d., 0000–2364.01 78, 1341C, MUA.
87 Arthur Blakely, "McGill Discovery Will Benefit Military," *Gazette,* 26 April 1956, 1, 0000–2364.01 78, 1341C, MUA.
88 The Canadian Cabinet was responsible for cancelling the project. McCoy, "Science in Dachau's Shadow," 406.
89 John Zubek, "Behavioural and Physiological Effects of Prolonged Sensory and Perceptual Deprivation (NATO Lecture)," c. 1972, John Zubek Papers, Collection No. MSS 85, box 3 of 7, folder 20, University of Manitoba Archives and Special Collections (UMASC).
90 Brownfield, *Isolation: Clinical and Experimental Approaches* (New York: Random House, 1965), 92.
91 Brownfield, *Isolation,* 92; Richard Farrell and Seward Smith, "Behaviour of Five Men Confined for Thirty Days: Psychological Assessment during Project Mesa," Engineering Psychology Bioastronautics, Boeing, June 1964, John Zubek Papers, Collection No. MSS 85, box 5 of 7, folder 6, UMASC.
92 Brownfield, *Isolation,* 92.
93 Zubek CV, 17 October 1973, John Zubek Papers, Collection No. MSS 85, box 1 of 7, UMASC; Rosner, "Isolation"; Elliot Stellar, Johns Hopkins, to Hebb, 8 February 1950, 0000--2364.01. 127 1341C, MUA; Hebb to C.T. Morgan, Chairman, Department of Psychology, Johns Hopkins, 16 February 1950, 0000--2364.01. 127 1341C, MUA.
94 Rosner, "Isolation."
95 Rosner, "Isolation"; D.O. Hebb to Dr. Gillson, President of University of Manitoba, 18 November 1953, 0000--2364.01. 127 1341C, MUA.
96 Zubek CV, UMASC.
97 Rosner, "Isolation," 32; John Zubek, "DRB: Application for a Grant for Research, 1959," RG 24, acc. 1983–84/167, box 7564, file 9425–08, pt. 1, LAC.
98 John Zubek, "DRB: Application for a Grant for Research, 1959," RG 24, acc. 1983–84/167, box 7564, file 9425–08, pt. 1, LAC.
99 Rosner, "Isolation."
100 Zubek, "DRB: Application for a Grant for Research, 1959," LAC.
101 Rosner, "Isolation," 29.
102 "At U of M: 'Space Man' Tests Here," *Winnipeg Free Press,* 3 October 1959, 1, John Zubek Papers, Collection No. MSS 85, box 5 of 7, folder 2, UMASC.
103 Ross Henderson, "10 Days of Sheer Monotony," *Winnipeg Tribune,* 3 October 1959, 1, John Zubek Papers, Collection No. MSS 85, box 5 of 7, folder 2, UMASC.

104 John Zubek, "Annual Progress Report 1960, Effects of Adverse Environmental Conditions on Intellectual and Perceptual Processes," 1960, RG 24, acc. 1983–84/167, box 7564, file 9425–08, pt. 1, LAC; John Zubek et al., "Perceptual Changes after Prolonged Sensory Isolation (Darkness and Silence)," c. 1960, RG 24, acc. 1983–84/167, box 7564, file 9425–08, pt. 1, LAC; John Zubek et al., "Perceptual Changes after Prolonged Sensory Isolation (Darkness and Silence)," n.d., John Zubek Papers, Collection No. MSS 85, box 1 of 7, folder 10, UMASC; John Zubek, G. Welch, and M.G. Saunders, "Electroencephalographic Changes during and after 14 Days of Perceptual Deprivation," *Science* 139, 3554 (8 February 1963): 490–92.

105 "Effects of Severe Isolation on Human Behaviour," *Image* Photo Reports, Roche 7, March 1964, 5, John Zubek Papers, Collection No. MSS 85, box 2 of 7, folder 1, UMASC.

106 Zubek, Welch, and Saunders, "Electroencephalographic Changes," 490.

107 "Effects of Severe Isolation on Human Behaviour," 6, UMASC.

108 Raz, "Alone Again," 382.

109 Peter Suedfeld, DRB, "Referee Report on Application," 1971, John Zubek Papers, Collection No. MSS 85, box 6 of 7, folder 7, UMASC.

110 Suedfeld, "Referee Report," UMASC.

111 Austin Riesen, ed., *The Developmental Neuropsychology of Sensory Deprivation* (New York: Academic Press, 1975), xiii.

112 Heron, Bexton, and Hebb, "Cognitive Effects of a Decreased Variability," 1.

113 Principal Personnel Officers' Committee Meeting, 7 March 1955, WO 32/20493, TNA.

114 Principal Personnel Officers' Committee, Advisory Panel on CAC, "Training in Resistance to Interrogation and Indoctrination: Report by War Office," 10 December 1954, WO 32/20493, TNA.

115 App to AC 8/2/362B, "Report by Lt. Seeger," TNA.

116 Brigadier Vickers, Inspector of Intelligence, "Report on Interrogation Phase of March Hare III," April 1965, ADM 201/126, TNA.

117 C.H. Owen, "Evasion and Escape," 7 August 1954, TS 28/572, TNA; Ministry of Defence, Naval Personnel 1, "Security—Resistance to Interrogation," 23 January 1967, DEFE 69/395, TNA; "Exercise Exe Meet: Joint Exercise Instructions," 1963, ADM 201/126, TNA; B.T.V. Cowey to Brigadier Hackett, HQ Middle East Command, June 1963, ADM 201/126, TNA; "Report on Interrogation Phase of Exercise Silent Tread in Metz, France, 23–30 May 1962," DEFE 69/395, TNA; LCdr Abraham, Royal Navy, to Naval Liaison Officer, Intelligence Centre, Maresfield Camp, "Report on Interrogation Phase of Exercise Bad Jest in Aden, 11 to 15 February 1963," 27 March 1963, ADM 201/126, TNA; Head of DS6, "Resistance Training after Parker Report," 22 March 1972, WO 32/21776, TNA; Joint Services Interrogation Division, "Research into Interrogation Methods Report on Exercise Hardnut Wanderer, 30 May 1969–1 June 1969," WO 32/20490, TNA.

118 Joint Services Interrogation Division, "Research into Interrogation Methods on Exercise Hardnut Wanderer," TNA.

119 F.H. Lakin to J.C. Penton, "Exercise WHITE KNIGHT," 11 July 1959, WO 342/2, TNA.

120 Gentner, "Understanding the POW Experience," 156.

121 Quoted in Susan Carruthers, *Cold War Captives: Imprisonment, Escape and Brainwashing* (Berkeley: University of California Press, 2009), 211.

122 Carruthers, *Cold War Captives*, 211.

123 R.N. Gilbey to Christopher Soames, MP, Home Office, 11 March 1960, WO 32/17501, TNA; Cabinet Office, Extract from Hansard (Commons), Columns 1481–82, 17 March 1960, CAB: 21/3184, TNA; Oral Answers, House of Commons, Brainwashing and Nerve Gas, 21 March 1960, CAB: 21/3184, TNA; Revd. Hopcraft to Miss Jennie Lee, MP, 1 January 1961, WO 32/17501, TNA; Mrs. W.G. Agnew to Sir Charles, 22 March 1961, WO

32/17501, TNA; MI11, n.d., WO 32/17501, TNA; APS/S of S to MA/CIGS through PS/ PUS, 29 March 1961, WO 32/17501, TNA; App to AC 8/2/362B, "Report by Lt. Seeger," TNA; "Annex A to RM 8/19/175 (A), Rules for Conduct of Resistance to Interrogation," 10 January 1962, ADM 201/126, TNA; Major Stevenson for Director of Army Training, "Combat Survival Training Directive," 14 February 1969, WO 32/20490, TNA.

124 Raz, "Alone Again," 387–89.

125 Lord Parker of Waddington, *Report of the Committee of Privy Counsellors Appointed to Consider Authorized Procedures for the Interrogation of Persons Suspected of Terrorism* (London: Her Majesty's Stationery Office, March 1972), 17.

126 European Court of Human Rights, *Judgment: Case of Ireland v. The United Kingdom, Application no. 5310/71*, 18 January 1978, 9.

127 European Court of Human Rights, *Judgment*, 1.

128 William O'Donohue et al., "Ethics of Enhanced Interrogations and Torture: A Reappraisal of the Arguments," *Ethics and Behavior* 24, 2 (2014): 109–25; Samantha Newberry, "The UK, Interrogation and Iraq, 2003–2008," *Small Wars and Insurgencies* 27, 4 (2016): 659–80.

129 Cooper, *Opinion of George Cooper*, 127.

130 Cooper, *Opinion of George Cooper*, 88.

131 Cooper, *Opinion of George Cooper*, 75.

132 Chief Superintendent of Defence Research Medical Laboratories, 20 January 1965, RG 24, acc. 1983–1984/167 GAD, box 7559, 9400–1, LAC.

133 W.F. Cockburn to Mr. Watson, 7 August 1964, RG 24, acc. 1983–1984/167, box 7559, 9400–1, LAC.

134 Gentner, "Understanding the POW Experience," 151–52; Ruth Hoyt—SSO/HRR, "Travel Report," c. 1955, DRBSG 9400–1, vol. 24062, LAC.

135 Hoyt, "Travel Report," LAC.

136 Joy Rohde, "Gray Matters: Social Scientists, Military Patronage and Democracy in the Cold War," *Journal of American History* 96, 1 (June 2009), 99.

137 Mescaline is a naturally occurring hallucinogen.

138 It is worth noting that John Zubek did screen his volunteers at the University of Manitoba, but like Hebb, he was not required to monitor his subjects after the study was complete. "Effects of Severe Isolation on Human Behaviour," UMASC; McCoy, "Science in Dachau's Shadow," 406–7.

139 McCoy, "Science in Dachau's Shadow," 407; J. Marks, *Search for the Manchurian Candidate: The CIA and Mind Control* (New York: Times Books, 1979), 23–25, 32–33, 106, 137–38, 201–2; R.E. Brown, "Alfred McCoy, Hebb, the CIA and Torture," *Journal of the History of the Behavioral Sciences* 43, 2 (2007): 209.

140 McCoy, "Science in Dachau's Shadow," 407.

141 Stuart W. Leslie, *The Cold War and American Science: The Military-Industrial-Academic Complex at MIT and Stanford* (New York: Columbia University Press, 1993), 2; Rohde, *Armed with Expertise*, 37–41.

Part 3
Politics and Procurement

5

The Honest (Arms) Broker
Promoting the Military-Industrial Complex during the Golden Age of Canadian Foreign Policy

Asa McKercher

IN WHAT WAS THE LARGEST single weapons export in its history, Canada sold $15 billion worth of light armoured vehicles (LAVs) to Saudi Arabia in 2014, a move that upset many Canadians. That Ottawa was arming a regime with a notorious human rights record, that sponsored the puritanical Wahhabi branch of Islamism, and that was embroiled in armed conflict with neighbouring Yemen seemed at odds with Canada's reputation of promoting stability and championing liberal democratic values. Fundamentally, the LAV sale challenged Canadians' self-image of their country and its role in the world.[1] Yet Canada has a long history of selling arms, often to dubious buyers. The role of arms broker is as Canadian as maple syrup.

Beginning in the late 1940s, military exports became an important element of Canadian foreign and defence policy. Driven by a mix of motives, including pursuing commercial interests, offsetting military procurement costs, and shaping global events, Canada actively became an arms dealer. It undertook this role amid the so-called golden age of Canadian foreign policy. Lasting roughly a decade after the end of the Second World War, this period saw Canada, a newly anointed middle power, embrace multilateral institutions, sign on to collective security pacts, and implement foreign aid programs. Its history as an arms exporter has received scattered attention, even though it represented a significant aspect of Canadian foreign policy during the golden age.[2] This era is mythologized as a time when Canada sought to bridge global divides in pursuit of peace, but recent scholarship has emphasized that policymakers were far less idealistic than myth-making would have it.[3] This conclusion certainly applies to arms sales, where the pursuit of economic and narrowly defined strategic interests took precedence.

The arms broker role emerged amid the transition from a wartime to peace-time military and munitions industry, and in this regard can be viewed as a key component in the advent of Canada's military-industrial complex (MIC). As the editors of this volume note in their Introduction, the Canadian MIC extended beyond the economic and political ties that bound the armed services with private defence industry. Tracing the direct links between arms exports and Canada's domestic munitions industry, in particular, demonstrates the prime importance that sales to foreign buyers played in maintaining (and arguably growing) Canada's distinct MIC that arose during the mid-twentieth century. Initially, following the Second World War, Canadian officials sold off demilitarized equipment but otherwise proved reluctant to export munitions. However, the unfolding Cold War changed matters. Defending North America and Western Europe necessitated both the buildup of Canada's military and its maintenance in a constant state of readiness. This effort was an expensive one, and the small size of the Canadian armed forces meant that foreign markets were vital to providing economies of scale, in turn benefitting Canada's manufacturing sector. Pursuing this complex of economic and military goals was important to the Canadian government, but the resulting search for foreign buyers was a source of dispute among policymakers. Notably, officials in the Department of External Affairs (DEA) had doubts about the new arms broker role. This chapter focuses primarily on these diplomats, showing that whatever concerns they had about the international impacts of munitions exports tended to be outweighed in senior government circles by the perceived economic and military benefits of selling materiel abroad. As a result, the role of arms broker became an important element of Canadian foreign and defence policy.

An Evolving Export Sector

Canada's role as arms exporter grew out of the Second World War. Throughout the conflict, Canada produced huge amounts of equipment and munitions for its own use, as well as for its allies through the Mutual Aid Board. In late 1943, with war's end in sight, the government created the War Assets Corporation (WAC) to dispose of surplus materiel, both domestically and to foreign buyers: several dozen naval vessels, stripped of armaments, were sold to various Latin American governments; the Canadian Army in Britain and the Netherlands transferred much of its munitions and vehicles to the Dutch; and other vehicles were given to the newly formed United Nations to assist with postwar reconstruction.[4] Saving on the costs of shipping equipment back to Canada, these efforts recouped money sunk into wartime production. Limited manufacturing continued into peacetime, with the federal government opting to maintain a rump military and to continue selling materiel to its two major allies, the United States and Britain. To this end, in 1946, Ottawa created the Canadian Commercial Corporation (CCC) to handle direct sales to foreign governments. Whereas the WAC dealt with surplus, the CCC contracted for new equipment. Under a regime formed through an Order-in-Council in 1941 (P.C. 2488), exports of Canadian arms were subject to permits authorized by the Department of Trade and Commerce (DTC). In a reciprocal arrangement, this export permit regime did not apply to the United States or Britain.[5] Given the sensitive nature of arms exports, in 1946 the DEA sought to exert control over the permit process.

The issue achieved prominence in spring 1946, when Chile and the Dominican Republic tried to buy guns for the demilitarized naval vessels that they had previously purchased from Canada. Having insisted that the ships be sold without weapons, the DEA then opposed selling the armaments. It also blocked Mexico's effort to purchase twelve armed frigates. Opposing the sale, Norman Robertson, the under-secretary of state for external affairs (USSEA), explained in a memorandum that permitting these sales would break new ground, putting Canada in the same position as the United States, the region's major arms exporter.[6] Robertson's report was circulated at a May 1946 Cabinet meeting, where ministers accepted his position. Further, they agreed on a general policy of restricting sales on a case-by-case basis pending Cabinet review, excepting exports to the United States and Britain. Under this system, recommendations were to reach Cabinet through the DEA, which would consult the Department of National Defence (DND) and the DTC on the advisability of selling either surplus materiel from the WAC or new weaponry via the CCC.[7] In line with this new procedure, the following month, Cabinet approved the sale of 6 million rifle cartridges to the Netherlands, ammunition for the surplus weapons transferred by the Canadian Army at the war's end.[8]

In early 1947, Ottawa began fielding an increasing number of inquiries regarding surplus equipment. Given this interest, Lester Pearson, the new USSEA, reviewed the issue. Pointing to a faltering UN initiative to establish an international arms control convention – growing Cold War rivalry prevented agreement – and to an Anglo-American disagreement over selling weaponry to Argentina's authoritarian regime, he remarked that it was "necessary for the Canadian Government to make up its own mind on the proper policy for Canada to pursue."[9] This pursuit of a more independent position was in keeping with the approach that Pearson and other golden age officials adopted on a range of issues, and at his direction, Escott Reid, his deputy, drafted a memorandum on arms exports. A leading figure in the DEA who, the following year, would articulate the ideological reasoning for Canada's adherence to the Western cause in the Cold War, Reid produced a report largely skeptical of the value of Canadian entry into the international weapons market. While admitting to the commercial benefit, he laid stress on political factors, including the matter of whether foreign governments might use arms supplied by Canada in ways "repugnant to a large number of Canadians," either in civil wars or in "pacifying rebellious colonial peoples." Beyond harming the government's standing with voters, the end use of Canadian weaponry in repugnant ways could feed Soviet propaganda about the evils of the West, arouse anti-Canadian feeling abroad, and damage relations with post-colonial states. Turning to the United States and the United Kingdom – both major arms exporters – Reid highlighted

Anglo-American differences over sales to certain countries and warned about becoming involved in disputes pitting Canada's closest allies against one another. Comparing Ottawa's restrictive policy to Washington and London's positions, he emphasized that supplying arms to foreign governments was the role of a "great power" and not "a power of the dimensions of Canada."[10]

Reid's memorandum made the case for caution, a position evidently supported by Pearson, who signed off on it and sent it to Louis St-Laurent, the foreign minister. St-Laurent presented the report to a small group of ministers delegated to handle trade policy, who considered the paper in relation to specific matters: an Argentinian request for 150 surplus de Havilland Mosquito bombers; the Republic of China's demand for anti-aircraft guns and machinery to build a small-arms factory; the Dutch colonial administration in Indonesia's effort to secure small-arms ammunition; and the WAC's petition to solicit bids for surplus naval vessels. Although St-Laurent sought agreement on a general policy, his colleagues opted to address the requests individually: on Argentina, Canada would consult with the United States, which was imposing an arms embargo; on China, where a civil war was waging, they recommended a "complete embargo," with the exception of machinery for the arms plant; on the Dutch request, they deferred a decision pending information on whether the ammunition would be used against anti-colonial insurgents; and on the surplus vessels, they authorized the WAC to find foreign buyers.[11]

As for overall policy, the committee reasserted DEA oversight. The wider Cabinet then approved their recommendations.[12] Subsequently, the ammunition sale to Dutch forces in Indonesia proceeded, while in line with a US recommendation, Canada nixed selling the Mosquitos to Argentina. Meanwhile, the DEA asserted its authority to stop an effort by C.D. Howe, the minister of reconstruction and supply – overseeing the WAC – to sell a surplus destroyer and a bevy of small arms to the Dominican Republic, home to a dictatorship dismissed by SSEA St-Laurent as "one the most corrupt in Latin America." More importantly, he added, with an insurgency raging in the country, it would be "embarrassing" for a Canadian destroyer to be used in the Dominican regime's counterinsurgency efforts.[13] Caution still prevailed in Ottawa.

Early 1948 saw the Canadian government reconsider its position in light of both increasing demand and the deepening Cold War. Although a small order, The Hague's request for ten thousand submachine gun assemblies took on wider significance. Reporting on the Dutch order, Reid addressed arms sales in relation to the growing standoff with the Soviets in Europe. On the positive side of the ledger, he outlined the deal's economic rationale, emphasizing – in a point that became central to Canadian policy – that arms exports would better allow Canada to equip its own forces and maintain a domestic arms industry that could be expanded in wartime. Moreover, a less restrictive policy would allow Canada "to provide our friends with arms, and thus strengthen them against the Soviet Union." On the negative side, Reid outlined how arms exports created new and avoidable problems, particularly the possibility that by restricting sales to certain governments while allowing sales to others, Canada risked straining relations with countries to which it denied arms. As for the specific Dutch request, he asserted the need to ensure that the weapons would not be used to reassert colonial control over Indonesia.[14]

Guided by this advice, Pearson pushed for a more formal policy review, a recommendation accepted by the DTC, whose deputy minister agreed that political implications outweighed commercial ones and that munitions exports should be limited "to those friendly countries which are likely to be allied with us in the event of trouble."[15] The DEA proposed a policy reconfirming its control over the vetting process in sending requests to Cabinet and containing two new points. First, sales should be made only to governments – a stipulation necessitated by evidence that surplus wartime equipment sold to private organizations had been transferred to Jewish insurgents fighting British rule in Palestine – and second, exports should proceed only if the equipment in question was either surplus to Canadian requirements or its manufacture supported the Canadian military's own procurement efforts.[16] The export-procurement connection signified officials' sense of the importance of maintaining peacetime armed forces, particularly amid the unrest that characterized the late 1940s. As one DND official put it in 1950, by offsetting procurement and recouping costs, an export program was "the only way the Army could afford to obtain essential new equipment."[17] Overall, arms exports reflected new trends apparent in postwar Canadian foreign and defence policy, especially the buildup of Canada's own military.

Presenting the DEA proposal at an April 1948 Cabinet meeting, St-Laurent highlighted the changing international scene, where, for instance, the United States and the United Kingdom had decided to sell weapons to China's Nationalist government, backing it against Communist forces. With Canada's allies relaxing their own export controls, he reported that the DND favoured ensuring the existence of "the nucleus" of a Canadian munitions industry, which could not be maintained on domestic orders alone. St-Laurent recommended sales of arms from current production to "potential allies" and countries "whose regimes were, generally speaking, democratic" so long as orders "would serve to develop the Canadian munitions industry along lines desired." Cabinet approved this policy, as well as the export of 10,000 submachine gun assemblies to the Netherlands and 100,000 rounds of ammunition to China.[18]

Informing Canadian missions abroad of this policy change, Pearson stated that, due to the "progressively worsening international situation," the government was being inundated with arms requests and was looking for sales that would help "develop the Canadian arms industry." Although striking a cautious note about the evolution of the government's position and noting that care would be taken to avoid sales to "international trouble spots," he defended the policy, stressing that with other states pushing their own exports, "it appeared that the Canadian Government, though it might lose much by an embargo on the export of arms, could not hope, by adopting such an embargo, to make any major contribution to world peace."[19] Over subsequent decades, the position that Canada alone could not effect outcomes through virtuous action so long as other countries prioritized their economic interests would be used by government officials to deflect criticism of trade with human rights abusers, from apartheid South Africa to Saudi Arabia. Ottawa's own prioritization of economic factors lay behind the adoption of the arms broker role, but military and political issues were also of importance.

Arms Exports to India and Pakistan

Canada did exercise restraint over exports to India and Pakistan, which had gained independence from Britain in August 1947 amid terrible internecine violence. Despite the tension created by partition, that December, London informed Ottawa that all reasonable arms requests from India and Pakistan would be met. The following July, the Indians and Pakistanis each requested Canadian materiel. Ottawa approved the sale of several dozen trainer aircraft to both countries. More contentious were requests for rifles and ammunition. In a report to St-Laurent, Pearson opposed this sale, recommending a moratorium pending a "radical change" in the situation on the subcontinent.[20] Although St-Laurent accepted this view, Karachi and Delhi pressed the matter, and in September the issue came before Cabinet, one of the last meetings presided over by William Lyon Mackenzie King, who soon stepped down as prime minister. St-Laurent, King's eventual successor, continued his opposition, warning that by fulfilling Pakistan's demand for 20 million rifle rounds and India's for 100,000 rifles and 100 million rounds, Canada risked "an encouragement to war between two members of the Commonwealth." Given Canadian economic interests, as well as a desire not to offend two new Commonwealth members, who might resent being treated differently from the old, white dominions, he outlined a need to differentiate between small arms and heavy weapons, the latter geared for extensive military operations. King was skeptical, emphasizing the need to refrain from creating grounds for criticism that "the government were engaged in the manufacture and sale for profit of armaments for aggressive purposes." In the end, Cabinet opted to permit arms exports to India and

Pakistan with several caveats: only defensive weapons would be sold; Canada would seek to balance its exports to both countries; and each government would be informed of Canadian munitions sales to the other. Ministers also approved India's request for rifles and ammunition.[21] Soon after, they refused an Indian request for mortar shells on the grounds that they could be used in offensive operations, and in the name of balance, they approved Pakistan's outstanding application for rifle ammunition.[22]

The policy of balancing exports to India and Pakistan came amid the worsening Cold War situation, which included negotiations leading to the formation of the North Atlantic Treaty Organization (NATO). This context informed Canada's response to a renewed Indian request for 289,000 mortar rounds, as well as a Pakistani order for a long list of goods including anti-tank rockets and anti-aircraft guns. In a Cabinet submission, Defence Minister Brooke Claxton urged approving larger-scale military exports to both countries. While admitting to Indian-Pakistani hostility, he contended that the prevailing issue was to support the building of a "nucleus" of a domestic arms industry that could be expanded in a conflict. Further, given the possibility of a Communist victory in China's civil war, arming India and Pakistan was "strategically of great value" to the West. In the resulting Cabinet discussion, Howe backed Claxton, emphasizing that sales to both Commonwealth members, as well as Nationalist China, "would result in substantial savings" for military procurement. Cabinet approved the requests and continued to support arms sales to India and Pakistan over subsequent years.[23] Canadian goals were to assist these fellow Commonwealth members and as Claxton affirmed, to "see the maximum productive capacity possible maintained in Canada for military supplies," considerations that outweighed DEA concerns about the "very awkward position" in which Canada would find itself should the two countries go to war.[24] Again, economic and military considerations took precedence.

Ottawa continued to prioritize balance. In 1956, for instance, the sale of $3,880 worth of spare parts for trainer aircraft to India was held up due to the "balance between shipments" to both countries.[25] However, there were occasions when achieving balance proved impossible. After Communist China's attack on India in 1962, Ottawa rushed support to the Indians. Given the need for speed, the John Diefenbaker government required India to affirm that the arms being transferred would not be used against Pakistan.[26] Where Canadian policy failed was with nuclear technology: in 1974, India tested a nuclear bomb that utilized plutonium from a Canadian-built reactor exported in the 1960s, a blow to nuclear non-proliferation. As with arms sales, exporting nuclear technology had been seen as key to offsetting the costs of Canada's domestic nuclear industry.[27]

Arms Exports to China

The Canadian government's boost in exports to India and Pakistan occurred alongside increased sales to the Republic of China. The sales had begun through a March 1944 agreement whereby Canada undertook to transfer military equipment for the Chinese war effort against Japan. The two allies also concluded several commercial agreements, including a February 1946 contract in which Canada extended a $60 million credit to China, $25 million of which could be used for armaments. This credit agreement was made just as the long-simmering civil war between China's Nationalist government and its Communist opponents – largely paused amid the war with Japan – began anew. In June 1946, the Nationalists sought 100 million rounds of ammunition and 11 armed frigates. The Canadian government balked at both requests, in part because the Americans were withholding arms and also because fighting had accelerated since the signing of the February credit agreement. As Cabinet ministers concluded, they had no desire to see their government "accused of backing one side against the other" in China's civil war.[28] Violating the spirt of this decision, Howe secretly drafted an agreement allowing the Chinese government to construct an ammunition plant utilizing surplus Canadian equipment. After learning of the plan, the DEA protested against it, warning that with war raging, establishing the factory "would not be likely to commend itself to the Canadian public and would likely become the subject of propaganda abroad which would disturb Sino-Canadian relations."[29] Matters came to a head at an April 1947 Cabinet meeting: ministers put in place a "complete embargo" on arms exports to China, rejecting a Chinese government request for anti-aircraft guns. However, due to cajoling from Howe, Cabinet approved the sale of machinery for the munitions plant, concluding that selling manufacturing equipment did not violate the letter of the embargo.[30]

Over the summer of 1947, the Communist forces achieved several successes, leading Washington to lift its arms export ban to the Chinese republic. Desperate, China's government sought a range of weaponry from Canada, and Howe seized the opportunity. Citing the change in US policy, he pushed St-Laurent to approve instructions to the WAC "that the door is open" to military exports.[31] DEA officials reacted with considerable skepticism, judging that the Nationalist position was "deteriorating very rapidly indeed" and that Canadian arms would do little to improve the situation.[32] As a further report later that summer concluded, due to the military incompetence of the Nationalist force, there was "little evidence" that it could succeed against the Communists. What was needed, officials told St-Laurent, were domestic reforms, whereas arms sales would simply strengthen "the militarist clique" within the regime. Worse, abandoning the embargo would sully "Canada's name" among the Chinese people.[33] China's request from Canada centred on 211 surplus de Havilland Mosquito bombers and ammunition for their guns, a large sale worth $5 million, half of which would be drawn from the credit agreement and the other half paid for in American dollars, an important consideration given Ottawa's need for convertible currency. In a report to his ministerial colleagues, St-Laurent recommended rejection on the grounds that the benefit of payment in US dollars did not offset "political objections."[34] However, during another skirmish in what one diplomat later called the "running argument" between the DEA and the DTC, Howe convinced his Cabinet colleagues to agree to an exception to the embargo.[35] With China, Canadian economic interests proved imperative.[36]

The situation soon soured, with the Chinese opting to pay for the Mosquitos wholly on credit. As Pearson mused to St-Laurent, ministers had approved the sale on the basis of accessing US dollars, which was no longer the case.[37] At the same time, China's government sought more weaponry: 6 million rounds of machine gun ammunition, 1 million rifle rounds, and several dozen artillery pieces. Given the embargo, DEA officials considered denying the request, but there was uncertainty in light of whether the Mosquito exception constituted a precedent. Predictably, Howe pushed to conclude the sale. St-Laurent, though, saw the request as "a further extension" of Canada's wider arms export policy in that it involved sales to a conflict zone, and he sought Pearson's advice. With the growing Cold War situation in mind, Pearson replied that the basic issue was "whether the Canadian Government wishes to send arms to the Nationalist Government of China to be used against the Communists." Asserting that months earlier "I would myself have argued strongly against" the arms deal, he noted the change in US policy, which made him question adhering to the embargo.[38] Ultimately, St-Laurent approved the ammunition sale, as the rounds were for guns that were already in the Nationalists' possession. As for the Mosquito sale, he grew increasingly worried because it was drawing negative attention from both the Chinese Communists and critics in Canada.[39]

Beyond opponents of Canada's arms exports, the Mosquito sale was also a *cause célèbre* for communists and other leftists who were angered by Canadian support of the Nationalist government. In the House of Commons, M.J. Coldwell, leader of the Co-operative Commonwealth Federation (CCF), asked St-Laurent whether, since wartime mutual aid was meant to assist China against Japan, did its continuation not mean that Canada was "now 'mutual aiding' in the civil war in China?" In reply, St-Laurent referred only to the 1946 credit agreement and the portion accorded to weapons purchases, contending that the Mosquito sale was proper, given that it involved a government recognized by Canada.[40] Opponents inundated the government with letters and petitions. For instance, one United Church of Canada official urged Prime Minister

Mackenzie King to refrain from "unwarranted interference in the internal affairs of the Chinese nation."[41] In late 1947, word that a ship in Vancouver was being loaded with munitions destined for China led to protests at the port by labour, clergy, and CCF members, as well as local communists.[42] By the new year, the situation was resolved and the shipment left for China. Collectively, these protests created hesitancy in Ottawa. At a Cabinet meeting, King urged that "great care" should be taken in regards to arms exports, especially to China. Privately, regarding munitions sales to China, he reflected that "Canada should keep out of matters affecting domestic affairs of foreign countries."[43] Ever cautious about seeing Canada embroiled in foreign disputes, King was hardly a supporter of the arms broker role, but his time as prime minister was ending.

Official opinion was divided on the question of actively backing the Nationalists. From China, Canadian ambassador T.C. Davis urged support for "containing the Communist movement."[44] Meanwhile, Arthur Menzies counselled rejecting a Nationalist request for rifle ammunition. Fulfilling the order, he warned, could create "untoward effects" on the Canadian missionary and business communities in China, particularly if the Communist side won, an increasingly likely outcome.[45] Nonetheless, the ammunition sale was approved, and as an accounting of arms sales to China up to October 1948 recorded, over the past year Canada had shipped the surplus Mosquitos with accompanying ammunition, 125 Pratt-Whitney aircraft engines, 100,000 rifle rounds, and 200 Harvard trainer aircraft. The Nationalists sought an additional 2,000 submachine guns and $5 million worth of ammunition. In a memorandum for Cabinet, Pearson, now foreign minister, highlighted several reasons for refusing the request, including potential damage to Canada's reputation in China, with a resulting impact on the missionary community and commercial interests, and the likelihood of criticism from Canadians. On the plus side, he emphasized that Canada recognized the Nationalist government, that assistance to that government would boost its chances of military success whereas the denial of arms extended indirect aid to the Communists, and – in somewhat of a contradiction – given the huge amount of American military aid, that Canada's exports were "insignificant" to the overall outcome of the conflict. At his recommendation, Cabinet approved the sale on credit.[46]

Two months later, as Nationalist forces experienced heavy reversals, Canadian ministers reconsidered their decision. In light of what St-Laurent referred to as the possibility of Canadian goods "falling into the hands of a Communist-dominated government" and China's difficulty with financing purchases, Cabinet froze China's credit in December, although munitions already purchased by the Chinese, mainly ammunition, could still be exported.[47] Within weeks, Nationalist resistance largely collapsed, and Cabinet halted all shipments.[48] The stoppage proved temporary: with the Nationalist government escaping to Taiwan, ministers approved rerouting shipments of ammunition and airplane parts to the island. Still, Ottawa refused even to consider further Chinese arms requests, and in May, Cabinet placed a moratorium on military exports to China.[49] The sole exception was an order of 78 million rifle rounds, already purchased by the Nationalists and scheduled to be manufactured and shipped in monthly allotments ending in September 1950.[50] In August 1949, Ambassador Davis cabled Pearson that although pockets of Nationalist forces were still fighting, overall they were "licked," and Canada might avoid joining the Americans in perpetuating the civil war. Concurring, Pearson suggested in Cabinet that Canada taper off the ammunition production and shipments. Ministers agreed, setting an end date of November, ten months early.[51]

By November, the civil war had largely come to an end, with the Communists having declared the creation of the People's Republic on 1 October. Advising Pearson on China policy, USSEA Arnold Heeney suggested writing off the Nationalists from a military viewpoint and continuing the moratorium lest Canadian weapons "ultimately find their way into Communist hands." In December, Cabinet suspended military sales to the Nationalists in Taiwan.[52] Summing up the decision, one diplomat emphasized that whereas Ottawa would continue to recognize the Republic of China as the country's legitimate government, it would avoid becoming embroiled in the dispute between Taiwan and the Communist mainland.[53] In subsequent years, Canada relaxed its embargo somewhat, allowing sales of items of indirect military value such as radios, but otherwise the moratorium persisted, a policy in accord with that of Britain but not of the United States, which backed Taiwan to the hilt.[54] This position reflected a sense of caution pervading much of Canada's stance on arms exports, but the fact remained that to advance economic interests, Ottawa had armed the Nationalist side in China's civil war. Canadian diplomat Chester Ronning received a vivid reminder of this fact during a visit to Shanghai in June 1949, when he had witnessed Canadian-made Mosquitos strafing the city, shell casings from their machine guns raining down on his afternoon tea.[55]

Arms Exports to NATO

Canadian exports to China were largely of surplus wartime equipment, but as the Cold War situation worsened Ottawa expanded Canada's military, and the Canadian arms industry ramped up production. The result was a need to achieve economies of scale, with Canada's alliances providing a prime conduit for munitions exports. A key development was the formation of NATO in 1949 and the revival in 1950 of the Second World War–era Mutual Aid Program (MAP) to build up NATO's military forces (the United States undertook a parallel program). MAP provided Canada with a destination for surplus munitions and a larger market to offset procurement costs. In a memorandum setting out the motivations behind MAP's relaunch, USSEA Arnold Heeney traced how the growing Cold War demanded that Canada break with its "tradition of extremely small peacetime forces and correspondingly low defence budgets." Any effort to maintain a large military would be hamstrung by the small size of Canadian forces, and so exports would offset this limitation while helping "to maintain a high level of employment in Canada."[56] For instance, the sale of over two hundred Canadair F-86 Sabres to the West German government in 1956 was a prime example of MAP's domestic benefits: in his 1950 memo, Heeney had predicted the closure of the Montreal Canadair plant in 1952, lest Ottawa find foreign buyers.[57] This direct link between arms exports and the viability of Canada's domestic munitions industry showcases that sales to foreign buyers played an important part in maintaining the Canadian MIC. As General Charles Foulkes, chief of the general staff, had remarked to an intra-governmental panel in 1950, since "we made 70% of our last war production for our allies, we could not afford to ignore Western European requirements."[58]

Beyond its considerable economic import, the NATO program played a larger role for the alliance, with Canada helping, as Pearson explained in 1955, to bolster psychologically and militarily the "fragile" Western position in Europe through the building of "an effective collective defence system."[59] Yet, MAP posed a problem: many of Canada's NATO partners were colonial powers embroiled in suppressing independence movements. Wanting their allies to focus on defending Western Europe, Canadian officials had little desire to see Canadian weaponry used in colonial conflicts. The French war in Indochina was a particular worry, given its severity and France's importance to NATO defence efforts. In 1948, the French Ministry of Overseas Colonies sought ammunition for its colonial garrisons. Diplomats judged that acceding to the request would damage Canadian "impartiality" on the UN Security Council – Canada was then serving as a non-permanent member – where colonial matters were prominent. Furthermore, with "the tide of nationalism" in Asia "in full flood," propping up French imperialism risked harming Canada's reputation with newly independent states.[60] Four years later, with France now a NATO ally, the calculus had evidently changed. When Pearson informed Cabinet that Paris proposed diverting materiel received via MAP to Indochina, ministers resolved to permit it to do so provided it found a "replacement in kind to their NATO forces in Europe."[61] In short, as long as the French maintained adequate forces directed toward deterring the Soviet threat – MAP's purpose and Ottawa's chief concern – Canada's government was willing to continue selling arms to France even as those weapons ended up in Southeast Asia.

This position was at odds with stated Canadian policy. As a 1953 DEA study on Indochina stressed, Canada's position was "sharply defined": No military involvement "and no direct military aid" to the French colonial regime. Indirectly, the report continued, the French army in Saigon had procured a modest amount of Canadian "radios, aircraft, military vehicles, and spare parts" from private firms, with clearance from Ottawa. More importantly, since 1950, Canada had transferred $2.5 million worth of materiel to France, some of which had been siphoned to the war effort in Asia (an accounting was difficult since Ottawa did not monitor the end use of MAP exports).[62] This attitude was typical. As historian David Webster observes, "alliance-driven thinking" was a major determinant of Canadian policy toward decolonial conflicts.[63] Certainly, with MAP and Indochina, support for France trumped avoiding arms exports to an international hot spot.

Whether Canadian policymakers' concerns about MAP munitions being diverted to colonial conflicts extended to Britain is unclear, as arms sales to the British were approved automatically without reference to Cabinet or requirement for the interdepartmental export permit review process. The same was true of Canadian arms sales and transfers to the United States, which were exempt from any controls. During the 1960s, in an exceptional move and in order to comply with UN resolutions, Canada barred arms sales to NATO ally Portugal, embroiled in vicious fighting in southern Africa.

Policy Changes

NATO provided one outlet for arms exports, but the Canadian government was keen to find other foreign buyers. In 1954, now serving as minister of trade and commerce, Howe pushed to reform the export permit regime governing arms sales in order to streamline the export process. On friendly terms with many industrialists, Howe had long championed the Canadian munitions industry.[64] Citing delays that had cost Canada sales, he urged his Cabinet colleagues to authorize the DTC to approve sales to NATO members and their colonies or to Commonwealth countries – India and Pakistan excepted – without consulting the DEA. He added several caveats: No sales to countries under a UN embargo; no sales to Communist bloc countries except Yugoslavia, which was seeking to become neutral in the Cold War; and no sales, without Cabinet approval, to areas of "political unrest or local conflict," which included Indochina and Malaya, where the French and British respectively were waging counterinsurgencies. The Americans and the British would continue to require no export permit, whereas permits to other countries would be granted with Cabinet approval. The DEA would be consulted regarding sales to "politically sensitive" regions only, principally the Middle East and North Africa, but also Cold War hot spots West Germany, Hong Kong, and South Korea. In cases where a new policy was being fashioned, then Cabinet approval would be necessary. Recognizing the need to streamline the export permit process, ministers approved Howe's recommendations, praised within the DEA for bringing "much needed clarity and consistency."[65]

A new case of policy emerged in 1956, when the Colombian government inquired about purchasing six Canadair F-86 Sabres. Up to that point, Ottawa had been cautious about selling arms in Latin America; this sale therefore represented a new step, triply so because the aircraft were not from surplus but would have to be manufactured and because Canada had sold F-86s – advanced jet aircraft – only to fellow NATO members West Germany and Belgium, and to South Africa, a Commonwealth member. Given the request's unprecedented nature, the DEA initially counselled against gratifying it.[66] Howe protested this cautious decision. In a note to the DEA, his department emphasized that the Department of Defence Production favoured the sale because it would offset the costs of producing similar aircraft and spare parts for Canada's air force.[67] DEA and DTC officials met to review the matter, with diplomats emphasizing that Colombia's government, "a military dictatorship of an unpleasant type," was unpopular at home, as were many regimes in the region. By supporting such governments, DEA officials maintained, Canada risked alienating "the liberal and progressive forces with which Canadian opinion is disposed to be sympathetic."[68] In the end, economic interests won out, and Pearson overruled his advisors. When the issue came before Cabinet, he stressed the extent to which the sale would help reduce costs and could lead to sales elsewhere in the region. Admitting to the precedents being set, he nonetheless recommended that the sale proceed, noting that though the Colombian regime was "not exemplary" in its conduct toward its own people, it had no recent history of conflict with its neighbours. Furthermore, Bogotá could presumably find other suppliers, so a Canadian decision not to sell the planes would have little impact. Ministers agreed, approving the export permit.[69]

Although Cabinet had acted to secure economic advantage regarding Canada's own procurement efforts, one of Pearson's senior advisors hoped that the government would avoid developing "anything like a vested interest in competitive armaments programmes of various military dictatorships."[70] The F-86 sale to Colombia demonstrated both the low priority accorded to human rights as a factor in determining arms sales and the extent to which Canada's export policy was evolving as more countries sought Canadian arms. The caution that had prevailed after the war was increasingly outmoded. In Cabinet, soon after the Colombian deal was concluded, and with a similar sale to Israel pending, Pearson urged his colleagues to consider a policy of continuing to reject exports "if they were likely to increase international or domestic tension, or lead to violence."

Still, he urged that the mere fact that an "area was a 'sensitive' one" should not preclude arms sales. Cabinet approved the measure, paving the way for advanced weapons sales in the Middle East, undeniably a sensitive area.[71]

Arms Exports to the Middle East

Like Canadian arms sales overall, exports to Middle Eastern countries had evolved in response to demand and to Ottawa's growing willingness to enter the munitions market. Furthermore, as with sales to India and Pakistan, Canadian exports reflected a sense of balance, in line with Ottawa's approach to the region, as summed up by one diplomat: "Israel had a right to exist and Canada would deal with Israel and the Arabs in an even-handed manner."[72] The Middle East was of little direct interest to Canada, which lacked a diplomatic presence there until 1954, when embassies were established in Cairo and Tel Aviv – a testament to the Canadian emphasis on balance. Even so, Canada had a considerable impact on the region through its involvement in the partition of the British mandate of Palestine and subsequent efforts at the UN to create the state of Israel. The resulting war between Israel and its Arab neighbours led to caution over arms exports, as did Canadian Zionists' purchase and transfer of equipment to Jewish fighters in Palestine during the uprising against British rule. In January 1949, both Israel and Egypt approached Canada about purchasing trainer aircraft. Although the requests came literally weeks into a ceasefire between the two belligerents, Ottawa agreed, requiring them to assert that the aircraft would be used for peaceful purposes.[73]

Whereas balance in the India-Pakistan context meant weighing Canada's exports equally, in the Middle East it encompassed the total balance of forces in the region, eventually leading to an imbalance in Canadian munitions sales favouring Israel. Initially, in the wake of the 1948–49 Arab-Israeli war, the Canadians had pursued sales to Egypt, which was then ruled by a British-backed monarchy. One diplomat advocated arms exports as a means of "developing closer political relations" with the Egyptians, dismissing possible Israeli concerns about any sales on the grounds that Canada was also likely to sell munitions to Israel. An assessment by the Joint Intelligence Committee likewise praised the benefits of supplying arms to Egypt, which should be built up "as a bastion against Communist aggression in the Middle East."[74] However, a coup against the monarchy in 1952 and the subsequent transformation of Egypt into an epicentre of anti-colonial agitation under Colonel Gamal Abdel Nasser put paid to these hopes. In 1955, Ottawa rejected an Egyptian request for forty F-86 Sabres, which would tip the military balance.[75] This rejection proved portentous: within weeks, Nasser concluded a massive weapons deal with Czechoslovakia, raising Western fears that Egypt was slipping into the Soviet bloc.

In the wake of the Egyptian-Czechoslovak deal, which included the transfer of fifty Ilyushin-28 bombers and two hundred MiG-15 fighters, Israel sought its own Sabres from Canada, a request that Ottawa eventually met to preserve the regional military balance. Preserving this balance was the basis of the May 1950 Tripartite Agreement whereby Britain, France, and the United States committed to avoiding a Middle Eastern arms race and to selling only weapons that could be used primarily for defensive purposes. Although Canada was not a signatory, Canadian officials felt bound by the pact, authorizing exports to Israel of weapons of a "defensive character," such as ammunition, machine guns, and anti-aircraft guns.[76] As the regional situation evolved, Canada became a prime supplier of munitions for Israel, partly because Arab states received arms from the British and French.[77] Partly, too, Canadian authorities felt a sense of attachment to Israel. "It is a simple act of justice to enable Israel to defend itself," one senior diplomat concluded in 1956, adding that "we share the responsibility for the establishment of that State and we share the obligation to see that the Israelis are in a position to defend themselves."[78] In 1951, the Cabinet Defence Committee reviewed an Israeli request for artillery, classed as offensive weapons. Pearson urged relaxing Canadian policy, contending that with "the Arab world in a state of internal unrest and mounting anti-Western hysteria, Israel was emerging as the one stable element in the area." Agreeing, St-Laurent judged that additional sales to the Israelis would have a "stabilizing effect" on the region.[79] This calculus guided Canadian arms sales to Israel over the next few years. Even so, Canada was cognizant of the regional balance, rejecting an Israeli request for F-86 Sabres in 1954 and doing the same with Egypt in 1955.[80] Canada, Pearson told the House of Commons in early 1956, "should not contribute to the development of an arms race in the Middle East."[81]

Weeks after this statement, with the Egyptian-Czechoslovak arms agreement, Pearson made the case in Cabinet for lifting restrictions. Since Arab governments were receiving advanced weapons from the great powers, Canadian controls amounted to "an embargo against Israel only." Cabinet agreed to relax restrictions, insisting, though, that arms sales to Israel be made following consultation with Canada's allies.[82] Pearson and St-Laurent duly raised the issue with their British and American counterparts, who emphasized growing concern over Soviet involvement in the Middle East and worry about boosting their own arms exports to Israel lest doing so would turn Arab opinion against the West. Throughout these discussions, Pearson was adamant, as he told British prime minister Anthony Eden, that Israel could not be expected to act peacefully while its neighbours prepared for war. With Arab states rearming, he added, the danger lay in the Israelis hitting their enemies before they found themselves in a weaker position.[83] Although Pearson told US secretary of state John Foster Dulles that

Canada "was not any more anxious than the United States to become identified with one side or the other," it was within the context of potential Israeli weakness, and the instability that the situation created, that he pushed Cabinet to approve selling twenty-four Sabres to Israel.[84]

The Israeli request for the F-86s came amid mounting regional tensions: In April 1956, Cairo and Prague concluded a second arms deal, prompting Washington to pull its funding for the Aswan Dam, in turn causing Nasser to nationalize the Suez Canal in July. The very day that Nasser took this momentous step, Canadian ministers met to consider Israel's request. Given the Suez situation, they deferred a decision, but a month later, with the prospect of a diplomatic resolution to the standoff over the canal, Cabinet approved the sale. Twelve F-86s would be released in the autumn, and the remaining dozen would follow by the end of 1956.[85] Events intervened, however. In October, Israel attacked Egypt, an action taken with the connivance of Britain and France, which dispatched troops to take control of the canal zone under the pretext of keeping the waterway open to international shipping. Ottawa halted the Sabre shipments and suspended arms sales to the Middle East, moves in keeping with a UN embargo imposed amid the violence. Early the next year, Canada's moratorium was loosened somewhat: exports to Egypt, Israel, and Syria remained suspended; other Middle Eastern countries could receive materiel apart from weapons and ammunition; and vehicle parts were soon sold to the Lebanese military.[86] Among the reasons for the continuance of the moratorium was the presence of Canadian soldiers on the United Nations Emergency Force (UNEF). This peacekeeping force's creation had helped end the Suez Crisis, cementing Canada's position as an honest broker and earning Pearson a Nobel Peace Prize. As Pearson told his advisors in May 1957, "it would be hard for us to send any arms to either [Egypt or Israel] so long as UNEF remained in its present position and role." Even so, he wondered about the possibility of exporting items of "marginal" military value.[87] Here, the dichotomy between Canada as peacekeeper and arms broker is vividly displayed.

Conclusion

This contrast became more pronounced amid the Vietnam War, putting paid to many young Canadians' ideas about Canada's mythic role as an honest broker in world affairs. Through the 1956 Defence Production Sharing Agreement (DPSA) negotiated with Washington to help offset the costs of equipping Canada's military, Canadian arms manufacturers and other companies were able to compete for Pentagon contracts. Proving lucrative for Canadian industry, the arrangement became a source of criticism from opponents of the Vietnam War, who decried Canada's complicity in the American military campaign.[88]

Yet even as journalists revealed that US forces in Vietnam were utilizing Canadian-made materiel, Canadian officials claimed ignorance of the end use of exported munitions. "There is, so far as I am aware," Lester Pearson, now prime minister, explained in 1967, "no way in which the Canadian government, and perhaps even the US government, could ascertain the present whereabouts of all military equipment purchased in Canada by the USA." In private, there was more candour. Warning his Cabinet colleagues about the growing criticism of the DPSA, Paul Martin, Pearson's secretary of state for external affairs, offered the assurance that, officially, "items were being shipped from Canada to United States inventory and therefore Canada had no formal knowledge of or control over the ultimate destination." In actuality, he admitted, Canadian-made aircraft and ground vehicles were indeed being used by American forces in Vietnam.[89] Despite such evidence, there was no impetus in government circles to end the DPSA. Failing to honour it, Pearson explained in 1967, "would have far-reaching consequences which no Canadian government could contemplate with equanimity. It would be interpreted as a notice of withdrawal on our part from continental defence and even from the collective defence arrangements of the Atlantic Alliance."[90]

For many Canadians, the situation could not be made to accord with their image of their country: incongruously, even as the DPSA ensured market access for Canada's arms manufacturers, Canadian officials were serving on the International Control Commission, the quasi-peacekeeping body whose purpose was to enforce the 1954 Geneva Accords that had ended French rule in Indochina. As Pearson put it publicly in 1966, Canadian arms shipments to the United States were "incompatible with our role in the International Control Commission."[91] But the reality of the DPSA arrangement conflicted with this assurance, leading one critic to characterize Canada's approach to Vietnam as "profit-oriented objectivity."[92] This situation reflected in microcosm the nature of Canada's postwar arms export policy, where caution about fuelling conflict or arming repressive regimes frequently lost out to economic concerns. During the so-called golden age of Canadian foreign policy, arms exports emerged as a tool for policymakers to strengthen the manufacturing sector, reduce procurement costs, and support the country's allies and other important states. Just as other golden age developments became bedrock elements of its long-term foreign policy – NATO membership, support for the UN, international development spending – Canada continues to act as an arms broker.

Critics of Canada's 2014 weapons sale to Saudi Arabia should not be surprised at Ottawa's prioritization of economic factors. From the golden age to the present, successive Canadian governments have been willing to sell arms, creating a tension between self-aggrandizing rhetoric about Canada as a middle power and the reality of policymakers' hardnosed decisions.[93] From an initial desire to offload surplus wartime materiel but otherwise tread cautiously, the Canadian stance on the issue evolved to a more fulsome export-oriented position. The latter was meant to help offset the costs of arming and maintaining Canada's own military forces and to ensure a functioning munitions industry, and thus to benefit the country's MIC.

The Cold War was the context for this development, as was Canada's adoption of more globally engaged foreign and defence policies. As one senior official crowed after the 1956 Sabre sale to Colombia, the unprecedented deal was "in keeping with our increase in international importance and military strength," with additional exports of high-value materiel bound to "enhance respect for Canada." Or, as Mackenzie King had complained several years earlier in regard to what arms exports to China portended for the direction of Canada's shifting postwar foreign policy, "We have been too eager to play a role in world affairs ... like a child with a new toy."[94] These statements are reminders that the role of arms broker was a new one for Canada, the result of Cold War imperatives that transformed its foreign and defence policy.

Worth noting, though, is that in 2019 Canada adhered to the UN Arms Trade Treaty, regulating international arms sales. The move necessitated legal and regulatory changes to export controls, including a stipulation requiring the foreign minister to assess whether exported arms could be used to violate humanitarian law or threaten international peace. This development was an important one, even as arms sales remain vital to Canada's defence industry. A 2021 House of Commons report noted that half of Canadian arms companies' revenue stems from foreign sales, with exports sustaining the industry in light of a domestic market that is too small to do so on its own. So long as that reality persists, the goal, as the report put it, is to maintain an "elusive balance," or "middle ground," between exporting arms and upholding international law or not fuelling conflicts.[95] In other words, Canada will remain an honest arms broker.

Notes

1 Jennifer Pedersen, "'We Will Honour Our Good Name': The Trudeau Government, Arms Exports, and Human Rights," in *Justin Trudeau and Canadian Foreign Policy*, ed. Norman Hillmer and Philippe Lagassé (Basingstoke: Palgrave, 2018), 207–32; Srdjan Vucetic, "A Nation of Feminist Arms Dealers? Canada and Military Exports," *International Journal* 72, 4 (2017): 503–19; Ellen Gutterman and Andrea Lane, "Beyond LAVs: Corruption, Commercialization and the Canadian Defence Industry," *Canadian Foreign Policy Journal* 23, 1 (2017): 77–92.
2 Charles Taylor, *Snow Job: Canada, the United States and Vietnam* (Toronto: Anansi, 1974), 121–24; Victor Levant, *Quiet Complicity: Canadian Involvement in the Vietnam War* (Toronto: Between the Lines, 1986), 51–62; Michael Oren, "Canada, the Great Powers, and the Middle Eastern Arms Race, 1950–1956," *International History Review* 12 (1990):

280–300; Chris Kilford, *The Other Cold War: Canada's Military Assistance to the Developing World, 1945–1975* (Kingston: Canadian Defence Academy Press, 2010), 69–93.

3   Adam Chapnick, "The Canadian Middle Power Myth," *International Journal* 55 (2000): 188–206; Hector MacKenzie, "Golden Decade(s)? Reappraising Canada's International Relations in the 1940s and 1950s," *British Journal of Canadian Studies* 23 (2010): 179–206.

4   Alex Souchen, *War Junk: Munitions Disposal and Postwar Reconstruction in Canada* (Vancouver: UBC Press, 2020), 156, 162.

5   Pearson to St-Laurent, 2 April 1947, RG 25, vol. 7582, file 11044–40-pt. 1, Library and Archives Canada (LAC).

6   Robertson to King, "Sale of Armaments to Foreign Governments," 30 April 1946, RG 25, vol. 4440, file 50000–40-pt. 1, LAC.

7   Cabinet Conclusions, 24 May 1946, RG 2, vol. 2638, LAC.

8   Cabinet Conclusions, 27 June 1946, RG 2, vol. 2638, LAC.

9   Pearson to Mills, 21 March 1947; Pearson to St-Laurent, "Export of Armaments," 29 March 1947, both in RG 25, vol. 7582, file 11044–40-pt. 1, LAC.

10 Pearson to St-Laurent, "Export of Armaments," 2 April 1947, RG 25, vol. 7582, file 11044–40-pt. 1, LAC.

11 Cabinet Committee on External Trade Policy, 3 April 1947, RG 25, vol. 7582, file 11044–40-pt. 1, LAC.

12 Cabinet Conclusions, 16 April 1947, RG 2, vol. 2640, LAC.

13 St-Laurent to Howe, 24 September 1947; DEA to Washington, tel. EX-3039, 27 November 1947, both in RG 25, file 11044-BU-40, LAC.

14 Reid, "Manufacture of Arms in Canada for Export," 12 February 1948, RG 25, vol. 7582, file 11044–40-pt. 1, LAC.

15 Mackenzie to Pearson, 9 March 1948, RG 25, vol. 7582, file 11044–40-pt. 1, LAC.

16 Moran to Pearson, 21 March 1948; and attached St-Laurent, Memorandum for Cabinet, "Export of Arms from Current Production," 25 March 1948, RG 25, vol. 7582, file 11044–40-pt. 1, LAC.

17 Interdepartmental Meeting on Export of Arms, 31 January 1950, RG 25, vol. 7582, file 11044–40-pt. 2.1, LAC.

18 Cabinet Conclusions, 7 April 1948, RG 2, vol. 2641, LAC.

19 Pearson to Heads of Post Abroad, 1 May 1948, RG 25, vol. 7582, file 11044–40-pt. 1, LAC.

20 Pearson to St-Laurent, "Sale of Arms to India and Pakistan," 26 July 1948, RG 25, vol. 4442, file 50000-H-40-pt. 1, LAC.

21 Cabinet Conclusions, 1 September 1948, RG 2, vol. 2642, LAC.

22 Pearson, Memorandum for Cabinet, 4 October 1948; Pearson, Memorandum for Cabinet, "Sale of Arms and Ammunition to Pakistan," 7 October 1948, both in RG 25, vol. 4442, file 50000-H-40-pt. 1, LAC; Cabinet Conclusions, 12 October 1948, RG 2, vol. 2642, LAC.

23 Memorandum for Cabinet, "Export of Military Equipment to India and Pakistan," 7 December 1948, RG 25, vol. 4442, file 50000-H-40-pt. 1, LAC; Cabinet Conclusions, 8 December 1948, RG 2, vol. 2642, LAC.

24 Cabinet Conclusions, 5 April 1950, RG 2, vol. 2645, LAC; Cabinet Conclusions, 5 January 1949, RG 2, vol. 2643, LAC.

25 Ritchie to Léger, "Export of Aircraft and Aircraft Parts," 20 March 1956, RG 25, vol. 7581, file 11044–40-pt. 5, LAC.

26 Cabinet Conclusions, 6 and 20 November 1962, RG 2, vol. 6193, LAC; Ryan Touhey, *Conflicting Visions: Canada and India in the Cold War World, 1946–76* (Vancouver: UBC Press, 2015), 145–47.

27 Duane Bratt, *The Politics of CANDU Exports* (Toronto: University of Toronto Press, 2006).

28 Memorandum for Heeney, "Sale of 100,000,000 Rounds of Bren Gun Ammunition to the Chinese," 27 June 1946, RG 25, vol. 4301, file 11044-BS-40-pt. 1, LAC; Cabinet Conclusions, 27 June 1946, RG 2, vol. 2638, LAC.

29 Pearson to St-Laurent, "Export of Arms to China," 20 March 1947, RG 25, vol. 4301, file 11044-BS-40-pt. 1, LAC.

30 Cabinet Conclusions, 16 April 1947, RG 2, vol. 2640, LAC.

31 Howe to St-Laurent, 2 June 1947, RG 25, vol. 4301, file 11044-BS-40-pt. 1, LAC.

32 Moran to Pearson, "Export of Arms to China," 10 June 1947, RG 25, vol. 4301, file 11044-BS-40-pt. 1, LAC.

33 Beaudry to St-Laurent, 23 August 1947, RG 25, vol. 4301, file 11044-BS-40-pt. 1, LAC.

34 St-Laurent, Memorandum for Cabinet, 23 August 1947, RG 25, vol. 4301, file 11044-BS-40-pt. 1, LAC.

35 John W. Holmes, *The Shaping of Peace: Canada and the Search for World Order* (Toronto: University of Toronto Press, 1982), 2:133; Cabinet Conclusions, 25 August 1947, RG 2, vol. 2640, LAC.

36 Kim Richard Nossal, "Business as Usual: Canadian Relations with China in the 1940s," *Historical Papers/Communications historiques* 13, 1 (1978): 146.

37 Pearson to St-Laurent, 10 September 1947, RG 25, vol. 4301, file 11044-BS-40-pt. 1, LAC.

38 Pearson, quoted in Beaudry to St-Laurent, "Sale of Arms and Ammunition to China," 22 October 1947; Beaudry to St-Laurent, "Sale of Arms and Ammunition to China," 10 November 1947, both in RG 25, vol. 4301, file 11044-BS-40-pt. 1, LAC.

39 Burwash to file, 10 November 1947; Moran to Menzies, 24 November 1947, both in RG 25, vol. 4301, file 11044-BS-40-pt. 1, LAC.

40 Canada, *House of Commons Debates*, 19 December 1947, 494.

41 Rev. McGookin to King, 31 March 1948, RG 25, vol. 3814, file 8505-A-40, LAC.

42 "Protests Mount Because Canada Sends China Arms," *Globe and Mail*, 18 December 1947; "Shipload of Arms Bound for China Picketed by Union," *Globe and Mail*, 19 December 1947; "$1 Million in Arms Shipped to China; B.C. Dispute Ends," *Globe and Mail*, 3 January 1948.

43 Cabinet Conclusions, 15 January 1948, RG 2, vol. 2641, LAC; King Diary, 19 December 1947, LAC.

44 Davis to St-Laurent, 19 December 1947, RG 25, vol. 4301, file 11044-BS-40-pt. 1, LAC.

45 Menzies, "The Sale of .30 Calibre Cartridges to China," 3 June 1948, RG 25, vol. 7582, file 11044-40-pt. 1.2, LAC.

46 Pearson to Cabinet, "Sale of Arms to China," 7 October 1948, RG 25, vol. 7582, file 11044-40-pt. 1.2, LAC; Cabinet Conclusions, 12 October 1948, RG 2, vol. 2642, LAC.

47 Cabinet Conclusions, 16 December 1948, RG 2, vol. 2642, LAC.

48 Cabinet Conclusions, 25 January 1949, RG 2, vol. 2643, LAC.

49 See Cabinet Conclusions, 17 February, 7 March, and 23 March 1949, RG 2, vol. 2643, LAC.

50 Cabinet Conclusions, 3 May 1949, RG 2, vol. 2643, LAC.

51 Nanking to DEA, tel. 137, 27 August 1949, RG 25, vol. 4717, file 50055-40, LAC; Cabinet Conclusions, 31 August 1949, RG 2, vol. 2643, LAC.

52 Heeney to Pearson, "Policy towards Communist China," 4 November 1949, RG 25, vol. 4719, file 50055-B-40, LAC; Cabinet Conclusions, 21 December 1949, RG 2, vol. 2643, LAC.

53 Ronning to Economic Division, "Sale of Arms and Ammunition to Nationalist China," 13 March 1953, RG 25, vol. 4301, file 11044-BS-40-pt. 2, LAC.

54 Wilgress to Acting Minister, "Export of Military Equipment and Strategic Materials to Nationalist China," 13 April 1953, RG 25, vol. 4301, file 11044-BS-40-pt. 2, LAC.

55   Chester Ronning, *A Memoir of China in Revolution* (New York: Pantheon, 1974), 138.

56   Heeney to Pearson, "North Atlantic," 20 February 1950; and attached memorandum, "North Atlantic Treaty: Canadian Mutual Aid," 20 February 1950, RG 25, vol. 4506, file 50030-L-40, LAC.

57   Cabinet Conclusions, 10 August 1956, RG 2, vol. 5775, LAC. On Canada's F-86s, see Randall Wakelam, *Cold War Fighters: Canadian Aircraft Procurement, 1945–54* (Vancouver: UBC Press, 2011).

58   "Minutes, Tenth Meeting of Panel on Economic Aspects of Defence Questions," 11 July 1950, in *Documents on Canadian External Relations 1950*, ed. Greg Donaghy (Ottawa: Canadian Communication Group, 1996), doc. 519.

59   Pearson to Campney, 18 January 1955, RG 25, vol. 4504, file 50030-L-40, LAC. For a later incident of Canadian arms procurement playing a similar role in the NATO context, see Frank Maas, *The Price of Alliance: The Politics and Procurement of Leopard Tanks for Canada's NATO Brigade* (Vancouver: UBC Press, 2017).

60   Johnson to Economic Division, 8 March 1948, RG 25, vol. 4075, file 11044-A-40-pt. 1, LAC.

61   Cabinet Conclusions, 31 July 1952, RG 2, vol. 2651, LAC.

62   Blanchette, "Canada's Policy on Indochina," 16 November 1953, RG 25, vol. 4627, file 50052-40, LAC.

63   David Webster, *Fire and the Full Moon: Canada and Indonesia in a Decolonizing World* (Vancouver: UBC Press, 2009), 4.

64   On Howe, see Don Nerbas, *Dominion of Capital: The Politics of Big Business and the Crisis of the Canadian Bourgeoisie, 1914–1947* (Toronto: University of Toronto Press, 2013), 201–41.

65   Howe, Memorandum for the Cabinet, "Control over the Export of Military Equipment," 21 January 1954, RG 25, vol. 7581, file 11044-40-pt. 5, LAC; Cabinet Conclusions, 10 March 1954, RG 2, vol. 2654, LAC; McKay to Pearson, "Authority to Approve Export of Arms," 26 May 1954, RG 25, vol. 6607, file 11044-40-pt. 3.2, LAC.

66   Léger to Pearson, "Possible Sale of F-86 Aircraft to Colombia," 13 February 1956, RG 25, vol. 7704, file 12001-40, LAC.

67   Department of Trade and Commerce note, "Sale of F86s to Colombia," 27 February 1956, RG 25, vol. 7704, file 12001-40, LAC.

68   Léger to Bull, "Possible Sale to Colombia of F-86 Aircraft," 28 February 1956, RG 25, vol. 7704, file 12001-40, LAC.

69   Pearson, Memorandum for the Cabinet, "Proposed Export of F-86 Aircraft to Colombia," 20 March 1956, RG 25, vol. 7562, file 11044-40-pt. 5, LAC; Cabinet Conclusions, 22 March 1956, RG 2, vol. 5775, LAC; Stefano Tijerina, "One Size Fits All? Canadian Development Assistance to Colombia, 1953–1972," in *A Samaritan State Revisited: Historical Perspectives on Canadian Foreign Aid*, ed. Greg Donaghy and David Webster (Calgary: University of Calgary Press, 2019), 123–43.

70   DEA to Argentina, tel. X-348, 23 October 1956, RG 25, vol. 7704, file 12001-40, LAC.

71   Cabinet Conclusions, 2 August 1956, RG 2, vol. 5775, LAC.

72   Arthur Andrew, *The Rise and Fall of a Middle Power: Canadian Diplomacy from King to Mulroney* (Toronto: James Lorimer, 1993), 76.

73   Pearson, Memorandum for Cabinet, 22 January 1949, RG 25, vol. 4444, file 50000-C-40-pt. 1, LAC; Cabinet Conclusions, 25 January 1949, RG 2, vol. 2643, LAC.

74   Macdermott to Economic Division, 28 June 1949; Joint Intelligence Committee, "Export of Arms to Egypt," 9 August 1949, both in RG 25, vol. 4444, file 50000-C-40-pt. 1, LAC.

75   Cabinet Conclusions, 16 September 1955, RG 2, vol. 2658, LAC.

76 Cabinet Conclusions, 27 April 1950, RG 2, vol. 2645, LAC; Cabinet Conclusions, 13 September and 25 October 1950, RG 2, vol. 2646, LAC.

77 Wilgress to Pearson, "Export of Arms to the Middle East," 19 January 1953, RG 25, vol. 4440, file 50000-A-40, LAC.

78 Macdonnell to Pearson, "Political Factors Governing a Decision to Export Jet Interceptor Aircraft to Israel," 14 May 1956, RG 25, vol. 4442, file 50000-B-40, LAC.

79 "Cabinet Defence Committee Minutes," 30 August 1951, RG 2, Cabinet Defence Committee Records, vol. 244, file C-10-9-M, LAC.

80 Cabinet Conclusions, 13 July 1954, RG 2, vol. 2655, LAC.

81 Canada, *House of Commons Debates*, 24 January 1956, 468.

82 Cabinet Conclusions, 3 February 1956, RG 2, vol. 5775, LAC.

83 DEA to Washington, tel. K-237, 9 February 1956, RG 25, vol. 6098, file 50359–40-pt. 2, LAC.

84 Pearson to St-Laurent, 10 May 1956, MG 26 N1, vol. 38, LAC.

85 Cabinet Conclusions, 27 July, 31 July, and 29 August 1956, RG 2, vol. 5775, LAC; Oren, "Canada, the Great Powers, and the Middle Eastern Arms Race."

86 Reece to file, "Canadian Arms Policy for the Middle East," 8 October 1963, RG 25, vol. 4442, file 50000-A-40-pt. 9, LAC.

87 Meeting of Heads of Canadian Posts in the Middle East, 5–7 May 1957, RG 25, vol. 7204, file 10170-C-40-pt. 16.2, LAC.

88 "We're Making Millions Out of Vietnam," *Maclean's*, May 1967; Levant, *Quiet Complicity*, 51–62; Taylor, *Snow Job*, 121–24.

89 "Canada, the United States and Vietnam," DEA *Statements & Speeches* 67/8, 10 March 1967; Cabinet Conclusions, 8 September 1965, RG 2, vol. 6271, LAC.

90 "Canada, the United States and Vietnam," DEA *Statements & Speeches* 67/8, 10 March 1967.

91 "Pearson Says Canada Cannot Stop Arms Being Used in War," *Globe and Mail*, 8 January 1966.

92 Walter Stewart, "Proudly We Stand the Butcher's Helper in Southeast Asia," *Maclean's*, March 1970, 13.

93 Ernie Regher, *Arms Canada: The Deadly Business of Military Exports* (Toronto: James Lorimer, 1987).

94 DEA to Argentina, tel. X-348, 23 October 1956, RG 25, vol. 7704, file 12001–40, LAC; King Diary, 19 December 1947, LAC.

95 Canada, House of Commons, Standing Committee on Foreign Affairs and International Development, *Assessing Risk, Preventing Diversion and Increasing Transparency: Strengthening Canada's Arms Export Controls in a Volatile World* (Ottawa: House of Commons, 2021), 9, 10, 21.

6

"This Seems Pie in the Sky and Most Unlikely"
The Origins of General Dynamics Land Systems–Canada

Frank Maas

FOR THE PAST THREE DECADES, General Dynamics Land Systems–Canada, in London, Ontario, has been Canada's largest defence exporter and has outsold all comparable manufacturers by a wide margin. Governments, both Liberal and Conservative, have celebrated the plant's successes, though it has also been subject to controversy, especially with the sale of armoured vehicles to Saudi Arabia in 2014.[1] Few people, however, are aware of the beginning of armoured vehicle production in London, which sheds light on the origins and international character of Canada's defence-industrial base. From 1950 to 2002, the plant was owned by General Motors; originally called Diesel Division General Motors (DDGM), it was rebranded as General Motors Defense in the 1990s. The American defence conglomerate General Dynamics bought the plant in 2002 and gave it its current name, General Dynamics Land Systems–Canada. For the sake of simplicity, I will refer to it as DDGM, its name during the period discussed in this chapter.

Production of armoured vehicles at DDGM began in the 1970s when a Swiss manufacturer, Mowag, offered a licence to DDGM to produce its Piranha design, a lightly armoured wheeled vehicle that was well suited to patrolling and rapid movement on roads. As a result, DDGM built nearly 500 Piranhas for the Canadian army. As that order ended, the US Marine Corps bought more than 750 throughout the 1980s, which allowed the London plant to develop into a full-fledged defence contractor. More achievements for DDGM came during the 1990s when it sold and distributed thousands of vehicles around the world. DDGM was successful because it started with a reliable and durable design, and in the 1980s, developed that into one of the best wheeled armoured vehicles in the world. It also responded to engineering and production challenges and met its delivery schedules with few problems. DDGM's sales ensconced it in two critical markets, Canada and the United States, which have been a base for global exports. Finally, the plant capitalized on unexpected changes in procurement processes and the global strategic context as the Cold War ended. Its success, however, is unique and not easily replicable.

Before delving into the history documented in this chapter, DDGM must be situated in relation to definitions and descriptions of the military-industrial complex (MIC). The American MIC has been defined as a "network of public and private forces that combine a profit motive with the planning and implementation of strategic policy."[2] The armed forces and defence contractors figure prominently in this relationship, but Congress and universities participate as well. Members of Congress want military funding to be directed to their districts and can exert considerable sway over defence allocations, and universities are eager for research funding.[3] The Canadian MIC operates differently, however. Political scientists Alistair Edgar and David Haglund offer a strong analysis of Canada's MIC in their survey of the Canadian defence industry in the 1990s. They point out that Canada's defence-industrial base possessed nowhere near the clout or influence of the United States or European countries. It was simply too small. Edgar and Haglund also note high export dependence in Canada's MIC, as the equipment needs of the Canadian military cannot sustain domestic industries alone. Therefore, Canadian companies have been reliant on exports since at least the 1950s, meaning that their prospects have been "strongly influenced – and even determined, at times – by the impact of changes in the international demand and supply for defence equipment." This export focus has resulted in what one participant called "Canada, Inc.," in which Canadian companies are supported, not only by the armed forces, but by other government departments interested in international relations, economic development, and trade.[4] A critical, but challenging, market for Canadian companies is the United States. Canadian defence contractors have privileged access to the American market but must also contend with American industries and politics, and this chapter will reveal the pathways to success under these circumstances.

The Search for a Light Armoured Vehicle

The Canadian army began looking for a light wheeled armoured vehicle in the 1960s. Inspired by the American Flexible Response strategy and efforts to develop globally mobile forces, it developed plans for a light force that could be rapidly deployed around the world.[5] It required a vehicle for fire support and transport, and army planners thought that the American Cadillac Gage V-100 Commando was the best option. However, the army never bought the Commando in quantity because of budgetary constraints and frequent changes in defence policy. It tested an improved version, the V-150, in 1972, and General Jacques Dextraze, a Second World War and Korean War veteran who was appointed chief of the defence staff in 1972, took an interest in its possible purchase.[6] His priority was to buy new equipment to replace Canada's aging materiel, especially its main battle tanks. In 1969, Pierre Trudeau's government announced that all Canadian tanks, even those stationed in Europe as part of the North Atlantic Treaty Organization (NATO) forces to deter the Soviet Union and its Warsaw Pact allies, would be withdrawn from service because there was no concrete military need for them at home.[7] Most army officers felt that this was a foolish idea. They argued that Canadian troops based in Europe needed the tanks to be effective and that the Canadian army would not be capable of waging modern warfare without them. Dextraze did everything possible to get tanks for Canadian troops in Europe and eventually succeeded with the help of NATO allies. He knew, however, that he did not have enough political capital to convince Trudeau to supply tanks for the forces at home too.[8] As a result, he sought a compromise by either developing, or at least adopting, the idea of a group or "family" of armoured vehicles, also known as an armoured vehicle general purpose (AVGP). Dextraze believed that the AVGP family would be useful for internal security operations at home, but more importantly, it would enable more realistic training in Canada. He commented later that "if we are not going to have any tanks in the country to train the troops on but we are going to have them if we go to war I have got to have something in the country that's going to be useful for internal security and so on, and at the same time to train the crews."[9] An AVGP with a gun in a turret could substitute for a tank and ameliorate the effects of its withdrawal from service.

The AVGP family was composed of four variants: a fire support vehicle, an armoured personnel carrier, a missile carrier, and a maintenance vehicle. Its requirements were modest and rooted in the idea that it would be used for training, not operations. Its armour needed only to withstand small-arms fire and light-artillery shell fragments and to provide some protection for the crew against armour-piercing and heavy machine guns from longer range. The centrepiece of the family was the fire support vehicle – the tank substitute – intended to support infantry and to destroy lightly armoured enemy vehicles. It required a turret with a gun ranging from 75 to 105 mm – the army's project team tasked with the AVGP acquisition eventually preferred the British 76 mm gun produced by Alvis. The armoured personnel carrier required a turret with two machine guns to provide limited fire support, and space for nine people including a driver and a gunner. The missile carrier required an anti-tank missile launcher, and the maintenance and recovery vehicle needed specialized equipment to tow, lift, and retrieve broken-down vehicles. Initial plans called for 715 units in total: 440 infantry carriers, 204 fire support vehicles, 28 missile carriers, and 43 maintenance vehicles.[10]

Through 1973, the army tested the now familiar Cadillac Gage Commando V-150, Dextraze's personal favourite and the early front-runner for the purchase. With its head offices in Warren, Michigan, close to Canada's manufacturing heartland, Cadillac Gage had established an effective network of Canadian suppliers and was eager to develop it to improve the appeal of its bid.[11] In the mid-1970s, the Canadian government was on the cusp of introducing an "offset" policy to develop and protect its industrial base and acquire new technologies. The core of the policy was that all major procurements from foreign companies would require either part of the contract's value to be spent in Canada or arrangements for production licences and technology transfers to Canadian firms.[12] Cadillac Gage offered up to 30 percent Canadian content for a possible contract, which later expanded to 50 percent.[13] Satisfied with this plan, the army's project team decided in early 1974 to procure the Commando without holding a competition. The team opened negotiations with the aid of the civilian Department of Supply and Services (DSS), the purchasing arm of the federal government, which requested that Cadillac Gage disclose its costing, a measure required for sole-source procurements. However, Cadillac Gage did not comply, so the DSS and the army gave it an ultimatum: if it did not disclose costing by 15 June 1974, the project team would put out a competitive tender for similar vehicles. Cadillac Gage decided not to provide the costing, so the army sent out its request for proposals to other manufacturers.[14] In the following months, the team made a whirlwind tour of five similar producers in Europe and one in Brazil, after which it concluded that the Swiss company Mowag's Piranha was the best technical vehicle, followed by the Brazilian company Engesa's Urutu, with the Commando in third place.[15]

The Competition: Procurement Meets Politics

In early 1974, the team sent out its request for proposals to five manufacturers and invited Canadian manufacturers, notably Bombardier, to partner with foreign companies, only to find that they were uninterested in the scheme. The government, however, was adamant that provisions for Canadian industrial participation must be built into the final agreement.[16] By September 1974, the team had chosen to test the Cadillac Gage, Engesa, and Mowag vehicles in Alberta in early 1975. The Commando was the cheapest at $66,000 apiece, but Ottawa still wanted Cadillac Gage to disclose its costing. The company provided a good benefits package, with a well-developed network of Canadian suppliers, and could offer 50 percent offsets, or up to 100 percent, given that it was about to sell several hundred vehicles to Saudi Arabia.[17]

Engesa, based in São Paulo, had been founded in 1963. Its Urutu was expensive, coming in at $113,000 per vehicle, but the DSS asked for a price reduction, and the Brazilians promised to do their best.[18] The Department of Industry, Trade and Commerce (ITC), responsible for developing Canadian industry and trade opportunities, and the Department of External Affairs were both enthusiastic about the Urutu purchase and hoped that the Brazilians would buy more Canadian products in exchange, notably the de Havilland Canada Buffalo utility transport aircraft.[19] They also thought that a purchase from Engesa would improve Canada's image in the so-called Third World, as the director of the Defence Programs Branch at ITC, F.T. Jackman, wrote: "Politically, as well as commercially, the favourable repercussions throughout the underdeveloped world would be incalculable. It would mark what is probably the first time that any developed country had ever purchased sophisticated equipment from a developing country."[20] For the Brazilians, the prospect of a sale to Canada was a validation of their industry and a source of pride, and they made the potential sale a high priority. Rumours spread that the president of Brazil had pushed the company to "participate regardless of technical problems."[21]

The final candidate was Mowag, based in Kreuzlingen, Switzerland. Although the project team preferred the Piranha, it was also expensive – at $109,000 each – and it was nearly excluded from the competition until Mowag came forward with a plan to produce the vehicle under licence in Canada, and the owner and founder, Walter Ruf, came to Ottawa to make his case for the Piranha.[22] Mowag had been founded in 1950, and its major customers were in Africa and Latin America. The firm was small – only around 350 employees in 1975 – with a limited production capacity of just ten vehicles per month. It had a tradition of setting up licence production arrangements with local companies to strengthen the political and economic appeal of its bids.[23]

Mowag had designed the six-wheeled Piranha for export in 1972, and when it heard of the Canadian program, it started looking for suitable Canadian partners. It found DDGM, which had been established in London, Ontario, in 1950 to manufacture locomotives, trucks, buses, and other heavy equipment. Steve Moyse, a DDGM employee responsible for the engineering side of transplanting production, noted that Mowag pursued DDGM because it had the expertise and workforce to conduct specialized welding.[24] Curtis Locke, who worked in the DDGM finance department at the time and was later a program manager, recalled that Ruf came unannounced to DDGM, where he knocked on the door and requested a partnership to produce the Piranha in Canada. This was known in Mowag circles as the "knock on the door," and DDGM was interested. Subsequent discussions resulted in a plan that would make DDGM the prime contractor. The engine and transmission of the Piranha would be American, but its suspension and some of the electronic components would be imported from Mowag and assembled in Canada.[25] A central problem was the production of hardened ballistic steel for the vehicle, and after some testing, steel produced by Canadian Heat Treaters in Richmond Hill was found to be better than that of the competitors. Clearing this hurdle made effective licence production a real possibility.[26]

Canada's Department of National Defence (DND) tested two vehicles each from Cadillac Gage, Engesa, and Mowag from 15 January to 15 March 1975. The testing revealed the excellence of the Piranha design, which was clearly superior to the Commando and the Urutu, and the only one to satisfy all of the army's requirements. It also impressed Dextraze, who visited the trials.[27] The Urutu was deemed acceptable, "with certain deficiencies," and the Commando was judged the worst of the three contenders.[28] Officials in the DND wanted to purchase the Piranha immediately, but ITC and External Affairs questioned the decision, noting that licence production of the Piranha in Canada was desirable, but that it involved mostly assembly work rather than the production of high-technology components and that long-term export prospects for the vehicle were unlikely.[29] The possible markets were limited because most countries had either their own domestic plants or access to competitive vehicles. One aide-memoire concluded that the DND was "looking for justification to spend the extra money and preferably to have some of the money from another government department. This seems like pie in the sky and most unlikely."[30]

The French company Saviem, initially excluded because one of its variants was not ready, tried to enter the project, lobbying DSS Minister Jean-Pierre Goyer and Prime Minister Trudeau. Saviem's proposal, however, was rejected because it would not be ready in time, and Cadillac Gage's Commando was declined because it was inferior to the others.[31] The completion of the Defence Structure Review in 1975 – a wide-ranging reappraisal of Canada's commitments and forces – put the program on hold until late in the year, but after that Cabinet decided that the AVGP program should proceed.[32]

The army's project team and Dextraze were set on the Piranha for the AVGP program. In a January 1976 meeting of the Defence Management Committee, the DND's highest committee, Dextraze helped shepherd the program on to Cabinet. He emphasized the tank-training role of the vehicle and stated that "no capability now exists for training forces in Canada in direct fire support techniques which involve the employment of both infantry and tanks. This deficiency is particularly evident ... since the tank has now been phased-out in Canada." The meeting concluded with the resolution that the DND would seek "immediate approval in principle" for the AVGP purchase.[33] The DSS and the DND, partially supported by External Affairs, wanted to start negotiations for a sole-source procurement of the Piranha from Mowag, but ITC was still hesitant.[34]

Aware of the deal and of the Brazilian interest in it, External Affairs recommended that Canada suspend negotiations on offsets to avoid leading the Brazilians on. The Brazilians correctly interpreted this as a prelude to rejection, and their messages in support of the Urutu became more strident.[35] At the instruction of their president, Brazilian officials notified the Canadian ambassador, Barry Steers, that they were eager to go forward with purchases of

Canadian products if there were movement on the AVGP decision.[36] Trudeau was frustrated with the slow progress of the purchase, which came to a head in a Cabinet meeting on 8 April 1976. Pointing out that the French government had been advised that their vehicle had been excluded from the competition due to time constraints, Trudeau asked Defence Minister James Richardson for an explanation as to why no decision had yet been reached. Richardson responded that his department had made its choice, that its submission was waiting at the Treasury Board, and that other ministers were responsible for the delay. External Affairs had noted the Brazilian objections, "with the knowledge and support of the President of Brazil himself," and Trudeau remarked that the government was now in an awkward position with regard to the Brazilians. Richardson replied that there were two possible options – decide immediately or grant a thirty-day extension – but DSS Minister Jean-Pierre Goyer recommended the former. Trudeau supported him, and Cabinet agreed to the immediate purchase of the Piranha family and to inform the Brazilians that the Urutu had not been selected.[37] There was little parliamentary discussion over the AVGP, and it was quickly overshadowed by the larger purchases in the 1970s: the Leopard main battle tank, new fighter aircraft, and ships.[38]

Two days later, External Affairs Minister Allan MacEachen sent a lengthy memorandum to Trudeau in which he outlined Brazil's grievances and suggested that a final evaluation be conducted to show that the Urutu had received due consideration. He stated that the Brazilians had "assigned almost undue importance to this sale as a symbol of their capacity to produce sophisticated equipment and sell it competitively on the international market." Trudeau rejected MacEachen's plan and wrote on the memo, "I find it incredible that a parallel concern for Canada-France relations appears nowhere in this paper ... How can your Department prepare the present memo without even mentioning the problem it creates for us with France?"[39] On 15 April 1976, the Treasury Board approved the purchase of the Piranha, and on 5 May, a lengthy message informed the Brazilians that the Urutu had not won the competition.[40]

In June, the AVGP project team began negotiating with DDGM for the purchase of the Piranha, and with Alvis for the purchase of the turret with the 76 mm gun. The number of vehicles to be ordered fluctuated during the negotiations because the first phase of spending was limited to $150 million, and the total number therefore increased or decreased in accordance with cost estimates for the vehicles. The army dropped the missile carrier because it planned to field the launcher on its M113 armoured personnel carrier, and adapting it for a few AVGPs would be too costly. In January 1977, the three variants were christened: the fire support vehicle was the Cougar, the personnel carrier was the Grizzly, and the maintenance and recovery vehicle was the Husky.[41] By the time the contract was signed on 18 February 1977, the deal was for 350 vehicles, which could increase to 715 with subsequent purchases, and DDGM would manufacture most of them. First deliveries would be in October 1978, with production completed by April 1981.[42]

This was a major sale for Mowag, its first to a Western army and the largest in total numbers. DDGM invested $9.5 million in improvements to its main plant and equipment to produce armoured vehicles.[43] The DND displayed some hesitation about transferring European production to Canada, but this was allayed by the vehicle's significant amount of North American content. DDGM would do the basic assembly of the hull with ballistic steel produced in Canada, installing a commonly used engine and transmission. Mowag would supply the suspension and driveline, and DDGM would install it.[44] To resolve production issues, the two companies decided that the first fifteen vehicles would be built in Switzerland with jigs and tooling that would then be used by DDGM in London to "permit validation of all production processes and standards."[45] The first six vehicles built in Switzerland arrived in London in early 1978, and Steve Moyse recalled that DDGM invited its subcontractors to bid on the production of items that were easy to substitute, such as fans, pumps, or propellers, and sought out Canadian companies to do the work.[46] The biggest obstacle during production and initial fielding was oil leaks in the driveline caused by faulty seals. DDGM called in a retired expert, who designed a replacement for the faulty seal.[47] Otherwise, production went smoothly and the relationship between the two companies was mutually beneficial. Canadian ballistic steel proved both superior to and more economical than Mowag's supply, so the Swiss company agreed to use Canadian steel in future production.[48] The planned follow-on purchases fluctuated as well, but all told the army bought 491 AVGPs – 195 Cougars, 269 Grizzlys, and 27 Huskys – and production was completed by September 1982 (Figure 6.1).[49]

The project team may have thought highly of the Piranha, but the Canadian army as a whole had little affection for it because it preferred tracked armoured vehicles. The armoured corps disliked the Cougar, which paled in comparison to a tank, particularly the Leopard C1, also introduced in the 1970s. To be fair, the Cougar was an improvement over previous tank alternatives, such as an M113 with a stovepipe, and it did facilitate more realistic training.[50] The infantry preferred the tried-and-tested M113 over the Grizzly, although the Grizzly was complementary to the M113 instead of a substitute. The two had comparable armour protection, but the M113 had better off-road mobility and more carrying capacity, whereas the Grizzly was faster on good ground and easier to maintain, and its turret was superior to the M113's armament.[51] AVGPs, although purchased as training vehicles, were pressed into service on numerous operations, ranging from domestic policing actions to

Figure 6.1 An AVGP Cougar on display at Wolseley Barracks in London, Ontario. | Photographer Frank Maas.

1990s peacekeeping missions in the former Yugoslavia and Somalia. Critics found fault with the thin armour of the AVGP family and the weakness of the Cougar's main gun.[52] These points were valid, but they obscure a more complicated story. The real problem was the cancellation of new armoured vehicle programs in the late 1980s, which forced the army to deploy in the 1990s with under-armoured vehicles. By 2004, all AVGPs had been withdrawn from Canadian service, although some soldier on in other countries or Canadian police services.[53]

The AVGP had been one of Dextraze's personal priorities, and he was proud of his role in bringing it to fruition.[54] Although the army was lukewarm about the AVGP, the quality of the original design came to the fore quite quickly. DDGM's vehicles impressed at trials in Indonesia and Malaysia, but they did not win any orders.[55] DDGM would need exports to keep armoured vehicle production alive in London, and that opportunity came from the United States, a critical market for Canadian defence industries. Piranhas impressed the US Marine Corps when it borrowed some AVGPs for testing rapidly deployable vehicles in 1980, a result of turmoil in the Middle East.[56]

The End of Détente and American Interest in the Piranha

In the late 1970s, the United States became increasingly concerned about the safety of the Persian Gulf. The Soviet invasion of Afghanistan in December 1979, hard on the heels of the fall of the shah in Iran, caused serious alarm in Washington.

This was aggravated by the Soviet Union's friendly relations with other states in the region, including Yemen and Ethiopia. The United States had few forces of its own in the area and had relied instead on regional "policemen" such as Iran to maintain order and keep the Soviets out.[57] This policy was in a shambles as détente came to an abrupt end, and in the early 1980s, the US military attempted to bolster its capabilities in the region through the Rapid Deployment Force (RDF).

The key to maintaining the safety of the gulf was the ability to deploy quickly. Unlike in Western Europe or Korea and Japan, there was no existing network of bases, so US forces would need to be transported to trouble spots to counter Soviet moves and airlifted to challenge them with speed. The other problem for American military planners was the sheer number of combat vehicles, especially tanks, in both Soviet and Soviet-supplied armies. The United States needed to be prepared to fight effectively against a panoply of Soviet armoured vehicles, but apart from the flawed Sheridan light tank, it possessed nothing that was easily deployable by air and armed with a main gun that could destroy Soviet light armoured vehicles, let alone tanks. This challenge was particularly acute for the Marine Corps, which had historically operated and trained as light infantry.

The Marine Corps had identified this deficiency in the early 1970s, especially for its initial landing forces, and it wanted a "lightweight, highly mobile and agile, helicopter-transportable weapons system capable of supporting the infantry against armor, materiel, and personnel targets."[58] The US Army also started its own program to equip mobile forces. The Marines borrowed Cougars and Grizzlys to test out the concepts for their mobile force, but fielding a vehicle that met the requirement would take years – they would not be ready until 1986 if the Marines chose to develop an existing vehicle and 1988 if they chose to develop a new one.[59] But in early 1980, both the US Senate and the House of Representatives pressured the army and the Marine Corps to buy an "off-the-shelf, airliftable, lightweight armored vehicle which would provide mobility, protection, and firepower in support of the rapid deployment force."[60] The Marines concluded that they would be interested in purchasing four to six hundred vehicles based on multiple variants to equip a brigade for the RDF, and they would work out the doctrine and tactics afterward. The army was less enthusiastic, preferring a limited purchase for study purposes. The Marine Corps set up its Light Armored Vehicle Directorate in September 1980 and hoped to have its "Light Assault Vehicles" in the inventory by late 1982 or early 1983.[61]

The purchase of the light armoured vehicle (LAV), as it became known, quickly tapped into a divisive debate within the Marine Corps over the adoption of more armoured vehicles. For some Marines, keeping the infantry on foot was central to the corps' distinctiveness and ethos. One contributor to the *Marine Corps Gazette* decried the purchase of a LAV, arguing that the "best light armored vehicles for the Marine Corps are attack helicopters and combat boots with infantrymen inside of them, not bore-sighted iron boxes waiting to become light-armored victims."[62] However, other Marines were in favour of mechanization; one wrote that "there exists among us a vocal minority of officers who are either resistant to innovative change or who are less-than-thoroughly familiar with the extraordinary intensity and lethality that Marines are likely to encounter on the modern battlefield."[63] Another contributor to the *Marine Corps Gazette*, Richard Stewart, commented that the LAV and other purchases were first steps in developing "medium" forces that had more staying power than light infantry but were "optimized for strategic and intra-theater airlift."[64]

On 14 April 1981, planning to start producing vehicles in 1982 and to field them in 1983, the Marine Corps issued a request for proposals for an off-the-shelf vehicle.[65] In late 1981, its program merged with that of the army, and the army's Tank-Automotive and Armaments Command (TACOM) took overall responsibility for the project due to its experience in armoured vehicle acquisition. There were problems from the outset, however, in co-operation between the army and Marine Corps. The army had two planning centres, each with different plans, and it dropped one of the variants that the Marines wanted.[66] The key requirements of the LAV, which would form the basis for ten possible variants, were that it be fast, amphibious, and light enough to be carried by helicopter. The need for portability limited its armour, with the result that it would be proof only against small-arms fire and small-calibre shell fragments, with some protection against heavier fire. Its primary weapon would be the excellent 25 mm Bushmaster cannon. The procurement plan was to buy 969 vehicles – 680 for the army and 289 for the Marine Corps, although the total number could rise to 2,350 for the army and 744 for the Marines.[67]

US Orders "Drive the LAV"

When DDGM received the Marine Corps request for proposals, it realized that its six-wheeled AVGP would not have the required payload or carrying capacity to meet the specifications, so it consulted with Mowag, which was working on eight-wheeled prototypes.[68] Out of seven responses, the Marines selected four: DDGM for an eight-wheeled vehicle based on the Piranha; Cadillac Gage for two vehicles, a lengthened four-wheeled V-150 and a new six-wheeler, the V-300; and Alvis from England for a tracked vehicle.[69] The program was supposed to be an off-the-shelf purchase, but all the submissions involved modified or new designs, so testing for the prototypes was required.

The American project team awarded DDGM a $3.1 million contract to supply four eight-wheeled LAVs for evaluation. The decision to increase the wheels from six to eight was an easy one, and it significantly increased the payload of the vehicle, with a minor design modification that represented only 5 to 6 percent of its total cost.[70] DDGM had not produced turrets before – the turrets for the Cougar and Grizzly had come from other contractors – so it installed some examples supplied by Arrowpointe, a Michigan company. The weight limit of 14.5 tons posed some problems. Constructing three prototypes from the steel used to build the AVGP, DDGM discovered that they were 2,000 pounds overweight. This steel was relatively soft and flexible, relying on thickness rather than hardness to provide armour protection against small-arms fire and fragments. To reduce the weight, DDGM used a harder, but thinner and lighter steel to construct the top half of the hull, reserving the thicker steel for the bottom, where its flexibility could better accommodate stresses. By October 1981, it had supplied one LAV equipped with a 25 mm cannon and another with a 90 mm gun.[71]

When the army and Marine Corps tested the prototypes in California, they discovered that, although DDGM's submission was more expensive than the others, it was also the best technical vehicle, "substantially and significantly superior to all other candidates."[72] A central strength of the DDGM prototype was its reliability and durability. It had an average of 1,449 mean miles between mission failures, which was well in excess of the requirement of 1,250 and far superior to the 398 miles of the V-150 and the 158 of the V-300.[73] During testing, DDGM brought in Delco Systems Operations from outside Santa Barbara, California, to assist with finishing the turret system and electronics.[74] The program ran into a political roadblock during 1982 when the US Senate and House committees cut funding for the army, so the LAV project office had to do three rounds of best and final proposals. Although the DDGM LAV was the most expensive, it was clearly the best, and DDGM was awarded the contract on the basis of best value for money.[75]

The federal government supported the sale through the Canadian Commercial Corporation (CCC), a Crown company that was responsible to Parliament and tasked with "helping Canadian exporters gain access to foreign government procurement markets." The CCC lent the credibility and weight of the federal government by signing the contract on behalf of DDGM and guaranteeing its performance.[76] The CCC's other role was to justify and certify costs for the program to the US government and to satisfy Washington's labyrinthine defence procurement cost regulations, an area in which DDGM had little experience. It began assisting DDGM in this role in 1981 during the proposal phase, and the government established a permanent office in London to aid DDGM. CCC personnel worked closely with plant personnel for the duration of the Marine Corps order and other foreign sales.[77]

Although DDGM was a Canadian company, it was largely insulated from political criticism as a foreign defence contractor because it was owned by GM, with its powerful lobbyists and contacts in Washington. It also enjoyed the benefits of the Defence Production Sharing Agreement. First signed in 1956 between Canada and the United States, and renewed several times since, the agreement stipulated that Canadian companies were, in effect, to be treated no differently from American companies when bidding for military contracts, and vice versa.[78] The agreement has been extraordinarily successful for Canada because it gives Canadian companies privileged access to the American defence market without subjecting them to the restraints of the Buy American Act, which is not the case for other nations. Despite the agreement, however, DDGM employee Curtis Locke recalled that DDGM broadened its supplier base to win as much support as possible from members of Congress and Senate who served on the House and Senate Armed Services Committees. It chose Lukens Metals in Pennsylvania to produce the harder ballistic steel for the top half of the hull, and Rockwell, a reliable and cost-effective supplier, to produce the suspension and drivetrain.[79]

In late 1983, complications resurfaced between the army and the Marine Corps. The House and Senate Armed Services Committees deleted all funding for army vehicles in the 1984 contract, ostensibly because of dissatisfaction with the army's requirement, and the army's funding was reduced, which posed major problems for the contract. Reports circulated that, according to a major lobbying campaign by a rival manufacturer, Food Machinery Corporation, the army had no need for light wheeled vehicles and that the money should go to further upgrades to its current vehicles, the M113 and the Bradley. The next year, the army withdrew from the LAV program, putting it in danger, but the Marine Corps wanted the vehicle, so DDGM and the Marines worked together over two months to restructure the contract and keep it alive.[80]

The Marines eventually bought 758 LAVs from 1983 to 1988: 422 LAV-25s armed with a 25 mm cannon and a 7.62 mm coaxial machine gun, with a driver, gunner, crew commander, and space for six marines; 46 recovery vehicles, with a crane, winch, and repair equipment; 94 logistics variants, with a high roof to accommodate cargo and a crane; 50 mortar variants, with an 81 mm mortar; 50 command vehicles; and 96 anti-tank vehicles, with an anti-tank missile launcher. The supporting vehicles were also armed with a 7.62 mm machine gun.[81] There were plans to develop an assault gun variant armed with a 60 to 90 mm gun to destroy tanks and provide fire support, and an air defence variant, but these required extensive and costly development, and were deferred in the original purchase.[82]

DDGM Becomes Part of the North American Defence-Industrial Base

The sale was a major achievement for DDGM, but it also posed challenges and demanded major changes to the company as it transitioned from a licence producer to a defence contractor in its own right. Locke noted that few DDGM employees had any experience with defence procurement, so the plant asked for help from corporate oversight, which sent in William King. He had dealt with American regulations and TACOM from the Sheridan light tank project, and he brought some engineers to London. To strengthen DDGM's management of the LAV program, he established departments that mirrored TACOM's, such as logistic support. This ensured that DDGM would meet all its contract requirements and that the US representative would have a DDGM counterpart at any negotiations or meetings. King was also familiar with the regulations and standards applicable to American defence procurement, and he understood how DDGM needed to organize its accounting practices to meet US requirements. There was some resistance from the senior managers on the civilian locomotive side of DDGM, but under King, the plant developed an organization to support the LAV program within several months of winning the contract.[83]

Production of the first LAVs went smoothly, although some minor problems arose with the fire-control system and new components.[84] The original turret supplier, Arrowpointe, could not meet production deadlines, so DDGM bought the company and eventually moved fabrication to London. It assigned full responsibility for the 25 mm turret to Delco, which also assisted with the installation of the anti-tank missile system.[85] The biggest problem occurred partway through production. As employees walked past finished vehicles, they sometimes heard them emit loud bangs; inspection of the top hull revealed cracks in the thinner and harder armour plate that could be anywhere from six to twenty-two inches long. DDGM promptly shut down production and worked around the clock, bringing in metallurgists from around the world to help explain why the steel had cracked. After two weeks, they identified the problem. A batch of the steel had been produced according to the military's standards, but some of the required elements to meet the chemical composition were at the lower end of the scales. The steel could not bear the stresses from the design of the hull and started to crack. DDGM changed suppliers and developed its own proprietary steel mixture for armour plate, which resolved the issue. This problem occurred on 35 percent of the Marine Corps vehicles. Once DDGM developed its own specifications and had more experience with welding high-hardness steel, there were no further problems for subsequent vehicles.[86]

The LAV was not replacing any Marine Corps vehicle in service, and the corps had little experience with similar vehicles. Because of the rapidity of the purchase, LAV units' doctrine and structure changed multiple times.[87] However, the Marines were proud that they were pioneering light armour in the US military. One commented in the *Marine Corps Gazette* that "it is clearly evident that the U.S. Army may never enthusiastically endorse the concept of wheeled, light armored vehicles in light of its preoccupation with fielding the M2 Bradley fighting vehicle."[88] The US Army, like the Canadian, was rooted in fighting the land war in Central Europe with heavily armed and armoured tracked vehicles, which it saw as the only option to challenge the preponderance of Soviet and Soviet proxy armoured fighting vehicles. There was no real lobby in the army for a light armour force, and in the 1980s the army did not buy an equivalent to the LAV, choosing instead to test out Humvees and other light vehicles as part of rapidly deployable forces.[89] By contrast, the Marine Corps, with no role in Central Europe and no deeply ingrained tradition of tracks, was prepared to accept the LAV. The major stumbling block was that the LAV would make the Marine Corps too *heavy*, but its leadership deemed that the vehicle was needed to fight mechanized opponents.

Although the Marines fielded the LAV in the 1980s, they never fielded the assault gun variant whose powerful gun was intended to destroy enemy tanks, which was what they had originally wanted. The plan was resurrected in 1987, and the Marine Corps began working with the army once more, with two candidates to mount a 105 mm gun on a wheeled or tracked vehicle.[90] Again, tension regarding requirements resurfaced with the army, and budget cuts endangered the program. The Marine Corps persisted and stuck to the weight limit of 14.5 tons, the same as the LAV. DDGM successfully mounted the gun on a LAV chassis, and a competitor produced three prototypes in 1995, but the Marine Corps never bought them in quantity.[91]

On exercise, the LAV's speed and manoeuvrability were valuable assets, and one report noted favourably that "LAVs are tremendously versatile in reconnaissance, counter reconnaissance, and screening missions, and in a variety of other ad hoc roles."[92] A great strength of the LAV was its low cost of operation. Marine Corps figures from the late 1980s put its cost at just $5,616 a year, far less than the $42,412 required to run the M113.[93] The LAV was first deployed operationally in 1989 during the invasion of Panama (see Figure 6.2), after which it saw widespread use during Desert Shield and Storm and the intervention in Somalia. It was also deployed in the invasions of Iraq and Afghanistan, where it acquitted itself well, with its main strengths being durability, mobility, and firepower. It did require more armour, however, to improve protection against improvised explosive devices.[94] The Marines' affection for the LAV was a far cry from the lukewarm response of the Canadian army to the AVGP, and by the time of its retirement, it will have been in service for roughly fifty years.[95]

Figure 6.2 A Marine Corps LAV-25 patrols along a road in Panama in 1989. | Photo no. 330-CFD-DF-ST-90-02945, US National Archives.

DDGM's Success in the Canadian Defence-Industrial Base

The sale to the Marine Corps led to DDGM's development as a fully fledged defence contractor. William Kienapple, DDGM executive director during the late 1980s and the 1990s, recognized this and officially separated the original locomotive business from the defence side in 1987.[96] Although its efforts for global sales were limited in the 1980s, DDGM had ensconced itself in two critical markets: Canada and the United States. In the 1990s, it sold thousands more vehicles to Australia, Canada, New Zealand, and Saudi Arabia, becoming one of the dominant producers of wheeled armoured vehicles in the world. The end of the Cold War weakened the argument for the preponderance of heavily armed and armoured tracked vehicles in Western and NATO militaries, and at the same time the capability of wheeled vehicles improved. The Canadian government continued to support the plant with sole-source purchases of capable vehicles, such as the LAV-III, a development of the Piranha design, which became the key fighting vehicle of the Canadian army. The US Army bought more than four thousand vehicles based on the LAV-III during the early 2000s.[97] After its purchase by the US defence giant General Dynamics in 2002, the plant became General Dynamics Land Systems–Canada and remains one of the most prominent manufacturers of armoured vehicles in the world. The original goal of the 1970s offsets policy – the maintenance and strengthening of the Canadian industrial base – was achieved by DDGM's success in producing armoured vehicles. Although locomotive production ceased in 2012, the London plant is a major employer in southern Ontario, and it continues to sustain a network of suppliers with advanced manufacturing capabilities across Canada.[98]

The success of DDGM over the past several decades in producing and selling armoured vehicles has been a unique feature for the Canadian defence-industrial base. Its development as a defence contractor took place over two phases. The first was the beginning of licence production of the AVGP and the mutually beneficial relationship with Mowag. The second was the sale to the US Marine Corps. There are some lessons, perhaps obvious ones, from the analysis of the early years. The first is that DDGM had an excellent product. The original AVGP was a good design, and the LAV was even better, perhaps the best in the world in the 1980s. The second is that DDGM exercised sound management in overcoming production and engineering challenges. Both DDGM and Mowag met the challenges, first, of transferring production to North America and producing a capable vehicle, and second, of meeting the Marine Corps requirement with an improved product. The third lesson is the need for Canadian defence companies to achieve success in multiple markets – at home, in the United States, and globally. The Canadian Armed Forces must buy from its domestic sources to support them and to demonstrate to foreign customers that it has confidence in them. Canada's purchases, however, are not enough to maintain an industry, and DDGM's history exemplifies the reliance of Canada's small defence-industrial base on exports, especially to the United States.

DDGM's success, however, was unique because it was facilitated by a series of favourable circumstances and good timing. If Cadillac Gage had disclosed its costing in 1974 or if Mowag's owner had not gone door-to-door in pursuit of a Canadian partner, there would have been no production by DDGM. If the US Congress had not made funding available to buy a light armoured vehicle in the early 1980s, DDGM could possibly have survived as a producer of light armoured vehicles but probably not for long. It also benefitted from the end of the Cold War when wheeled vehicles were a niche market. The Canadian army reluctantly purchased them because of Dextraze's plan, and the Marine Corps bought them because of their reliability and light weight. The end of the Cold War and the collapse of the Soviet Army broke the dominance of tracked vehicles and allowed wheeled vehicles to become a critical part of the Canadian army and a major component of the US Army. DDGM was prepared to capitalize on that opportunity.

Notes

1   Since the 1990s, the plant has accounted for more than 50 percent of all Western sales of 8x8 armoured vehicles. See Christopher F. Foss, ed., *Jane's Land Warfare Platforms Armoured Fighting Vehicles, 2017–18* (London: Jane's Information Group, 2018); Andrew Graham, "Ottawa to Buy 360 LAVs from London's General Dynamic Land Systems," *Global News London,* 16 August 2019, https://globalnews.ca/news/5775752/ottawa-lavs-london-general-dynamic-land-systems/; Norman DeBono, "Analysis: Cloud

Lifted from GDLS Saudi Deal, but Future Business Uncertain: Analyst," *London Free Press,* 10 April 2020, https://lfpress.com/news/local-news/analysis-cloud-lifted-from-gdls-saudi-deal-but-future-business-uncertain-analyst.

2   James Ledbetter, *Unwarranted Influence: Dwight D. Eisenhower and the Military-Industrial Complex* (New Haven: Yale University Press, 2011), 6.

3   Alex Roland, *The Military-Industrial Complex* (Washington: American Historical Association, 2001), 19–24, 37–40.

4   Alistair D. Edgar and David G. Haglund, *The Canadian Defence Industry in the New Global Environment* (Montreal and Kingston: McGill-Queen's University Press, 1995), xiv, 75, 140.

5   Canada, Department of National Defence, *White Paper on Defence* (Ottawa: Queen's Printer, 1964), 21–22, 24.

6   Chief of Operational Readiness, "General Purpose Armoured Vehicle for Special Service Force (IDP Data Code 679)," 30 June 1965, Robert Lewis Raymont fonds, 73–1223, series 1 and 2, box 9, file 140, Directorate of History and Heritage, National Defence Headquarters, Ottawa (DHH); William Johnston, *A War of Patrols: Canadian Army Operations in Korea* (Vancouver: UBC Press, 2004); Greg Taylor, email to author, 1 January 2019.

7   Warsaw Pact forces with thousands of tanks and armoured vehicles were based along the Iron Curtain and prepared to fight and overrun NATO forces in the event of war; their capabilities improved during the 1970s. See Vojtech Mastny and Malcolm Byrne, eds., *A Cardboard Castle? An Inside History of the Warsaw Pact, 1955–1991* (New York: Central European University Press, 2005), 40–49.

8   See Chapters 5 to 8 of Frank Maas, *The Price of Alliance: The Politics and Procurement of Leopard Tanks for Canada's NATO Brigade* (Vancouver: UBC Press, 2017).

9   Charles J. Gauthier, "Chapter VII: Important Equipment Acquisitions during the 1970–1990 Period," 43–46, Charles J. Gauthier fonds, 92–228, series 3, files 59 and 60, DHH. The quotation is from J. Dextraze, interview by Doug Bland, April 1992, transcripts, Military History Research Centre, Canadian War Museum, Ottawa.

0   H.G. Hunt to Automobile M. Berliet, "Re: Armoured Vehicles, General Purpose," 21 June 1974, Appendix, 1–5, Records of the Department of Industry, Trade and Commerce, RG 20, vol. 507, file 74714–2305–1, vol. 1, Library and Archives Canada (LAC).

1   Theodore J. Henke to D.H. Gilchrist, "Wheeled, Armored, Reconnaissance, Vehicle (WARV) Test and Evaluation Program," 1 October 1973, RG 20, vol. 512, file 74716–1520–6, LAC.

2   Maas, *The Price of Alliance,* 110–26.

3   A.L. McEachern, "Visit Report, Cadillac Gage Company, 17 Dec 73," 8 January 1974, RG 20, vol. 512, file 74716–4520–6, LAC.

4   Secretary of State of Canada, *Organization of the Government of Canada,* 9th ed. (Ottawa: Queen's Printer, 1978), 507; McEachern, "Visit Report, Cadillac Gage Company, 17 Dec 73," LAC; F.G. Johnson to R.F. Linden, "AVGP," 15 May 1975, RG 20, vol. 507, file 74714–2305–1, vol. 2, LAC; Hunt to Berliet, "Re: Armoured Vehicles, General Purpose," LAC.

5   J.M. Knowles to C.T. Charland, "Potential Armoured Car Procurement," 31 July 1974, RG 20, vol. 507, file 74714–2305–1, vol. 1, LAC.

5   H.G. Hunt to F. Jackman, 24 June 1974, RG 20, vol. 507, file 74714–2305–1, vol. 1, LAC.

7   D.W. Fulford to various, "Brazilian Armoured Vehicle Procurement February 10 Meeting," 17 February 1975, RG 20, file 74714–2305–1, vol. 2, vol. 507, LAC; External Affairs Ottawa to the Canadian Embassy in Brasilia, "Armoured Vehicle General Purpose," 13 September 1974, RG 20, file 74714–2305–1, vol. 1, vol. 507, LAC; H.A. Staneland, "Armoured Car Procurement - Cadillac Gage," 22 August 1974, vol. 507, RG 20, file 74714–2305–1, vol. 1, LAC.

    Fulford to various, "Brazilian Armoured Vehicle Procurement February 10 Meeting," LAC; External Affairs Ottawa to the Canadian Embassy in Brasilia, "Armoured Vehicle General Purpose," LAC.

19   Secretary of State of Canada, *Organization of the Government of Canada,* 287; Barry Steers, "Armoured Vehicle Sales to Canada," 2 September 1975, Alastair Gillespie fonds, R1526, vol. 113, file 25, LAC.

20   Canadian Embassy in Brasilia to External Affairs Ottawa, "DSS/DND Arms Purchasing Mission," 4 July 1974, RG 20, file 74714-2305-1, vol. 1, vol. 507, LAC. The quote is from F.T. Jackman to G.H. Pinfold, "Armoured Vehicle General Purpose Procurement," 23 August 1974, RG 20, vol. 507, file 74714-2305-1, vol. 1, LAC.

21   A.D. McArthur to various, "DND Acquisition of Armoured Vehicles," 1 May 1975, RG 20, vol. 507, file 74714-2305-1, vol. 2, LAC.

22   Fulford to various, "Brazilian Armoured Vehicle Procurement February 10 Meeting," LAC; External Affairs Ottawa to the Canadian Embassy in Brasilia, "Armoured Vehicle General Purpose," LAC.

23   Defence Programs Branch, "Aide Memoire: Armoured Car Procurement," 29 May 1975, RG 20, vol. 507, file 74714-2305-1, vol. 2, LAC; author interview with former Mowag employee, 22 April 2016; former Mowag employee, Summary of Mowag's history, emailed to author, 5 June 2015.

24   Author interviews with Steve Moyse, 17 September 2016 and 4 June 2019; Human Resources Management Department of Diesel Division, General Motors of Canada, "Diesel Lines," June 1990, paper copy given to the author by Karl Morgenroth.

25   J.M. Knowles to F. Johnson, "GM/MOWAG AVGP Proposal" (note: proposal attached) 14 February 1975, RG 20, file 74714-2305-1, vol. 2, vol. 507, LAC; W. Ruf to H.G. Hunt, "PIRANHA 6x6 Armoured Amphibious Vehicle in Its Version as Wheeled First Support Vehicle (WFSV)," 5 February 1975, RG 20, vol. 507, file 74714-2305-1, vol. 2, LAC; author interviews with Curtis Locke, 13 May 2016 and 13 May 2019, former Mowag employee, 22 April 2016.

26   Barnett J. Danson, "Canada's Military-Industrial Complex," (speech presented to the Empire Club, Toronto, 11 November 1982), http://speeches.empireclub.org/61457/data; H.A. Staneland to W.E. Grant, "Armoured Car Procurement - Reference My Memorandum of May 7," 13 May 1975, RG 20, vol. 507, file 74714-2305-1, vol. 2, LAC; author interview with Jim Fox, 5 May 2016. Fox was director armour for the Canadian army during the AVGP purchase.

27   Dextraze, interview by Bland, Canadian War Museum; author interview with Frank Lucano, 21 April 2016. Lucano was the army's engineer for the AVGP program.

28   R.J. Bradshaw to Danilo Zerwes, 17 July 1975, Records of the Department of Supply and Services, RG 98, vol. 390, file ERO-6500-31, LAC; "Deficiencies - Engesa Urutu EE-11," 16 July 1975, RG 98, vol. 390, file ERO-6500-31, LAC; "Aide Memoire: The Armoured Vehicle General Purpose (AVGP)," 23 September 1975, RG 98, vol. 390, file ERO-6500-31, LAC.

29   McArthur to various, "DND Acquisition of Armoured Vehicles," LAC; F.G. Johnson to R. Libby, 19 March 1975, RG 20, vol. 507, file 74714-2305-1, vol. 2, LAC.

30   "Armoured Vehicle General Purpose Procurement," [February?] 1975, RG 20, file 74714-2305-1, vol. 2, vol. 507, LAC; J.M. Knowles to F. Johnson, "AVGP Procurement - MOWAG Proposal," 25 February 1975, RG 20, vol. 507, file 74714-2305-1, vol. 2, LAC.

31   J.R. Richardson to J.P. Goyer, 17 April 1975, RG 98, vol. 390, file ERO-6500-31, LAC; "Aide Memoire: The Armoured Vehicle General Purpose (AVGP)," LAC; J.R. Richardson to J. Viot (French Ambassador to Canada), 17 October 1975, RG 98, vol. 390, file ERO-6500-31, LAC.

32   D. Gillett, "DND's Purchase of Armoured Vehicle, General Purpose," 11 November 1975, RG 25, vol. 10277, file 27-1-1-3, pt. 6, LAC.

33   "Minutes of the 186th Meeting of the Defence Management Committee," 20 January 1976, Defence Management Committee fonds, 79-560, box 3, file 2, DHH.

34 A.W. Allen to M.M. DesRoches, "Armoured Vehicle General Purpose (AVGP) Acquisition Program," 4 February 1976, RG 98, vol. 390, file ERO-6500–31, LAC.
35 Allan MacEachen to Pierre Elliott Trudeau, "Possible Purchase of Armoured Vehicle from Brazil," 10 April 1976, Pierre Elliott Trudeau fonds, MG 26 O7, vol. 524, file 0707, LAC; R.C.D. Laughton to J.M. DesRoches, "The DND Armoured Vehicle General Purpose Acquisition Program," 19 February 1976, RG 98, vol. 390, file ERO-6500–31, LAC.
36 B. Steers to External Affairs Ottawa, "General Purpose Armoured Vehicle - Brazilian Démarche," 18 March 1976, RG 98, vol. 390, file ERO-6500–31, LAC; W.B. Christie to R.C.D. Laughton, "DND Armoured Vehicle General Purpose Acquisition Program," 1 April 1976, RG 98, vol. 390, file ERO-6500–31, LAC.
37 Cabinet of the Government of Canada, "General Discussion: Armoured Vehicle General Purpose (AVGP)," Privy Council Office, 4 April 1976, Cabinet Conclusions Database, LAC, http://central.bac-lac.gc.ca/.redirect?app=cabcon&id=41994&lang=eng.
38 James Armstrong Richardson, "National Defence," 20 May 1976 (Canada, Parliament, House of Commons, Edited Hansard, 30th Parl., 1st sess.), https://lipad.ca/full/permalink/3035671/; James Armstrong Richardson, "National Defence-Inquiry Whether Canada Negotiating with Brazil in Purchase of Armoured Cars," 20 February 1975 (Canada, Parliament, House of Commons, Edited Hansard, 30th Parl., 1st sess.), https://lipad.ca/full/permalink/2947688/.
39 MacEachen to Trudeau, "Possible Purchase of Armoured Vehicle from Brazil," LAC.
40 Department of Supply and Services Ottawa to Engesa, 5 May 1976, RG 98, vol. 390, file ERO-6500–31, LAC.
41 J.G. Mumford, "Minutes of the 232nd Meeting of the Defence Management Committee," 31 January 1977, 7, Defence Management Committee fonds, 79–560, box 3, file 3, DHH; W.B. Christie to A.W. Allan, "Armoured Vehicle General Purpose," 28 May 1976, RG 98, vol. 390, file ERO-6500–31, LAC; author interview with Frank Lucano.
42 D.G. Lewis, "AVGP Project Briefing to PCB 9 Feb 78," 9 February 1978, briefing attached to the minutes of the Program Control Board meeting of 9 February 1978, RG 24, acc. 1997–98/625, box 3, file 1150–100/P15, pt. 1, LAC. See Sean Maloney, "A Proportion of Their Cavalry Might Be Converted: Light Armoured Force Development in Canada's Army, 1952–1976," *Army Doctrine and Training Bulletin* 2, 4 (1999): 85–105.
43 Author interview with former Mowag employee, 22 April 2016; Lewis, "AVGP Project Briefing to PCB 9 Feb 78," LAC.
44 Christopher F. Foss, ed., *Jane's Armour and Artillery: 1990–1991* (London: Jane's Information Group, 1991), 295; author interview with former Mowag employee, 22 April 2016.
45 "Minutes of the 186th Meeting of the Defence Management Committee," DHH.
46 Author interview with Steve Moyse, 17 September 2016; Graham Wragg, "AVGP Arrives!" *Sentinel* 14, 4 (1978): 18–20, Fort Frontenac Library, Kingston (FFL).
47 William King, email to author, 19 December 2016.
48 E.B. Creber, memo with key documents on the AVGP program, notably "GM Proposal, Benefits to Canada," 5 April 1976, RG 98, vol. 390, file ERO-6500–31, LAC.
49 Foss, *Jane's Armour and Artillery: 1990–91*, 291.
50 Dextraze, interview by Bland, Canadian War Museum; author interview with Jim Fox; Clive Milner, "Director of Armour's Foreword," *Armour Bulletin, 1981*, Armoured Department, Combat Arms School (Gagetown, NB), 6, FFL.
51 Author interview with Geoff Hutton, 3 May 2016; author interview with Colin Magee, 8 June 2016.
52 Scott Taylor and Brian Nolan, *Tested Mettle: Canada's Peacekeepers at War* (Ottawa: Esprit de Corps Books, 1998), 69; Auditor General of Canada, *Report of the Auditor*

General of Canada to the House of Commons - 1996 (Ottawa: Office of the Auditor General of Canada, 1996), 236, https://publications.gc.ca/collections/collection_2015/bvg-oag/FA1-1-1996-eng.pdf.

53 Auditor General of Canada, *Report of the Auditor General of Canada to the House of Commons - 1996*, 235; "Report on Plans and Priorities - 2010–11," Treasury Board of Canada Secretariat, https://publications.gc.ca/collections/collection_2015/bvg-oag/FA1-1-1996-eng.pdf; Edmonton Police Service, "Tactical," 2019, https://www.edmontonpolice.ca/CommunityPolicing/OperationalServices/Tactical; Auditor General of Canada, "ARCHIVED - Operation AUGURAL," Canadian Armed Forces, https://www.canada.ca/en/department-national-defence/services/operations/military-operations/recently-completed/operation-augural.html.

54 Gauthier, "Chapter VII," 43–46, DHH.

55 Author interview with Frank Lucano.

56 C.J. Gauthier, "Minutes of the 296th Meeting of the Defence Management Committee," 29 May 1979, 79–560, box 3, file 4, DHH.

57 Joseph Kostiner, *Conflict and Cooperation in the Gulf Region* (Wiesbaden: VS Verlag für Sozialwissenschaften, 2009), 143–44.

58 T.A. Bresnick, C.P. Annis, and D.M. Buede, *Concept Definition and Evaluation Criteria for the Mobile Protected Weapons System (MPWS) and the Light Armored Vehicle (LAV)* (McLean, VA: Decisions and Designs, 1981), B-3, https://apps.dtic.mil/sti/pdfs/ADA102879.pdf.

59 L.R. Williams, "Acquiring New Armored Vehicles and Weapons," *Marine Corps Gazette* 64, 12 (1980): 28.

60 W.H. Sheley Jr. to Caspar W. Weinberger, "Progress of the Light Armored Vehicle Program Should Be Closely Monitored," 10 August 1982, https://www.gao.gov/assets/masad-82-41.pdf.

61 Williams, "Acquiring New Armored Vehicles."

62 John P. Gritz, "Light Armored Vehicles or Light Armored Victims?" *Marine Corps Gazette* 66, 8 (1982): 36.

63 Richard G. Carter, "Mechanization: United or Divided?" *Marine Corps Gazette* 66, 8 (1982): 26.

64 Richard A. Stewart, "A Light, Medium and Heavy Approach to Marine Corps Operations," *Marine Corps Gazette* 65, 7 (1981): 31.

65 US Government Accountability Office, "B-203279" (Decision on Arrowpointe's protest to delay awards), 27 April 1982, https://www.gao.gov/products/b-203279.

66 Sheley to Weinberger, "Progress of the Light Armored Vehicle Program."

67 Sheley to Weinberger, "Progress of the Light Armored Vehicle Program"; James D'Angina, *LAV-25: The Marine Corps' Light Armored Vehicle* (Oxford: Osprey, 2011), 5.

68 Author interview with Curtis Locke, 13 May 2016.

69 US Government Accountability Office, "B-209102" (Decision on Cadillac Gage's protest over GM's selection for the LAV), 15 July 1983, https://www.gao.gov/products/b-209102; Editor, "Corps' Search Narrows for LAV," *Marine Corps Gazette* 65, 11 (1981): 10.

70 Foss, *Jane's Armour and Artillery: 1990–91*, 292; author interview with former Mowag employee, 22 April 2016.

71 Foss, *Jane's Armour and Artillery: 1990–91*, 292; author interview with Curtis Locke, 13 May 2016.

72 U.S. Government Accountability Office, "B-209102," 16, 25.

73 This was a metric used to assess reliability and durability in which the "number of mission failures was divided into the total number of miles traveled by a vehicle." US Government Accountability Office, "B-209102," 18–19.

74 Delco Systems Operations Retirees, *History of the Fire Control/Armament Programs* (Goleta, CA: privately printed by General Motors retirees, 2006), 59, 151. This history was shared with me by former Delco employee Herman Guenther.

75 Editor, "LAV Decision Is Delayed Again," *Marine Corps Gazette* 66, 10 (1982): 4.

76 The CCC "signs and manages contracts with foreign governments" and then "signs a sub-contract and flows the contractual commitments through to the qualified Canadian exporter." "Growing Canadian Export Business," Canadian Commercial Corporation, https://www.ccc.ca/en/ccc/about-ccc, accessed 13 February 2019; "Position Description for Director," Light Armour Vehicle Program for the Canadian Commercial Corporation [1993?], paper copy given to the author by Karl Morgenroth.

77 Author interview with Karl Morgenroth, 25 June 2019; author interview with Steve Moyse, 4 June 2019; "Overview of the CCC's LAV Program Office at Diesel Division" [1993], paper copy given to the author by Karl Morgenroth.

78 A copy of the 1956 agreement is available on the CCC's website, https://www.ccc.ca/wp-content/uploads/2019/05/defence-production-sharing-agreement-en.pdf.

79 Author interview with Curtis Locke, 13 May 2016.

80 Author interview with Curtis Locke, 13 May 2019; author interview with William Pettipas (executive director of the DDGM plant in the 1990s and early 2000s), 10 May 2016; Editor, "LAVs Closer, but Program Is Uncertain," *Marine Corps Gazette* 67, 10 (1983): 8; Editor, "Problems Cause Delay of FMF's LAV-25," *Marine Corps Gazette* 68, 1 (1984): 4.

81 Foss, *Jane's Armour and Artillery: 1990–91*, 292; C.F. Hamilton, "LAV and the Amphibious Assault," *Marine Corps Gazette* 67, 10 (1983): 67; Editor, "First of 95 LAV(L)s Delivered," *Marine Corps Gazette* 69, 10 (1985): 6.

82 Andrew R. Finlayson, "The Need for an Assault Gun," *Marine Corps Gazette* 71, 9 (1987): 57–60.

83 Author interview with Curtis Locke, 13 May 2019.

84 Editor, "Problems Cause Delay of FMF's LAV-25," 4.

85 Herman Guenther, email to author, 13 January 2017; Delco Systems Operations Retirees, *History of the Fire Control*, 73; Steve Moyse, email to author, 4 June 2019.

86 L.W. Hyttenrauch, "MILLAV SRB Briefing," 23 February 1989, RG 24, acc. 2004-00510-6, box 59, file 32460-100-003 pt. 1S, LAC; author interview with Curtis Locke, 13 May 2016.

87 D'Angina, *LAV-25*, 6; Richard G. Duvall, "Employment of the LAV," *Marine Corps Gazette* 72, 12 (1988): 35–36.

88 Richard G. Carter, "Modernizing Marine Armor," *Marine Corps Gazette* 70, 6 (1986): 61.

89 Edwin W. Besch, "Adding Perspective to the Light Armor Debate," *Marine Corps Gazette* 72, 4 (1988): 54.

90 Editor, "Commandant Calls for Assault Gun," *Marine Corps Gazette* 71, 10 (1987): 4.

91 Foss, *Jane's Armour and Artillery: 1990–91*, 273, 292.

92 Andrew R. Hoebn, "Force-On-Force at MCAGCC," *Marine Corps Gazette* 72, 7 (1988): 10.

93 Andrew R. Finlayson, "Marine Armor in Mid-Intensity Conflict," *Marine Corps Gazette* 72, 7 (1988): 40.

94 D'Angina, *LAV-25;* Christopher F. Foss, ed., *Jane's Armour and Artillery: 1995–1996* (London: Jane's Information Group, 1996), 271; Michael A. Micucci, "The Marine Corps Transitions the LAV for the Future," *Marine Corps Gazette* 91, 4 (2007): 18–20.

95 Matt Gonzales, "Marine Corps Plans to Replace LAV with New, 'Transformational' ARV," 16 April 2019, https://www.marines.mil/News/News-Display/Article/1817404/marine-corps-plans-to-replace-lav-with-new-transformational-arv/, accessed 10 October 2020.

96 Author interview with William Kienapple, 3 October 2018.

97 Foss, *Jane's Land Warfare Platforms,* 636–47, 964–67. Some scholars, such as J. Stone, observe that plants such as DDGM could distort the military's definition of requirements and limit its capabilities because it would choose the Canadian product to ensure political support. J. Craig Stone, "An Examination of the Armoured Personnel Carrier Replacement Project," *Canadian Military Journal* 2, 3, (Summer 2001): 65.

98 Progress Rail, "Progress Rail to Close London (ON) Locomotive Production," 3 February 2012, https://www.newswire.ca/news-releases/progress-rail-to-close-london-on-locomotive-production-509554411.html.

7
The Royal Canadian Air Force and the Military-Industrial Complex
A Figment of the Imagination

Randall Wakelam

THIS CHAPTER EXAMINES the history and evolution of Canadian fighter aircraft procurement throughout the twentieth century. It argues that the Royal Canadian Air Force (RCAF) did not, except for a brief period, have a permanent and cooperative relationship with the Canadian aircraft manufacturing sector. Only during the decade immediately following the Second World War (1945–55) did the RCAF purchase from Canadian producers and promote their products, but this was atypical over the long haul. At other times – during the interwar and late–Cold War periods – the RCAF procured aircraft in small numbers from foreign sources, and in some cases it settled for types that were not necessarily based on essential air force needs. Rather than being derived from purely strategic or operational factors, acquisition followed patterns of government-imposed budgetary constraints, often with associated technological compromises. In recounting these episodes, this chapter situates Canada's history of military aircraft procurement within the context of the country's unique defence requirements and security circumstances as a middle power and junior ally among the North Atlantic security partners. It also demonstrates the importance and pitfalls of international procurement strategies and the ways in which Canada depended on foreign military-industrial complexes (MICs) to defend its interests and security.

Before we examine the specifics of fighter aircraft procurement, a brief review of how Canada defines its aircraft and equipment needs is useful. Senior officers studying defence policy and questions of national security at the Canadian Forces College learn that defence spending, for personnel, operations and procurment, is the largest discretionary parcel of the government's annual budget. Other than personnel salaries and employment benefits, such as health care, the remainder of the defence budget, including for procurement, is more or less negotiable. Typically, there is sufficient money to conduct training and operations, with the balance going to infrastructure, which includes the acquisition of new or replacement equipment. This last figure hovers in the 15 to 20 percent range.[1] The procurement of new big-ticket items, officially known as "major Crown projects," is a long and involved process that sees reviews of specifications and costs at several levels in the Department of National Defence (DND) and the federal bureaucracy before a recommendation reaches Cabinet, where ultimately civilian members of Parliament make the final determination. What this means, in short, is that the military does not decide what it wants and purchases for new kit, regardless of the cost.

Military procurement needs – that is to say the weapons systems needed to fulfill mandated roles – are identified by leaders and staffers, both military and civilian, in the DND, by an examination of the government's defence policy, which lays out the priorities for the security of Canada, this security being achieved typically through coalitions and alliances. Over the past century, these associations have included the British Commonwealth and since 1945, the United Nations (UN), the North Atlantic Treaty Organization (NATO), and finally as of 1958 the North American Aerospace Defence Command (NORAD). Defence planners take the broad policy themes and distill them down to capabilities that would be needed to provide the associated level of defence. From these are identified specific types of units and the amount and functionalities of equipment required to carry out their roles. At this point, it is possible for these staffs to say "we need more of X" or "we need an entire new fleet of Y." Only then can the kit be defined (by function and quantity) and "costed" for the approvals described above. In short, it is the government and not the military that determines the broad security strategy for Canada and subsequently approves the purchase of equipment to allow the military to meet the associated defence capabilities.[2]

Although the government, both bureaucrats and politicians, has the deciding role on what equipment (and from here on I will use the term "aircraft") is purchased, in principle it is the military that defines the requirement for certain aircraft types with certain capabilities. A typical preliminary requirement might be, for instance, a fixed wing aircraft capable of transporting fifty tonnes over eight thousand kilometres. Over the past century, these definitions have often centred on the acquisition of aircraft that are already in use or are coming into use by Canadian allies; thus, in this example, the RCAF might be looking for an existing transport such as the C-17. Obtaining aircraft that allies are already using has several advantages. First, when the RCAF is deployed on operations with allied and partner nations that use identical aircraft types, it supports interoperability. One can only imagine the added convenience of using the same types of aircraft, so that spare parts and maintenance efficiencies can be had between various air units, particularly if they are deployed on the other side of the world. Second, the RCAF also allows for the use of the same sorts of tactical procedures because aircraft of various nations have the same capabilities. Beyond these considerations, buying types of aircraft that are already in service elsewhere means that savings can be negotiated with the manufacturer, who has already set up a production line and is hoping to maximize return on investments.

Two negative factors must be considered as well. First, buying from an existing production line typically means buying from a non-Canadian manufacturer, and thus there are fewer economic and employment advantages for Canadians. Second, offshore purchases can also create the illusion that a MIC exists in Canada by giving the impression that the RCAF is simply looking to make a deal with industry rather than finding the optimal aircraft and, perhaps, buying Canadian. These disadvantages are mitigated largely by the fact that the federal government negotiates manufacturing and other economic offsets with foreign manufacturers, whereby the companies buy products or services in Canada to counterbalance the government's spending outside of Canada. These products and services can either support the manufacture and operation of the aircraft in question or may be related to some other product lines. In terms of creating the impression that the air force appears to be in league with a certain manufacturer, scrutiny is placed on recommendations for purchase at all levels of government, including at the Cabinet table.[3]

A final characteristic in play through much of the past seventy years has been the lack of a competitive selection process, in either appearance or reality. Those who are familiar with the relatively recent attempts to find a replacement for the CF-18 Hornet might reasonably imagine that earlier acquisitions have also been made rigorously and fairly through a fully competitive practice such as described by Aaron Plamondon.[4] But this is inaccurate. As discussed below, the RCAF has twice made do with surplus postwar aircraft acquired by the government cashing in credits with the United Kingdom, and at other times, with used aircraft from the United States Air Force (USAF). When aircraft design and manufacture happened in Canada during the late 1940s and 1950s, there was no open competition. In those years, the RCAF and the government worked together to shape needs and designs for aircraft produced in Canadian plants. With this context established, we can now turn to the actual procurement history of fighter aircraft in Canada.

From Silver Dart to a Few of This and That: 1909–39

In 1909, the first aircraft built and successfully flown in the British Empire, the Silver Dart, took to the air in Baddeck, Nova Scotia, having been designed by Sir Alexander Graham Bell and a small team. Despite the Canadian first, there was no real interest in obtaining aircraft for the Canadian militia, and even with the rapid growth of military aviation during the First World War, Canada did not create an air service until 1918. What aircraft had been built in Canada during the war were the result of private ventures and were used for training. As the war drew to a close and the Canadian Air Force and Royal Canadian Naval Air Service (RCNAS) were formed, the two air force squadrons stationed in the

United Kingdom were provided with British aircraft already in production, whereas the RCNAS did not get airborne, for lack of aircraft and aircrew training, until well after 1918.[5] After the war, Canadians sought a rapid return to peace, but the advances in aviation led some to contemplate the creation of a permanent air force. There being no concrete military threat to Canada, the principal bureaucrats behind the plan opted for a concept that would foster a national "airmindedness" through the generation of air capabilities that were either directly relevant to civilian life (such as air mail and air ambulances) or paramilitary in nature (such as forest-fire fighting and drug enforcement).[6] All of these could initially be supported by surplus wartime aircraft, either trainers or twelve flying boats left behind by the US Naval Air Service.

The need for more capable aircraft was soon identified, particularly for work in the Canadian North, where the only landing surfaces were typically lakes. One manufacturer, Canadian Vickers, offered to meet air force needs, but only if it were given an exclusive contract. The government's answer was no; it would keep Vickers in mind but did not want to limit competition.[7] Over the two interwar decades, the RCAF procured small numbers of aircraft manufactured in Canada, but these were never a centrepiece of defence budgets and were often purchased at the end of the fiscal year, when money was left in the balance sheet. Thus, during the Great Depression, the RCAF was obliged to operate "a fleet of obsolescent aircraft which it was unable to replace."[8] We should also be aware that these manufacturers sold their products to civilian operators too, and here, prior to the Depression, the market had been relatively rewarding. In Montreal, Canadian Vickers built a range of flying boats for northern commercial operators, as well as the RCAF, and assembled Avro training aircraft and Fokker transports under licence. In Toronto, de Havilland sold 130 aircraft in 1929.[9] Overall, the RCAF was one of several outlets for Canadian manufacturers, which provided sufficient income for them to remain solvent.

While senior officials in the Canadian government were generally satisfied with the form of air power provided during these decades, RCAF officers had, like their army and navy counterparts, remained in contact with British colleagues, sending one or two officers annually to the Royal Air Force Staff College, where they were exposed to air force concepts and aircraft. Thus, as tensions grew with the resurgence of Germany after 1933, the RCAF leadership was able to ask for aircraft that would allow the air force to provide air capabilities as part of the approved defence "schemes" for both domestic and expeditionary operations. These aircraft were invariably off-the-shelf British models. But the government was loath to invest heavily in defence spending during the Depression, and thus by 1939, there were only 270 aircraft of twenty-three different types in the RCAF inventory, few of which were combat capable.[10]

Despite Ottawa's reluctance, there was acceptance in cabinet that Canada would need to contribute to the Commonwealth war effort and that this should include the production of aircraft and other weapons and equipment by Canadian industry. With this in mind, the British government sent a mission to Canada in early 1938 to determine its industrial capability. Although the mission saw that aircraft were already being manufactured from scratch, the British representatives were alarmed by the lack of industrial depth. They reckoned that if Canadian industry were given a "training order" of two hundred Wellington bombers, an admittedly complex state-of-the-art aircraft in 1938, it would take two years to establish a production line and two additional years to complete the modest numbers; this was based on a total workforce of just 1,500 technicians. Moreover, they noted that Canada had no capacity to produce aircraft engines.[11]

Wartime Expansion: Industrial-Scale Production

Despite these concerns, contracts did start coming to Canadian manufacturers, but the government quickly realized that the RCAF, like the other services and existing government organizations, did not have the experience or expertise to harness industry and manage large procurements.[12] Various central agencies were set up, culminating with the Department of Munitions and Supply under the direction of C.D. Howe, an industrialist in his pre-political years and now a senior Liberal minister. Howe and his deputies controlled procurement, not the air marshals.[13] But the process was not a straightforward one, either, as not even Howe decided what was acquired and for whom. That task was the purview of the Combined Munitions Assignment Board, which directed the flow of aircraft and all other war production among the Allies. The board, run jointly by the Americans and British, compared operational needs in all theatres of war with the planned and actual production of all the Western Allies and then directed the flow of weaponry to the theatre where it was most required. So tight was its control that in early 1942 the RCAF could not lay its hands on Hurricane fighters being built by Canadian Car and Foundry. The Hurricanes were needed for defence of the Pacific coast in 1942, but there were higher priorities in Europe.[14]

As the war progressed, Canadian manufacturers built some eleven thousand training aircraft to support the more than one hundred flying schools of the British Commonwealth Air Training Program located across the country. By 1945, they had also produced approximately five thousand combat aircraft of various types.[15] Howe, at one point, said that Canada really needed to get into the production of multi-engine heavy bombers, the most complex aircraft type in production bar none, as these would, in his words, "complete the industry."[16] By 1944, Victory

Aircraft in Toronto, a company set up at Howe's direction, was producing the Avro Lancaster, many of which did end up in Canadian squadrons.[17] Beginning in 1943, two major aviation manufacturing initiatives were under way. The first focused on bringing jet engine technology to Canada. A research and development (R&D) capability was created at Howe's instigation: Turbo Research Ltd. used technologies developed in Britain, replicating and advancing the concepts in Canada.[18] There was certainly interest in the RCAF, but as with every other aircraft decision, the government made the final decisions. As an aside, the jet engine initiative was, perhaps, a result of a major hole in Canadian production: though Canadian factories produced sixteen thousand aircraft, none of the engines were built in Canada. All would come initially from the United Kingdom and, once the Americans entered the war, from the "Arsenal of Democracy."[19]

Howe and his deputies had a second focus: What, if any, aircraft types would Canada want to build after the war? Howe thought the civilian transportation sector would need a large transport aircraft to open up the country.[20] On the other hand, RCAF leaders and in particular Air Vice Marshal (AVM) E.W. Stedman, the RCAF's most senior aeronautical engineer, argued strongly for a combat aircraft. His conviction was partly based on the cap-in-hand experiences of the interwar decades and partly on the frustrations of the Hurricane and other assignments of Canadian-made aircraft. After much discussion, it was agreed that the preliminary design of a combat aircraft could go ahead.[21] The RCAF had not made a deal with industry in an arrangement that mirrored the American MIC; rather, air force leaders had swayed decision-makers in Ottawa. It was Howe and his deputies who would lead the transition of wartime production toward a viable postwar aviation industry.

Cold War Beginnings: RCAF Requirements and Industry Capability

The results of these decisions were mixed. In terms of civilian transport aircraft, the newly formed Avro Canada, essentially Victory Aircraft with a new sign on the factory, set out to design and manufacture a jet-powered transport.[22] The Avro Jetliner first flew in 1949, only days after Britain's de Havilland Comet (the world's first commercial jet), but the Avro design was soon cancelled for want of sufficient engines. Meanwhile, to remain financially viable while the Jetliner was in design, Avro overhauled older Avro UK aircraft.[23] Similarly, in Montreal, Canadair, a new company based on Canadian Vickers, was refurbishing both C-46 and C-47 aircraft, as well as C-54 models, with all three being mid-long-range transports designed and built in the United States. Ultimately, the C-54 work would lead to a Canadair offshoot, the North Star, which combined the C-54 fuselage with British Rolls-Royce engines. Of the seventy-one North Stars built, the RCAF purchased just twenty-four, and a pressurized version of the aircraft became a mainstay for Trans Canada Airlines and Canadian Pacific Airways.[24]

At Turbo Research, work on a marketable jet engine continued. The project was sponsored by the government, with Howe's bureaucrats coordinating with Avro for the establishment of an engine division that would eliminate foreign dependence in this critical area. This exact problem unfolded as the Cold War intensified during the late 1940s and as the need for modern fighters and increased defensive capabilities against intercontinental bombers became a paramount concern in Western countries.[25] In 1945, however, the Canadian government was reluctant to fund significant defence spending, as postwar reconstruction and veterans' rehabilitation were priorities. By the end of the year, the RCAF was reduced to just over ten thousand personnel and a handful of squadrons; it had to be satisfied with the supply of eighty-three de Havilland Vampire jets secured through a trade-in and credit scheme with Britain.[26] The Vampires, at least, launched the RCAF into the jet age.

The service aircraft that AVM Stedman and others had wanted were still in the planning stages, but the government approved money only for the production of a prototype by Avro.[27] This work was done without competition and with collaboration between Avro managers, government bureaucrats and ministers, and RCAF leaders.[28] As the last half of the decade played out, the RCAF provided performance specifications, and the government approved money – first for development and, by October 1948, for ten preproduction aircraft.[29] If ever there was a distinct MIC arrangement in Canada, this was it, though it was not built on industry avarice and a military bid for empire, but rather by the growing likelihood of a threat to Canadian security and national defence.

As the decade ended, the RCAF was developing plans, largely in collaboration with NATO allies, for a massive buildup in the face of almost certain Soviet aggression by 1954. That year was the target for the establishment of NATO's Interim Force, which included a three-hundred-fighter RCAF Air Division to be stationed in France and West Germany.[30] Officials in the RCAF wanted to showcase the CF-100 by equipping the air division with Canada's world-class all-weather interceptor, but technical delays at Avro – namely, the challenges of designing, developing, and manufacturing Canada's first modern combat aircraft and the RCAF's constant tinkering with the specifications – meant that the interceptor was available neither in the numbers required by the RCAF nor for sales to the USAF or the Royal Air Force (RAF).[31]

What Canada could offer was the licence-built North American F-86 Sabre, which was happily accepted. The RCAF had sought the purchase of fifty-six Sabres as early as October 1948, as part of an enhanced overseas capability.[32] As tensions rose, the deal for licence production, like most others in the previous ten years, had been championed by Howe.[33] The licence manufacture was negotiated at the same time as efforts to purchase vintage Second World War–era North

American Mustang piston engine fighters in the weeks following the outbreak of the Korean War in June 1950. Acquiring about fifty Mustangs would allow the RCAF to equip squadrons hastily established for the purpose of defending, at best nominally, Canada's major cities should Soviet bombers arrive sooner than new fighters came off the production lines. Though the Mustangs were not jet fighters per se, they were the best that could be procured as a stop-gap.[34]

But leaders in the government and the RCAF needed jet fighters in the face of predicted Soviet aggression, which seemed more likely after the outbreak of hostilities in Korea. By this point, the agreement to manufacture the F-86 Sabre at Canadair in Montreal had been approved by both Ottawa and Washington, although the deal had taken extensive negotiations through much of 1948.[35] Initially, a number of crated aircraft "kits" were sent to Montreal for assembly, and once it was clear that the Canadian technicians were up to the job, the actual manufacture of parts and the production of complete aircraft was approved. They were initially powered by General Electric engines, but the use of Avro's Orenda engine soon followed, making the Canadian Sabre arguably the finest fighter of its type in NATO. USAF, RAF, and eventually German pilots would fly it. It was a fine daytime, fair-weather aircraft but in no way a match for the day-and-night capabilities of the all-weather CF-100.

The Avro CF-100 jet was a world-class interceptor, and both the RCAF and Avro were in contact with the RAF and the USAF on the matter of sales to those air forces. In the case of the RAF, it was the chief of the air staff, Sir Jack Slessor, who, when visiting Canada in October 1950, made it known that the British were interested.[36] Later that year, Avro took a sales team and aircraft to visit the USAF, who showed solid interest.[37] The problem with offshore sales was that there was no product ready. Design problems and manufacturing delays meant that the numbers of available CF-100s, even for RCAF needs, lagged behind deadlines. In the end, just 692 were built, with the major production model, the Mark 4, reaching prototype status only in 1952. And only three squadrons were eventually assigned to the RCAF Air Division, whereas the remainder served in Canada.[38] Attempts in 1954 to sell the jet to Colombia were stymied because the United States would not allow its American-made fire-control system to be sold to any country other than Canada or Britain.[39] Belgium received fifty-three CF-100s in 1957, and although a bit past their prime by that point, they were provided at no cost through the Mutual Aid Program.[40]

During these few years, there had been clear cooperation between the RCAF, the Canadian government, and Avro, and there might have been a reasonable chance of success in supplying the RAF with the CF-100. Had that happened, could we say that a MIC existed? Possibly, but this was not a case of rampant mutual aggrandizement for the sake of having the best and biggest air defence component, on the one hand, and excellent profits and financial strength, on the other. Rather, as stated earlier, leadership in the RCAF simply wanted to have a sufficient and effective defence against air attack while using the potential of Canadian industry to equip its squadrons. Avro did seek to maximize the return on its design efforts by selling the CF-100 to allied nations, but there was arguably a significant element of security imperative in the offer of a highly capable all-weather interceptor to air forces still seeking that capability.

The outcome of the CF-100/F-86 strategy was still to unfold when RCAF planners and leaders set Avro a new task of designing a supersonic interceptor that was to become the CF-105 Arrow. There was no competitive process to award the work: government officials went to Avro, in part to keep its design team together, although the Chiefs of Staff Committee did engage in some discussion about the merits of a shared project with the Americans.[41] Much has been written about the Arrow's amazing capabilities, as it would have done everything the RCAF wanted and might have been a suitable sales prospect for allied air forces.[42] But several factors thwarted such a scenario at the time, which gives pause for assessing this particular instance of industry/air force co-operation as being representative of a MIC in Canada. First, the Arrow, like its predecessor, was intended as a long-range interceptor to stop intercontinental bombers before they arrived over the industrial centres of Canada and the United States. However, once the Soviets demonstrated a successful missile threat with the launch of Sputnik in October 1957, the relative risk of a bomber attack lessened in defence planning, while the requirements for an anti-missile system increased. With only so much money available for defence needs, the government was right to cancel the Arrow program and to purchase (without delay) a ready-made alternative system from the USAF: the Bomarc missile.[43] On top of the change in defence requirements, there were also doubts concerning Avro's production record. Significantly, in late 1951, as Avro struggled with production of the CF-100 to meet the Interim Force and domestic air defence needs, Howe threatened to pull its contract because of the problems.[44] Indeed, they were manifest, as senior Avro manager Ken Smye would later comment: "If we had told Howe [how bad the situation was] he would have scrapped the CF-100 and the engine for sure."[45]

However, the cost of the Arrow program was an overwhelming concern, not only for Cabinet, but also for the public and even the RCAF. It was because of public concern over Soviet intentions that Canada's defence policy and its aircraft program were scrutinized in the press. As might be expected, the cancellation was controversial, and the government's decision came under strong criticism. For instance, a *Vancouver Province* article on 8 January 1952 criticized the aircraft program by pointing out its substantial price tag, with the F-86 costing $500,000 each and the CF-100 $1,000,000. If Ottawa were thinking of a supersonic fighter, why not buy them used? True, the current crisis had led to the decision for domestic production, but there was still the question of just how far the nation should carry this capability.[46] Significantly, on learning that the Americans were looking at similar requirements to those planned for the Arrow, Air Marshal Roy Slemon, chief of the air staff (CAS), was apparently not happy:

> The decision was made to proceed with the C105 project [when] it was assured no other country was planning on building an aircraft to meet the RCAF operational requirement. When governmental approval was granted for the C105, the CAS assured the Minister that if there was a possibility of procuring a new type to fill the RCAF requirements from other sources, the project would be curtailed.[47]

Arguably, with these factors in play, the government should not have hesitated to cancel the development of the Arrow. If, indeed, an aerospace MIC were functioning in Canada with the intent of creating a defence production colossus, it was not a particularly effective one.

After the Arrow: Abandoning a National Fighter Design and Manufacturing Capability

By the late 1950s, the RCAF had brought two squadrons of Bomarc missiles into service to defend the Windsor-Quebec industrial corridor. And the CF-100s that were still assigned to NORAD were deemed obsolete by 1960 and had to be replaced. The replacements were what might be called "gently used" USAF F-101 Voodoo air defence fighters, which were manufactured in the United States by McDonnell.[48] A decade later, they were exchanged with the USAF for yet another batch of less-used Voodoos.[49] Two rounds of accepting used aircraft in small numbers did not point to the existence of anything approaching a Canadian MIC; if anything, the pattern of purchases hearkened back to the interwar years and the acceptance of whatever reasonable solution might be available.

Similarly, the F-86s in Europe had reached the end of their service effectiveness. Moreover, as Canada now accepted a new nuclear strike role for the 1960s, the Sabres had to be replaced, and this was done by acquiring the American Lockheed F-104 Starfighter. Like the Voodoo, the F-104 was initially designed as an air defence interceptor, but it was deemed suitable for its new attack role. More importantly, it was not the favoured choice of the RCAF, as the final decision was made by Minister of Defence Production Raymond O'Hurley, who was able to negotiate a better offset package with the parent company Lockheed than that offered by the other contender, with licence production going to Canadair.[50] On 1 August 1959, the deal was announced for the manufacture of two hundred Starfighters, and the production of sixty-six additional sets of major components was also added to the contract.[51] In fairness, Canada was not alone in adopting the Starfighter: Norway, Germany, and Italy all flew it for many years. That considerable work went to Canadair meant that the enterprise could stay viable.

With the one limited exception being the CF-100, Canada's aircraft procurement experience in this period does not fit the standard definition of the MIC. A third small purchase from the United States came in the latter part of the 1960s, with the acquisition of the North American Freedom Fighter, which, built in the same fashion as its older cousin, the F-86, under licence by Canadair, was to equip two squadrons of tactical fighters assigned to NATO rapid deployment roles. This was not a good aircraft, but in this case, as in the other decisions of the previous decade, it was a politician, Minister of National Defence Paul Hellyer, who influenced the purchase.[52]

The final fighter procurement of the twentieth century occurred in the early 1980s, when the US-designed and -manufactured McDonnell Douglas CF-18 Hornet was purchased. A shipboard fighter, the CF-18 could serve in both interceptor and ground attack roles in NORAD and NATO. Here, a relatively open and rigorous process was conducted, with the air force setting the requirements after which various aircraft and industrial proposals were assessed by an interdepartmental project office and other federal agencies before Cabinet made a decision. As other chapters have shown, industrial offsets were developed and carefully assessed, so that Canadian firms could partner with international manufacturers to create jobs in Canada or facilitate technology transfers and other benefits for the Canadian economy.[53] The method has since been judged by several researchers as successful and rational, allowing both for a viable aircraft purchase for the air force and at the same time for an injection of money into some form of economic activity within the broader Canadian economy. Whether the economic activity is tied directly to the acquisition of the aircraft is of less importance in the greater scheme of ensuring work for Canadians. With respect to the CF-18, as Bezglasnyy and Ross observe, the process "produced a capable aircraft for the air force, a big boost to domestic aerospace manufacturing, and all at an acceptable cost."[54]

The same core process has ostensibly been used during the past two decades in the search for a replacement for the CF-18. But despite employing the same interdepartmental oversight structure, a lack of firm control by the Conservative government of Prime Minister Stephen Harper allowed the RCAF consistently to favour the F-35 Lightning.[55] Then came the volte-face pronouncements of the current Liberal government of Justin Trudeau – "anything but the F-35" – and the reset of procurement options, has, in my view, driven the selection toward the nonsensical, with a mere sixty-five or so aircraft supposedly filling fighter commitments for the next three or more decades. Recent years have seen the Liberal government decide that the purchase of what could be called "well-used" Australian F-18s as a stop-gap would allow more time to make a final decision. This was seen as largely pointless by many at the time, and only in the spring of 2022 was a final decision made to buy eighty-eight F-35s.

Given the current situation and the historical precedents, to say that the manufacturing segment of the Canadian economy or even the defence production segment are tilting toward a military-industrial relationship seems a stretch as regards fighter aircraft in particular. Even during the early Cold War years when numbers were not insignificant, the scale of Canadian fighter needs was such that there was really no chance of a big production run without international customers. As we have seen, there was interest in the CF-100, but that interest could not be converted to sales, whereas in the case of the F-86 it was NATO money that allowed Canada to pass on hundreds of aircraft. Following the cancellation of the Arrow project and the signing of the Defence Production Sharing Agreement, there have been no real considerations for producing and selling Canadian-designed and -built fighters.

A Different Kind of Relationship: de Havilland Canada and the US Army

By comparison, the only Canadian aircraft that have succeeded on the world market are the short take-off and landing (STOL) examples of de Havilland Canada (DHC). Having produced a variety of light aircraft in the interwar years and then trainers and the fabled Mosquito fighter-bomber during the Second World War, de Havilland returned to light aircraft production with its first Canadian design, the DHC-1 Chipmunk, a monoplane initial training aircraft that first flew in 1946. This design was deemed suitable for the RAF, and soon the Chipmunk was being produced under licence in the United Kingdom, which marked quite a reversal from the experiences of the previous twenty-five years.[56]

Designers at Downsview were well aware of the need for newer "bush aircraft" for the North, and after being invited to compete for a small order for the Ontario Department of Lands and Forests they crafted the DHC-2 Beaver in the winter of 1946–47.[57] The Beavers were not high on the list of RCAF needs, but they did come to the attention of the US Air Force and Army, as well as the British Army for their light transport and extreme short landing capabilities. Over the following twenty years, close to 1,000 Beavers were built for the Americans and 42 for the British Army.[58] Other militaries, but not the RCAF, operated smaller fleets.[59] The Otter sales story was similar, with 223 of the total production of 460 going to the US Army and the RCAF buying 66.[60] To say that this constituted a military-industrial collaboration, in the form of a MIC, between the RCAF and a Canadian aerospace company, is clearly not accurate, but these international sales figures were nonetheless remarkable for a Canadian firm.

Continuing to work closely with the US Army, de Havilland went on to design the DHC-4 Caribou in the closing years of the 1950s.[61] With two engines, it was faster and carried much more than the Otter; the US Army ordered 168 Caribou for battlefield transportation.[62] The Royal Australian Air Force ordered 18 for the same purpose.[63] The RCAF ordered 9.[64] In terms of any potential MIC, there was clearly no domestic connection or advantage to Canadian industry in the development of this aircraft type. A follow-on turboprop-powered development, the DHC-5 Buffalo, was initially intended for the US Army, but a realignment of military functions saw tactical air transport given to the USAF, which was already operating an equivalent aircraft, the Fairchild Provider, and as a result the American order was cancelled.[65] The RCAF did buy 15 Buffalos, hardly a major boon to de Havilland, initially for tactical transport, but soon after they were repurposed for domestic search and rescue.[66]

To what extent the STOL successes of DHC were the result of a close cooperation between industry and defence is hard to say. Ironically, however, what connection there was occurred between a US military service and a Canadian aircraft builder, not between the RCAF and de Havilland. And if de Havilland's connection with the US Army were part of President Dwight Eisenhower's powerful MIC, then the international factor and limited dollar value when compared to overall US defence spending certainly diminishes the relevance of these purchases in the greater US MIC argument.

This transnational interplay speaks perhaps to newer research, which recognizes that MICs and economic and industrial growth may not be limited to a nation's borders and to a government's purchasing.[67] In the case of DHC, which went on to produce the very successful Dash 8 series of turboprop short haul passenger aircraft, one has to assume that the relative depth of the design and manufacturing teams, nurtured through the contracts with the US Army, played a role in the firm's success. In the case of Canadair, which though not a design house still did much manufacturing in the 1950s and 1960s, it seems equally fair to say that this experience helped in the emergence of the Challenger series of aircraft that debuted in 1978. Ironically, it was Avro Canada, with support from government and products that were designed specifically with RCAF requirements in mind, that did not endure.

Conclusion

Returning to the central question of whether a MIC was/is associated with Canadian fighter procurement, we see that factors similar to those discussed continue to militate against the existence of such an arrangement. Government policy and often government direction determined what type and how many of any particular aircraft could be purchased, and with the exception of the Interim Force buildup, those numbers have been relatively miniscule. We have seen, too, that only the threat of communism prompted the politicians to give RCAF leaders a relatively free hand with setting the technical requirements and even shaping the size of the purchase. By comparison, there have been far more cases where the air force has been given whatever surplus aircraft could be had through wartime financial credits or where already in-service and used aircraft were acquired to fill a pressing need or where there was less than a fully competitive process. Only in the case of the CF-18 and the current quest to replace it have there been competitive processes (more or less) where the government, not necessarily the RCAF, sought to assure some degree of industrial benefits. Given this history, the idea that an effective and influential collaboration has existed between the RCAF and the aerospace industry is arguably, and perhaps demonstrably, a figment of the imagination.

Notes

1 For example, at the time of writing the "capital acquisition" figure of $3.9 billion represented 17 percent of the overall defence budget. See Canada, National Defence, "Defence Budget," https://www.canada.ca/en/department-national-defence/corporate/reports-publications/transition-materials/defence-101/2020/03/defence-101/defence-budget.html. The capital component of Canada's current defence policy, which was published in 2017, shows financial year 2021–22 capital at about 13 percent, with the capital portion growing to 22 percent at the end of the decade. See National Defence, "Strong Secure Engaged: Canada's Defence Policy," 2017, http://dgpaapp.forces.gc.ca/en/canada-defence-policy/docs/canada-defence-policy-report.pdf.

2 See discussions of Canadian procurement policy and practice in Aaron Plamondon, *The Politics of Procurement: Military Acquisition in Canada and the Sea King Helicopter* (Vancouver: UBC Press, 2010); Aaron Plamondon, "Equipment Procurement in Canada and the Civil-Military Relationship: Past and Present," *Calgary Papers in Military and Strategic Studies,* Occasional Paper No. 2 (2008): 1–47; Kim Richard Nossal, *Charlie Foxtrot: Fixing Defence Procurement in Canada* (Toronto: Dundurn, 2016).

3 The 2014 Defence Procurement Strategy, still in place at the end of 2019, was issued by Public Services and Procurement Canada – in other words, by a central purchasing department, not the DND. It states in part, "The Strategy has three key objectives: delivering the right equipment to the Canadian Armed Forces and the Canadian Coast Guard in a timely manner; leveraging our purchases of defence equipment to create jobs and economic growth in Canada; and streamlining defence procurement processes." Government of Canada, "Defence Procurement Strategy," https://www.tpsgc-pwgsc.gc.ca/app-acq/amd-dp/samd-dps/ssamd-adps-faq-eng.html.

4 See Plamondon, *The Politics of Procurement*, 1–15.
5 A full and excellent study of this first decade of Canadians and military aviation can be found in S.F. Wise, *Canadian Airmen and the First World War: The Official History of the Royal Canadian Air Force*, vol. 1 (Toronto: University of Toronto Press, 1980).
6 For an equal treatment of the first postwar developments of the Canadian Air Force and after 1924 the Royal Canadian Air Force, see W.A.B. Douglas, *The Creation of a National Air Force: The Official History of the Royal Canadian Air Force* (Toronto: University of Toronto Press, 1986), 2:1–119.
7 Douglas, *The Creation of a National Air Force*, 96.
8 Douglas, *The Creation of a National Air Force*, 89.
9 Larry Milberry, *Aviation in Canada* (Toronto: McGraw-Hill Ryerson, 1979), 105–10.
10 E.W. Stedman, *From Boxkite to Jet: The Memoirs of an Aeronautical Engineer*, Canadian War Museum Paper 1 (Ottawa: National Museums of Canada, 1972), 171.
11 H. Duncan Hall, *North American Supply* (London: HMSO, 1955), 28–31.
12 Fuller discussions on wartime procurement policies are in C.P. Stacey, *Arms Men and Governments: The War Policies of Canada 1939–1945* (Ottawa: HMSO, 1970), 285–301; Douglas, *The Creation of a National Air Force*, 343–72.
13 A.F. Plumtre, "Organizing the Canadian Economy for War," in *Canadian War Economics*, ed. J.F. Parkinson (Toronto: University of Toronto Press, 1941), 5.
14 Fred Gaffen, "Canada's Military Aircraft Industry: Its Birth, Growth and Fortunes," *Canadian Defence Quarterly* 15, 2 (1985): 51.
15 J. de N. Kennedy, *Canada in the Second World War*, vol. 2, *Controls, Service and Finance Branches, and Units Associated with the Department* (Ottawa: HMSO, 1950), 499.
16 J.W. Pickersgill, *The Mackenzie King Record*, vol. 1, *1939–1944* (Toronto: University of Toronto Press, 1960), 159.
17 Kennedy, *Canada in the Second World War*, 469–71.
18 James Eayrs, *In Defence of Canada*, vol. 3, *Peacemaking and Deterrence* (Toronto: University of Toronto Press, 1972), 102–5.
19 K.H. Sullivan and Larry Milberry, *Power: The Pratt and Whitney Canada Story* (Toronto: CANAV Books, 1989), 43; Pickersgill, *The Mackenzie King Record*, 86–87.
20 AMAE to CAS, Minute 2 to DGR 6 November 1942, n.d.; CAS to AMAS, Minute 3 to DGR 6 November 1942, 10 December 1942; AMAS to CAS, Minute 4 to DGR 6 November 1942, 18 December 1942; AMAE to CAS, Minute 5 to DGR 6 November 1942, 23 December 1942, all in Department of National Defence fonds, RG 24, vol. 6179, RCAF file 60-1-59, Aircraft Manufacture and Development in Canada, folder 1, Library and Archives Canada (LAC).
21 Randall Wakelam, *Cold War Fighters: Canadian Aircraft Procurement, 1945–54* (Vancouver: UBC Press, 2011), 19–21.
22 Greig Stewart, *Shutting Down the National Dream: A.V. Roe and the Tragedy of the Avro Arrow* (Toronto: McGraw Hill Ryerson, 1988), 37–44.
23 Stewart, *Shutting Down*, 40–41, 47–50.
24 Ronald Pickler and Larry Milberry, *Canadair: The First Fifty Years* (Toronto: CANAV Books, 1995), 31–51; Sullivan and Milberry, *Power*, 61.
25 Stedman to Brigadier F.C. Wallace, General Manager Turbo Research Ltd, 14 March 1945, RG 24, vol. 5404, RCAF file 60-5-26, Turbo Research Ltd., LAC.
26 "Report of the Post War Planning Committee: Proposed Post-War Plan for the Royal Canadian Air Force," revised 31 October 1945, 2, PARC RCAF, file 840-108, vol. 8, Directorate of History and Heritage (DHH); "Minutes of Air Council Meeting 1/1946," 3 January 1946, 2–3, PARC RCAF, file 840-108, vol. 8, DHH; AVM Wilf Curtis to Col. F.J. Graling, USAAF, 28 February 1946, CH3/9, DHH.

27   Stewart, *Shutting Down*, 59–69. More details are provided in Greig Stewart, "Canada and the Development of the Aircraft Jet Engine," *Canadian Defence Quarterly* 9, 1 (Summer 1979): 48–56.

28   C.D. Howe fonds, MG 27 III B20, vol. 48, file 9–85–30, folder 5, AV Roe Canada Ltd 1949–1951, LAC. Extract from James Hornick, "Flashbacks on the AVRO Story of Engines and Airframes," *Globe and Mail*, 10 October 1951, C.D. Howe fonds, MG 27 III B20, vol. 48, file 9–85–30, folder 5, AV Roe Canada Ltd 1949–1951, LAC.

29   "Minutes of Cabinet Defence Committee, Meeting 51," 30 October 1948, 4, Privy Council Office fonds, RG 2, vol. 2748, LAC.

30   "Minutes of Cabinet Defence Committee, Meeting 76," 29 June 1951, 2, RG 2, vol. 2748, LAC.

31   "Minutes of 482nd Meeting of CSC," 16 January 1951, 73/1223/1306, DHH. The minutes called for a fighter force in Europe, in which, by 1955, nine of twelve squadrons were to be equipped with the CF-100.

32   "Minutes of Cabinet Defence Committee" (various meetings in October 1948), RG 2, vol. 2748, LAC; Cabinet Document CD D-196, "Canadian Armed Forces Programme for Fiscal Year 1949–50," 5 October 1948, "Tab F – Royal Canadian Air Force," RG 2, vol. 2750, folder 6, LAC. See also Pickler and Milberry, *Canadair*, 88–90.

33   Order-in-Council P.C. 5700, 8 December 1948, 1–2, Department of Defence Production fonds, RG 49, vol. 1, Organization of Defence Production, folder 1, LAC. Howe's powers with respect to defence production were detailed in Order-in-Council P.C. 5700, of 8 December 1948, which was approved shortly after his return from the United States. It gave the minister of trade and commerce certain fundamental powers with respect to defence procurement. Specifically, he had control of funding for "research and development of jet engines and aircraft." Moreover, another section gave him the "powers, duties and functions" previously exercised during the Second World War by the Department of Munitions and Supply.

34   RG 49, vol. 136, file 13:11:5, Procurement of Mustang Aircraft from U.S.A. for R.C.A.F., LAC. The file contains a series of rapid-fire telexes back and forth between Canada's ambassador to Washington and various members of Cabinet.

35   Wakelam, *Cold War Fighters*, 66–67.

36   "Minutes of 482nd Meeting of CSC," 16 January 1951, 73/1223/1306, DHH. "Minutes of Special Air Members Meeting with Sir John Slessor, Chief of the Air Staff, RAF," 11 October 1950, 73/1223, DHH.

37   See MacDonald to Beaupre, 11 December 1950, covering "Memorandum of Meetings Held at the U.S.A.F. Materiel Command Wright-Patterson Fields, Dayton, Ohio, November 20–23, 1950," RG 49, vol. 136, file 13:11:6, United States Armed Forces Procurement Military Equipment from Canada, folder 1, LAC.

38   D. Glenn Cook and William Upton, "Canadian Aviation and Space Museum Aircraft AVRO Canuck 5D," https://documents.techno-science.ca/documents/CASM-Aicrafthistories-AvroCanadaCF-100.pdf.

39   "AVRO Aircraft Limited - Sale of Aircraft to Other Countries," n.d., RG 49, vol. 432, file 759-RA-12, LAC.

40   Larry Milberry, *The AVRO CF-100* (Toronto: CANAV Books, 1981), 152.

41   "Minutes of CSC Meeting 545," 6 October 1953, 73/1223/1307, DHH.

42   See, for example, Marc Andre Valiquette, *The Structure of a Dream*, 4 vols. (Winnipeg: Imaviation, 2009–12); Russell Steven Paul Isinger, "The Avro Canada CF-105 Arrow Programme: Decisions and Determinants" (master's thesis, University of Saskatchewan, 1997). Part of the mythology surrounding the Arrow focuses on the folly of cancelling the project. Criticisms of the cancellation, both at the time and almost constantly since, present the decision as a death sentence for Avro and a mighty blow against aerospace

manufacturing in Canada. Such might be true, but these same decisions point to the absence of any MIC-like influence of industry and air force over the procurement decisions of the nation.

43 John Boyko, "Bomarc Missile Crisis," *Canadian Encyclopedia,* https://www. thecanadianencyclopedia.ca/en/article/bomarc-missile-crisis.

44 Howe to Crawford Gordon, 12 November 1951, MG 27 III B 20, vol. 48, file 9–85–30, folder 5, LAC.

45 Stewart, *Shutting Down,* 146.

46 Ross Munro, "Why Millions for Super Planes?" *Vancouver Province,* 8 January 1952, Brooke Claxton fonds, MG 32 B5, vol. 94, Aircraft Clippings folder, LAC.

47 "Minutes of Air Members Meeting 194," 7 April 1954, 73/1223, DHH. See also Ray Stouffer, *Swords, Clunks and Widowmakers: The Tumultuous Life of the RCAF's Original 1 Canadian Air Division* (Ottawa: Department of National Defence, 2015), 108.

48 John Miller, "1200 Mph, 2,000-Mile Range: First of US Supersonic Voodoos Turned Over to RCAF at Uplands," *Globe and Mail,* 25 July 1961, 13.

49 Clyde Sanger, "Voodoos to Be Traded-in for U.S. Models, Defense Minister Tells House Committee," *Globe and Mail,* 11 March 1970, 31.

50 Stouffer, *Swords, Clunks and Widowmakers,* 105–11.

51 Canadian Starfighter Association, "Canadair CF-104 Starfighter," http://www. canadianstarfighterassociation.org/story.htm.

52 Ray Stouffer, "Cold War Air Power Choices for the RCAF: Paul Hellyer and the Selection of the CF-5 Freedom Fighter," *Canadian Military Journal* 7, 3 (2006): 63–73. Stouffer's presentation of the facts provides a fascinating and perhaps alarming examination of the tortuous and highly politicized nature of defence procurement, particularly as related to aircraft.

53 Kim Richard Nossal, "Late Learners: Canada, the F-35, and Lessons from the New Fighter Aircraft Program," *International Journal* 68, 1 (2012): 167–84.

54 Anton Bezglasnyy and Douglas Alan Ross, "Strategically Superfluous, Unacceptably Overpriced: The Case against Canada's F-35A Lightning II Acquisition," *Canadian Foreign Policy Journal* 17, 3 (September 2011): 241, quoted in Nossal, "Late Learners," 168.

55 Nossal, "Late Learners," 180.

56 Hugh Shields et al., *The de Havilland Canada DHC-1 Chipmunk: The Poor Man's Spitfire* (St. Thomas, ON: SBGB, 2009). See also Fred Hotson, *The de Havilland Canada Story* (Toronto: CANAV Books, 1987), 94–100.

57 Hotson, *The de Havilland Canada Story,* 104–7.

58 "U-6A/L-20 Beaver DHC-2," https://www.globalsecurity.org/military/systems/aircraft/u-6. htm; "United Kingdom, Army Aviation, Aircraft Types: de Havilland Canada Beaver AL. 1," http://www.aeroflight.co.uk/waf/uk/army/types/beaver.htm.

59 Hotson, *The de Havilland Canada Story,* 104–7.

60 Hotson, *The de Havilland Canada Story,* 109–22. Production numbers are available at "De Havilland Canada DHC-3 Otter," https://military.wikia.org/wiki/De_Havilland_ Canada_DHC-3_Otter; History Hangar, "DHC-3 Otter," https://www.thehistoryhangar. ca/aircraft---other/otter.

61 Hotson, *The de Havilland Canada Story,* 146–49, 158.

62 "De Havilland C7-A Caribou," https://www.nationalmuseum.af.mil/Visit/Museum-Exhibits/Fact-Sheets/Display/Article/196056/de-havilland-c-7a-caribou/.

63 Australian and New Zealand Military Aircraft Serials and History: RAAF A4 de Havilland DHC-4 Caribou, http://www.adf-serials.com.au/3a4.htm.

64 Hotson, *The de Havilland Canada Story,* 158–59.

65 Hotson, *The de Havilland Canada Story,* 165–70.

66 Hotson, *The de Havilland Canada Story,* 166.
67 See, for example, Michael A. Bernstein and Mark R. Wilson, "New Perspectives on the History of the Military–Industrial Complex," *Enterprise and Society* 12, 1 (2011): 1–9. See also Eugene Gholz, "Eisenhower versus the Spin-off Story: Did the Rise of the Military–Industrial Complex Hurt or Help America's Commercial Aircraft Industry?" *Enterprise and Society* 12, 1 (2011): 46–95.

Conclusion
"Insurance for Peace"

Matthew S. Wiseman

ON A LATE OCTOBER DAY IN 1953, several prominent figures from Prime Minister Louis St-Laurent's Liberal government convened in Ottawa with a large assembly of top industry executives at the annual meeting of the Canadian Industrial Preparedness Association (CIPA), an "organization encouraging active participation in industrial preparedness for the common defence of Canada."[1] Among the attendees were Minister of Defence Production C.D. Howe, Minister of National Defence Brooke Claxton, Minister of Finance Douglas Abbott, and Chairman of the Defence Research Board (DRB) Omond Solandt. The event included a visit to government research facilities and the opportunity to hear senior officials speak at a reception dinner. Solandt arranged two separate tours for the participants, with one group visiting DRB facilities and another visiting the local laboratories of the National Research Council (NRC). The DRB group toured the National Aeronautical Establishment, observing a state-of-the-art wind tunnel and related scientific equipment before visiting the Royal Canadian Air Force's (RCAF) Central Experimental and Proving Establishment at Rockcliffe to see equipment and methods used in aircraft trials. The NRC group visited an electronics laboratory and the Canadian Signals Research and Development testing facility.

A large, wealthy, and politically powerful group attended the CIPA meeting, including senior government officials, defence scientists, and prominent industry leaders from such large corporations as General Electric, Canadian Arsenals, Canadian Vickers, and the Ford Motor Company, to name only a few. The meeting also drew participants from south of the border, as top American executives representing the US National Security Industrial Association travelled from New York City. The day culminated with the annual CIPA reception dinner, keynote speeches by Abbott and Solandt, and closing remarks by Howe and Claxton. Howe paid tribute to CIPA, without which, in his view, Canada's "defence industry would be feeble."[2] Claxton's approach was more direct. Addressing the 292 CIPA members and guests, he espoused Cold War rhetoric to drum up support for the growing North American military-industrial base. "If there is a change in the behaviour of Russia and her satellites [after the conflict in Korea], there is no change in their design," Claxton stated boldly. "Any change in Red behaviour was because the free people had shown themselves ready to take action. You don't cut off your insurance because you haven't had a fire ... Defence payments are our premium on insurance for peace."[3]

Claxton's comments struck a chord with CIPA members. In a bulletin celebrating the meeting, the organization published a statement proclaiming Canada's responsibility to contribute to the military and industrial capacity of the North Atlantic Treaty Organization (NATO). The statement referred to defence as a "collective project" and suggested that each nation of the free world needed to work together to withstand Soviet aggression. For Canada and Canadians, this meant finding the will and resources to achieve maximum industrial output and the national capability to meet constantly evolving military needs. The solution was an unwavering belief in the need to prepare for conflict during peacetime, and in true Musketeerian fashion, the principle of "all for one and one for all" applied not only to the armed services but also to the physical and financial resources required for complete mobilization – the process of assembling and organizing national resources in preparation for emergencies or war.[4]

Calling on government and industry to recognize Canada's inability to defend its own interests without support, the CIPA bulletin paints a vivid picture of prevailing attitudes toward military-industrial partnerships in Canada during the early Cold War. As CIPA president T.R. McLagan, who was also president of Canada Steamship Lines, stated in his report, "Our Association has been attempting to point out through propaganda and by every other means possible, that in modern war the armed services are only part of the defence or striking force, and they are useless without properly equipped manufacturing plants behind them and staffed by well trained personnel."[5] CIPA represents the voice and opinions of major industrial executives who had clear political and economic motivations, but the strong and vociferous commitment of top government officials at the Ottawa meeting also speaks to the underlying concerns for national defence and the distinct sociocultural responses of Canadian leaders to the Cold War. From Ottawa's perspective, defence preparedness in peacetime necessitated permanent cooperation between the state and private industry. The political economy of Canada's military-industrial base was thus crucial to ensuring a safe and stable future for all Canadians – a message enthusiastically received, supported, and reciprocated by hundreds of corporate executives and their industrial brethren.

Today, few Canadians remember CIPA or know of the association and its members. It originated in 1948 under the name Canadian Ordnance Association, when top executives of leading manufacturers joined in a preparedness effort to cooperate with the federal government and mobilize national resources in the event of a major emergency or war. In standard military parlance, the phrase "defence preparedness" has close associations with the concept of mobilization.[6] CIPA surveyed large- and small-scale firms and tabulated equipment and facilities across Canada, helping to "marshal the industrial forces of the nation" and to produce "weapons of war" if necessary.[7] Members liaised with senior officials from several branches of the federal government, visited various military bases to witness weapons and equipment tests, and kept the wider industrial community informed of the country's military needs.

Over time, Canada's defence preparedness needs changed drastically as the weapons systems and strategic concepts of the Cold War evolved. After the Korean conflict, military and defence officials in Ottawa came to view preparedness through the prism of nuclear deterrence. In his examination of Canadian military strategy and nuclear weapons, historian Andrew Richter credits R.J. Sutherland and George Lindsey, two key strategic defence analysts, with the shifting paradigm. While studying nuclear strategy as DRB employees in the 1950s and 1960s, Sutherland and Lindsey wrote internal government reports and informed Canadian policy considerations on the US-Soviet nuclear balance.[8] Facing the possibility of a short and rapidly escalating nuclear war, analysts in the Department of National Defence calculated that there would be no time for extensive mobilization of soldiers or industry along the lines of the two previous global conflicts.[9] This meant that adequate military preparedness depended on Canada's ability to produce and supply the weapons and equipment required by the armed services well in advance of any future conflict. Under the looming spectre of atomic war, the Western democracies of the free world needed permanent military and industrial power. Just as the outgoing US president Dwight D. Eisenhower explained in his farewell address from the Oval Office in January 1961, post facto mobilizations were no longer an adequate or effective strategic doctrine.

In retrospect, mid-century Canada was a country deeply entwined with many recognizable military-industrial activities that marked the dawn of the Cold War. As historians Susan Colbourn and Timothy Sayle point out in a recent collection of essays on Canadian nuclear history, although never a nuclear power per se, Canada remains a "nuclear state" with a long and complicated history of participation in the military and civilian dimensions of the atomic age.[10] In the mid-1950s, for instance, Canadian soldiers deployed in Nevada and southern Australia participated in live nuclear-weapons trials that resulted in their direct exposure to dangerously high levels of radiation.[11] During the late 1960s, moreover, Canada was a member of NATO's Nuclear Planning Group, engulfed in the nuclear affairs and strategic policies of the alliance. As Ottawa planned and prepared for nuclear war, citizens across the country expressed their concerns and fears, many advocating nuclear non-proliferation, arms control, and disarmament.[12] Nevertheless, the federal government signed successive agreements giving the US Strategic Air Command access to Canadian bases and airspace for its bombers, and Canadian artillery and air units were equipped and trained to use nuclear weapons in Europe until the early 1970s. Canada also maintained combat-ready jet aircraft, three CF-101B Voodoo squadrons, with the capability of firing the Genie air-to-air atomic anti-bomber rocket against Soviet long-range bombers in the defence of North America.[13] The Canadian military received the Genies in the mid-1960s and maintained the rockets until their removal from Canada in June 1984.

Atomic weaponry represents only one part of Canada's overall Cold War–era nuclear story, though. Canada exported nuclear materials for peaceful purposes, but historian Ryan Touhey shows that India used the plutonium extracted from a Canadian reactor to detonate a nuclear device in 1974. Fraught with miscommunication, the incident strained bilateral relations between Canada and India, and it illustrated the political and moral consequences of the nuclear trade.[14] In the late 1980s, moreover, senior Canadian defence officials considered procuring nuclear-powered submarines capable of operating under Arctic ice and protecting the northern reaches of the continental shelf year-round.[15] Although the federal government never acquired the submarines, Canada developed close ties to the expanding global nuclear industry, extracting and exporting materials for international clients. Uranium mined from the Northwest Territories, Ontario, and Saskatchewan supplied the atomic age, nuclear reactors designed in Canada contributed to the emergence and installation of nuclear-powered electrical grids at home and abroad, and radioactive isotopes exported from Canada spurred global innovations in cancer treatment and medical procedures.[16]

Other elements of the Canadian experience in the Cold War speak to and inform the history explored in the preceding chapters as well. In addition to the military and civilian applications of nuclear technology, historians John Bryden, Donald Avery, and Susan Smith have lifted the veil on Canada's participation in the defensive aspects of biological, chemical, and bacteriological warfare research.[17] Academic and industrial researchers in various fields collaborated with federal authorities and military officials, using the most up-to-date information available to the Canadian government to study and defend against the threat of unconventional weapons, including deadly toxins and vector-borne attacks on the Canadian population and food supply.[18] Creating and sustaining a successful defence research program in the decades after the Second World War required extensive mobilization of resources and knowledge, which partly explains the deep political and financial entanglements at the core of Canada's military-industrial complex (MIC). Beyond weapons of mass destruction, historian Andrew Godefroy has documented the military's consistent presence and role in funding and facilitating Canadian space research between the late 1940s and the mid-1970s, and historian Jocelyn Wills has investigated Canada's private space industry and the export of Canadian-made satellite surveillance technologies to the United States during and after the Cold War.[19] Inextricably, these studies reveal the myriad *costs* of preparedness and the extent to which military and industrial partners in Canada worked together to defend, promote, and profit from investments in North Atlantic security and the maintenance of world order.

Canada's defence record runs contrary to the popular myth of the "peaceable kingdom," signalling the importance of studying history to interrogate and understand the scope and reach of the state's military-industrial base. Building on a strong foundation of scholarship that has explored Canadian investments in defence and international security, the chapters in *Silent Partners* reinforce Canada's deep history of direct participation in state-supported military research, development, and industrial production. As the editors articulate in the introductory chapter, determining whether Canada had or has a distinct MIC is a matter that extends beyond the limits of scholarly conjecture, but the interpretations and perspectives put forward by the contributing authors suggest that "silent partners" is an apt label indeed. In both domestic and international contexts, the twentieth century witnessed Canadian politicians, military leaders, academics, and industrialists contribute to the creation, growth, and expansion of a state-driven military-industrial base with ties to the political economy of warfare. Some Canadians protested government-sponsored military R&D during the mid–Cold War period, thereby nuancing (and even challenging) the "silent" partnership that we identify as crucial to understanding and investigating the MIC in Canada.[20] Nevertheless, the facade of Canada's so-called peaceful national image often resisted the military label and hid the depth and substance of relations among military, industrial, academic, and political interests. Indeed, historically the Canadian MIC developed silently because its participants, champions, and proponents operated largely free of dissent or opposition from within Canadian politics, business, and public life.

Arguably, however, this is a partial conclusion at best. The issue at the heart of the debate remains whether the people embroiled in and connected to Canada's military-industrial base constitute(d) a special interest group capable of bringing quantifiable power and influence to bear on Canada's political economy. By and large, the evidence gathered and explored in the preceding chapters casts doubt on the existence of a single group of such influencers in Canada. Instead, the historical case studies in this volume point at a largely disjointed but consistent record of state-supported activity directed toward encouraging and sustaining cooperation among political, military, industrial, and academic partners. Nevertheless, government and civilian partners in Canada have a documented history of nurturing the shared priorities and political and economic ties that make up the state's military-industrial base. Politicians and industry leaders have championed the benefits of defence preparedness for the national economy, for instance, advocating military and industrial growth and leveraging those relationships toward personal, economic, and political means. The scale and reach of Canada's military-industrial capacity certainly pale in comparison to those of the United States and other major powers, but size and scope are not the only factors in determining the existence and character of a Canadian MIC.

Consider the desire and effort on the part of senior Canadian defence officials to enmesh Canada in the military R&D activities of the United States and Britain, to name just two of Canada's prominent military and industrial allies. As Alex Souchen points out in Chapter 1, government officials in the Department of Munitions and Supply were at the centre of a mutually beneficial partnership between public and private enterprise that helped forge the foundations of Canada's MIC during the Second World War, with a staggering 70 percent of Canada's total wartime output generated for the British and other allies. Although demobilization, defence cuts, and changes in American and British domestic production at war's end radically affected the size and capacity of Canada's postwar armaments industry, officials in Ottawa continued to leverage Canada's military-industrial base to supply the evolving needs of the Canadian armed services, international clients, and the domestic economy.

Notwithstanding demobilization and the sharp reductions to Canada's munitions industry, the immediate and early postwar period introduced new opportunities for a fledging national MIC. The Cold War arrived on the front pages of Canadian newspapers in February 1946 when the revelations of the Gouzenko affair became public. Five months earlier, and only three weeks after Japan surrendered following the atomic bombings of Hiroshima and Nagasaki, Igor Gouzenko, a cipher clerk at the Soviet embassy in Ottawa, defected with more than a hundred documents incriminating the Soviet Union in espionage activities in the West.[21] The affair ignited national security concerns in Western capitals, inspired the 1948 Hollywood film *The Iron Curtain*, and represented the unofficial start of a new era in international tensions. By April 1949, the North Atlantic Treaty laid down the creation of NATO, and Canada officially committed to collective security, providing financial and military support to defend Western values and promote international peace and world order.[22] But preparations for any future conflict would be vastly different from those for the last.

In an era of atomic bombs and rapidly advancing weapons systems, science and engineering played an increasingly prominent role in postwar military preparedness. Senior Canadian defence officials created the DRB in April 1947, committing significant resources and personnel to manage the new and evolving R&D needs of the armed services. As several chapters in this volume explore, the scope and quantity of military R&D exploded in Canada during the earliest decades of the Cold War – owing predominantly to the large sums of defence funding distributed through the DRB – and the resulting implications extended well beyond the army, navy, and air force. The federal government expropriated large swaths of land to construct military training grounds and testing facilities, forcibly removing and displacing Indigenous people and settlers from their homes and territories. In Chapter 2, Brandon Davis focuses on the Suffield area in southern Alberta, describing the process of dispossession and displacement as sacrificial to the higher needs of national defence and permanent war-readiness. Defence officials surveyed and expropriated Suffield during the war, using the site in cooperation with British and American forces as a testing ground for various biological and chemical warfare agents. On-site experiments continued and expanded under the direction of DRB authorities during the early Cold War, introducing hazardous chemicals into the local environment and eventually drawing the ire of concerned citizens who protested military research at the experimental facility.

Matthew Wiseman and Matthew Farish explore similar issues in Chapter 3, discussing the expropriation of lands for military use in the Downsview area in Toronto's north end, where scientists and engineers at the DRB's newly constructed Defence Research Medical Laboratories carried out various experiments to develop equipment and techniques to support and improve upon the operational capabilities of military personnel. Several interconnected factors explain the DRB's foothold in postwar Toronto, including pre-existing facilities and experts at one of Canada's largest research universities, ample government support, and the commitment of influential scientists and academic colleagues who believed strongly in the application of science to contemporary military problems. What emerges from the history of military R&D at Downsview, not unlike Suffield, is the realization that powerful people connected with the Department of National Defence knowingly cultivated the mechanisms of Canada's MIC. The *inner ring* – a label that historian Mel Thistle once employed to describe the authorities at the heart of the NRC – seems apposite for defining and describing the select group of men who championed the government, corporate, and academic partnerships required to foster and grow Canada's postwar capacity for military R&D.[23] To be certain, though never a monolith, Canada's MIC represented the concerted efforts of a collection of like-minded individuals who aligned their shared values with national interests.

In addition to land expropriation and environmental degradation, Cold War–era military activity in Canada affected civilians and military personnel caught up in experimental research. Scientists and engineers employed by the DRB used its facilities to perform wide-ranging experiments on military personnel and equipment. Academics across the country also conducted experimental research for the DRB, using grant funding from the national defence budget to build laboratories, hire research assistants, and carry out projects with real and potential military applications. The startling sensory deprivation experiments performed on "volunteer" students at McGill University and the University of Manitoba, which Meghan Fitzpatrick documents in Chapter 4, occurred under the direction of leading psychologists Donald Hebb and John Zubek. Hopeful that sensory deprivation research would yield insights into mind control and attitudinal conversion, authorities in the DRB supported the experimental research of both scientists for more than twenty years between the early 1950s and mid-1970s. Unfortunately, the research, as Fitzpatrick makes clear, treaded on morally questionable grounds and resulted in negative impacts to some research subjects.

Canada's MIC was not limited to domestic R&D, however. As Asa McKercher investigates in Chapter 5, Canada has a long and complicated history of producing and exporting arms to international clients. While maintaining and strengthening the Canadian military to meet the escalating demands of the Cold War in North America and Western Europe, government officials in Ottawa sought foreign markets for Canadian-made materiel to offset high production costs. Although diplomats in the Department of External Affairs raised several concerns about Canada's new role as an international arms broker, the economic and military benefits of selling materiel abroad often outweighed altruistic notions of Canada's peaceful national identity. Despite seeking to enforce the 1954 Geneva Accords through membership on the International Control Commission, for instance, Ottawa signed the Defence Production Sharing Agreement with Washington in 1956, thus ensuring that Canadian arms manufacturers could compete for Pentagon contracts, and Canadian-made weapons ended up being used in Vietnam.

Frank Maas extends the discussion of military production and the economics of Canada's MIC in Chapter 6 by focusing on one major company: Diesel Division General Motors (DDGM), the forebear of today's General Dynamics Land Systems–Canada. During the 1970s, this corporation became a defence contractor that produced and sold light armoured vehicles to the Canadian Army and foreign buyers, including the US Marine Corps, Australia, New Zealand, Saudi Arabia, and other countries. As Maas points out, government and private interests overlapped to ensure success, as the maintenance and growth of Canada's domestic industrial base represented a key goal of economic and foreign policies aimed at supporting the production and sale of Canadian-made vehicles.

At the same time, Randall Wakelam's study of the RCAF in Chapter 7 reminds us that fulsome contextual understanding of Canada's MIC often requires independent analysis on a case-by-case basis. Unlike the Canadian Army, the RCAF has a limited history of direct cooperation with Canada's manufacturing sector. The first decade after the Second World War saw the RCAF purchase and promote Canadian-made aircraft, but during the mid-to-late Cold War period, it procured aircraft from foreign sources and did little to prop up or promote the Canadian aviation industry.

There is a greater need to investigate the history of Canada's MIC and the dynamic relationships forged among the federal government, military, and arms manufacturers, but novel research depends on open and unfettered access to archives and historical records. Unfortunately, historians, political scientists, journalists, and other researchers often encounter many obstacles and challenges stemming from Canada's convoluted and feeble information laws. In 1983, the Liberal government of Pierre Trudeau passed the current Access to Information Act, which permitted Canadians to retrieve government files for personal use.[24] Yet the act's name is extremely misleading. Canadian citizens do not have direct, unabated access to all types of information, and unlike other democratic countries, Canada has no default mechanism to release records. Citizens merely have the right to *request* access to what they want, and there is no default "thirty-year rule" for the review and release of government records.[25] Essentially, the Access to Information Act established what information can be accessed and mandated a systematic process for the consultation and review of information deemed to be potentially sensitive. Under the purview of the information commissioner of Canada, government departments cannot refuse to grant access to federal records without first authorizing a review of the documents requested for retrieval and release.

The list of files with exemptions from disclosure is quite expansive, especially when national security and defence are involved. Records containing information provided to the Canadian government in confidence by foreign governments are restricted, for instance. So, too, are files pertaining to public safety and security, provincial and federal relations, third-party companies, and information that may be used to undermine government operations. The list is not exhaustive, but nor is it black and white. Shades of grey permeate the Access to Information Act and disclosure process, negatively affecting the work of scholars who use federal records to research and write their topics, both historical and contemporary.[26] Jonathan Turner encountered access-to-information issues when attempting to research and write on the institutional history of the DRB; James Fergusson and Richard Goette faced similar hurdles when studying the history of Canadian involvement in North American air and missile defence; David Zimmerman overcame document restrictions while researching the Royal Canadian Navy and the history of maritime security on the West Coast; and Alex Souchen found many gaps in government records, as well as obstacles to accessing information about underwater munitions and their environmental impact.[27]

When in doubt about the sensitivity of records requested under the Access to Information Act, archivists and classification officers from Library and Archives Canada and other government departments must review the requested document(s) to determine the conditions of release. However, it is common for these reviews to take several months or years to complete, far surpassing the mandated thirty-day response times. Access-to-information analysts thus hold an impressive (and often daunting) amount of power and authority over the work of historians, political scientists, journalists, activists, and other public researchers. Some reviews receive a quick rejection, and most do not yield complete access to the files requested. Rather than providing important details and exciting new insights, records opened by review often contain heavily redacted information or facts of tertiary importance to the subject under examination by the requester. Newly opened archival documents from National Defence and External Affairs, for example, may contain references to administrative statistics or information already on public record rather than details about weapons procurement or executive government meetings on national security and foreign policy.

Perhaps, more than any other sub-field of the historical discipline, military history requires consistent and comprehensive access to declassified records. Indeed, without access to material sources, military history – especially when it intersects with national security – becomes an extremely difficult subject to research and write. The chapters in *Silent Partners*, then, represent a concerted first effort – the proverbial foot in the door – at tackling the history of Canada's MIC. Our goal, as editors and contributing authors, is to deploy historical perspectives and open new conversations about military, industrial, academic, and political relationships. We suggest that Canada has a MIC with traceable and quantifiable roots in the mid-twentieth century. Originating during the Second World War when Canadian industry supported the national war effort, it took hold and expanded in various ways during the Cold War, as a generation of military leaders, government officials, senior academics, and private executives recognized and pursued the many benefits of military-industrial cooperation. Understanding and contextualizing the implications and legacy of this history requires additional research, information, and constructive dialogue.

Access to information is by no means an issue unique to Canada or the Canadian historical discipline, but the current laws and enforcement structures impede and even curtail historical inquiry, research, and scholarship on the

MIC. Existing government legislation prioritizes the protection of information over transparency and accountability, and despite repeated calls for change, acceptance is the norm.[28] Consequently, articles and books on the history of Canada's political economy and military-industrial base go unwritten, as records critical to the research and writing process remain stowed away in archival repositories and closed to public consultation – thereby adding a further dimension to the "silent" partnership that we identified in this collection. To be certain, Canada's current information laws can and do affect the scope of research, shrouding important subjects in military history and national defence that have serious impacts on the health, safety, security, and livelihoods of Canadians.

Canada Declassified – an open-access web portal based at the University of Toronto that publishes newly opened records of the Canadian government – is an important and useful resource for students and scholars alike, but the burden and responsibility of requesting and then publishing declassified government records should not fall on the public.[29] As Alan Barnes, who spearheads the Canadian Foreign Intelligence History Project at Carleton University, explains, both researchers and government authorities have the responsibility to foster a better understanding of how the access-to-information process operates when dealing with historical records, especially those on foreign policy, defence, intelligence, and national security matters.[30] Increasing the accessibility of historical records will improve transparency and accountability, thereby reducing the pressure to "protect" sensitive information and easing the load and strain on the entire access-to-information system.

Understanding Canada's MIC ultimately requires additional quantitative and qualitative research on domestic and foreign activity, including the scale and substance of military R&D, industrial production, land use, defence lobbying, preparedness, procurement, and arms sales. Since the political economy of Canada's military-industrial base was and is unbounded by international borders, the empirical studies that aim to quantify and understand it should examine Canadian history at home and abroad. Furthermore, as McKercher and Maas both indicate in their chapters, Canada's MIC survives because of international exports and the offset policies for domestic production. Well after the end of the Cold War, Canadian manufacturers continue to participate in warfare's global economy, and all with the support of government officials and private lobbyists who leverage Canada's industrial capabilities to benefit the state's economic and political interests.[31] Canada's MIC originated and matured in response to the unique military and defence needs of the mid-twentieth century, but the strong economic and political ties created among government, corporate, and academic partners continue to grow and thrive in a manner that has and will affect Canadians and their country moving forward.

Notes

1 "T.R. McLagan Returned as President," *Bulletin,* 6 November 1953, 1, RG 24, vol. 2425, file Volume 1, Library and Archives Canada (LAC). *The Bulletin* was published in Montreal by the Canadian Industrial Preparedness Association.

2 "T.R. McLagan Returned as President," 1, LAC.

3 "T.R. McLagan Returned as President," 9, LAC.

4 "Defence a Collective Project: No Nation of Free World in Position to Withstand Aggression Alone," *Bulletin,* 6 November 1953, 9, RG 24, vol. 2425, file Volume 1, LAC. On mobilization, see Dan Middlemiss, "Canada and Defence Industrial Preparedness: A Return to Basics?" *International Journal* 42, 4 (1987): 707.

5 "The President's Report," *Bulletin,* 6 November 1953, 6, RG 24, vol. 2425, file Volume 1, LAC.

6 Middlemiss, "Canada and Defence Industrial Preparedness," 707.

7 "The President's Report," 6, LAC.

8 Andrew Richter, *Avoiding Armageddon: Canadian Military Strategy and Nuclear Weapons* (Vancouver: UBC Press, 2002), 63–68.

9 Middlemiss, "Canada and Defence Industrial Preparedness," 713.

10 Susan Colbourn, "Introduction: Nuclear If Necessary, but Not Necessarily Nuclear," in *The Nuclear North: Histories of Canada in the Atomic Age,* ed. Susan Colbourn and Timothy Andrews Sayle (Vancouver: UBC Press, 2020), 12; Timothy Andrews Sayle, "Conclusion: Nuclear Victorians," in Colbourn and Sayle, *The Nuclear North,* 231.

11 Matthew S. Wiseman, "'Baptism by Fire': Canadian Soldiers and Radiation Exposure at Nevada and Maralinga," in Colbourn and Sayle, *The Nuclear North,* 153–77.

12 Tarah Brookfield, *Cold War Comforts: Canadian Women, Child Safety, and Global Insecurity* (Waterloo: Wilfrid Laurier University Press, 2012); Andrew Burtch, *Give Me Shelter: The Failure of Canada's Cold War Civil Defence* (Vancouver: UBC Press, 2012).

13 John Clearwater, *Canadian Nuclear Weapons: The Untold Story of Canada's Cold War Arsenal* (Toronto: Dundurn Press, 1998), 178.

14 Ryan Touhey, *Conflicting Visions: Canada and India in the Cold War World, 1946–76* (Vancouver: UBC Press, 2015), 174–87.

15 Susan Colbourn, "Who's Going to Invade Arctic Canada, Anyway? Debating the Acquisition of the Nuclear Submarine in the 1980s," in Colbourn and Sayle, *The Nuclear North,* 133–52.

16 On uranium mining in Canada, see Robert Bothwell, *Eldorado: Canada's National Uranium Company* (Toronto: University of Toronto Press, 1984); Robert Bothwell, *Nucleolus: The History of Atomic Energy of Canada Limited* (Toronto: University of Toronto Press, 1988).

17 John Bryden, *Deadly Allies: Canada's Secret War, 1937–1947* (Toronto: McClelland and Stewart, 1989); Donald Avery, *Pathogens for War: Biological Weapons, Canadian Life Scientists, and North American Biodefence* (Toronto: University of Toronto Press, 2013); Susan L. Smith, *Toxic Exposures: Mustard Gas and the Health Consequences of World War II in the United States* (New Brunswick, NJ: Rutgers University Press, 2017).

18 On threats to the Canadian food supply, see also Amanda Kay McVety, *The Rinderpest Campaigns: A Virus, Its Vaccines, and Global Development in the Twentieth Century* (Cambridge: Cambridge University Press, 2018).

19 Andrew Godefroy, *Defence and Discovery: Canada's Military Space Program, 1945–74* (Vancouver: UBC Press, 2011); Jocelyn Wills, *Tug of War: Surveillance Capitalism, Military Contracting, and the Rise of the Security State* (Montreal and Kingston: McGill-Queen's University Press, 2017). Wills investigates the history of military contracting involving Canada's largest space company, MacDonald, Dettwiler and Associates.

20 In Chapter 3 of this volume, Wiseman and Farish identify one vociferous student protest at the University of Toronto during the late 1960s. Other scholars have documented examples

of anti-war protests and demonstrations against military R&D in Canada during the Cold War as well. See Brookfield, *Cold War Comforts,* 82–89; Avery, *Pathogens for War,* 124–27.

21 On the Gouzenko affair, see Reg Whitaker and Gary Marcuse, *Cold War Canada: The Making of a National Insecurity State, 1945–1957* (Toronto: University of Toronto Press, 1994), 27–30; Reg Whitaker and Steve Hewitt, *Canada and the Cold War* (Toronto: James Lorimer, 2003), 13–17; Dennis Molinaro, "How the Cold War Began ... with British Help: The Gouzenko Affair Revisited," *Labour/Le Travail* 79 (Spring 2017): 143–55.

22 Timothy Andrews Sayle, *Enduring Alliance: A History of NATO and the Postwar Global Order* (Ithaca: Cornell University Press, 2019).

23 Mel Thistle, *The Inner Ring: The Early History of the National Research Council* (Toronto: University of Toronto Press, 1966).

24 The Trudeau government also introduced the Privacy Act in 1983, which protects the privacy of individuals with respect to personal information held by the federal government. Federal records containing such information, therefore, also undergo review prior to disclosure.

25 Timothy Andrews Sayle, "Transparency, Access, and History in the 21st Century," *Canadian Historical Association Bulletin* 43, 3 (2021): 17.

26 Timothy Andrews Sayle and Susan Colbourn, "Canadians Will Be Glad to Know," *Policy Options,* 25 November 2021, https://policyoptions.irpp.org/magazines/november-2021/access-to-information-act-is-a-shambles/.

27 Jonathan Turner, "The Defence Research Board of Canada, 1947 to 1977" (PhD diss., University of Toronto, 2012); James G. Fergusson, *Canada and Ballistic Missile Defence, 1954–2009* (Vancouver: UBC Press, 2010); Richard Goette, *Sovereignty and Command in Canada–US Continental Air Defence, 1940–57* (Vancouver: UBC Press, 2018); David Zimmerman, *Maritime Command Pacific: The Royal Canadian Navy's West Coast Fleet in the Early Cold War* (Vancouver: UBC Press, 2015); Alex Souchen, "Missing from the Record: Historians, Archival Research, and Underwater Munitions," *Rethinking History: The Journal of Theory and Practice* 25, 3 (2021): 347–71. This list represents a very small subset of recent historical scholarship in Canadian military history and defence studies.

28 Timothy Andrews Sayle et al., "Canada's Information Laws Are Preventing Us from Understanding Our Own History," *Globe and Mail* (Toronto), 15 October 2022, https://www.theglobeandmail.com/opinion/article-canadas-information-laws-are-preventing-us-from-understanding-our-own/.

29 For more on Canada Declassified, see its homepage at https://declassified.library.utoronto.ca.

30 Alan Barnes, "Just What Are They Trying to Protect?: Redactions to Records on Intelligence and International Affairs and the Writing of Canadian History," Canadian Eyes Only, 15 November 2021, https://cihhic.ca/2021/11/15/just-what-are-they-trying-to-protect-redactions-to-records-on-intelligence-and-international-affairs-and-the-writing-of-canadian-history/. See also the homepage of the Canadian Foreign Intelligence History Project, https://carleton.ca/csids/canadian-foreign-intelligence-history-project/.

31 On 25 October 2022, amid the ongoing war in Ukraine and calls to remobilize the Canadian Armed Forces, the Canadian Global Affairs Institute hosted a one-day conference exploring some of the current challenges to defence procurement in Canada. Among the issues debated were the need to rebuild Canada's industrial base, implement NORAD modernization, and meet the myriad socio-economic challenges of the state's military commitments and responsibilities at home and abroad. Historians were strikingly absent from the program. See Canadian Global Affairs Institute, "Annual Defence Procurement Conference: Putting Canadian Defence Procurement on a War Footing," Ottawa, 25 October 2022, https://www.cgai.ca/annual_defence_procurement_conference_putting_canadian_defence_procurement_on_a_war_footing.

Contributors

Brandon Davis is a historian of environment, war, and science. He received his PhD in history from the University of British Columbia and is currently the CLASS Project Manager at Roehampton University. His work examines the origins of national sacrifice areas, the history of British, Canadian, and American chemical and biological weapons testing programs, and environmental underpinnings of permanent war.

Matthew Farish is an associate professor and associate chair, undergraduate, in the Department of Geography and Planning at the University of Toronto. He is the author of *The Contours of America's Cold War* (2010) and is working on a book about US military survival schools, climate laboratories, and proving grounds in the middle of the twentieth century.

Meghan Fitzpatrick is a strategic analyst and an adjunct professor of war studies at the Royal Military College of Canada. A graduate of King's College London, she is the author of numerous publications, including *Invisible Scars: Mental Trauma and the Korean War* (2017). Her work has also appeared in distinguished journals such as the *Social History of Medicine, War and Society,* and the US Army War College's *Parameters.*

Frank Maas researches Canadian defence policy and procurement and teaches writing and history at Fanshawe College in London, Ontario. His book *The Price of Alliance* (2017) examines Canada's relationship with NATO through the army's procurement of the Leopard tank in the 1970s. He is working on a history of General Dynamics Land Systems–Canada, in London, Ontario, Canada's largest defence contractor.

Asa McKercher is an assistant professor in the Department of History, Royal Military College of Canada, and a senior fellow of the Bill Graham Centre for Contemporary International History. He is the author of *Canada and the World since 1867* (2019), *Camelot and Canada: Canadian-American Relations in the Kennedy Era* (2016), and co-editor of *Undiplomatic History: Rethinking Canada in the World* (2019) and *Mike's World: Lester B. Pearson and Canadian External Affairs* (2017).

Alex Souchen is an assistant professor at the University of Guelph, cross-appointed between the Department of History and Bachelor of Arts and Science Program. He is the author of *War Junk: Munitions Disposal and Postwar Reconstruction in Canada* (2020), which won honourable mention for the 2020–21 C.P. Stacey Award. His research explores the history of science and technology, warfare, and the environment.

Randall Wakelam, col. (retd.), FRHistS, is an associate emeritus professor of history and war studies at the Royal Military College of Canada. He writes in the fields of air power, leadership, and military education and has published several books, including *The Science of Bombing: Operation Research in RAF Bomber Command* (2009), *The Report of the Officer Development Board: Maj-Gen Roger Rowley and the Education of the Canadian Forces* (2010), *Cold War Fighters: Canadian Aircraft Procurement, 1945–1954* (2011), and *Educating Air Forces: Global Perspectives on Airpower Learning* (2020). He is also the lead editor of *On the Wings of War and Peace: The RCAF during the Early Cold War* (forthcoming).

Matthew S. Wiseman is a Canadian historian whose research concentrates on science, technology, and medical research ethics in the Cold War. He is the author of a forthcoming monograph on the history of military research in northern Canada and the Arctic during the Cold War. His research on the history of military-sponsored science in post-1945 Canada has also appeared in such leading journals as *Canadian Military History* and the *Canadian Historical Review*. He received his PhD from Wilfrid Laurier University and is currently a lecturer in the Department of History at the University of Waterloo.

Index

Timothy Balzer, *The Information Front: The Canadian Army and News Management during the Second World War*

Andrew B. Godefroy, *Defence and Discovery: Canada's Military Space Program, 1945–74*

Douglas E. Delaney, *Corps Commanders: Five British and Canadian Generals at War, 1939–45*

Timothy Wilford, *Canada's Road to the Pacific War: Intelligence, Strategy, and the Far East Crisis*

Randall Wakelam, *Cold War Fighters: Canadian Aircraft Procurement, 1945–54*

Andrew Burtch, *Give Me Shelter: The Failure of Canada's Cold War Civil Defence*

Wendy Cuthbertson, *Labour Goes to War: The CIO and the Construction of a New Social Order, 1939–45*

P. Whitney Lackenbauer, *The Canadian Rangers: A Living History*

Teresa Iacobelli, *Death or Deliverance: Canadian Courts Martial in the Great War*

Graham Broad, *A Small Price to Pay: Consumer Culture on the Canadian Home Front, 1939–45*

Peter Kasurak, *A National Force: The Evolution of Canada's Army, 1950–2000*

Isabel Campbell, *Unlikely Diplomats: The Canadian Brigade in Germany, 1951–64*

Richard M. Reid, *African Canadians in Union Blue: Volunteering for the Cause in the Civil War*

Andrew B. Godefroy, *In Peace Prepared: Innovation and Adaptation in Canada's Cold War Army*

Nic Clarke, *Unwanted Warriors: The Rejected Volunteers of the Canadian Expeditionary Force*

David Zimmerman, *Maritime Command Pacific: The Royal Canadian Navy's West Coast Fleet in the Early Cold War*

Cynthia Toman, *Sister Soldiers of the Great War: The Nurses of the Canadian Army Medical Corps*

Daniel Byers, *Zombie Army: The Canadian Army and Conscription in the Second World War*

J.L. Granatstein, *The Weight of Command: Voices of Canada's Second World War Generals and Those Who Knew Them*

Colin McCullough, *Creating Canada's Peacekeeping Past*

Brandon R. Dimmel, *Engaging the Line: How the Great War Shaped the Canada–US Border*

Meghan Fitzpatrick, *Invisible Scars: Mental Trauma and the Korean War*

Patrick M. Dennis, *Reluctant Warriors: Canadian Conscripts and the Great War*

Frank Maas, *The Price of Alliance: The Politics and Procurement of Leopard Tanks for Canada's NATO Brigade*

Geoffrey Hayes, *Crerar's Lieutenants: Inventing the Canadian Junior Army Officer, 1939–45*

Richard Goette, *Sovereignty and Command in Canada–US Continental Air Defence, 1940–57*

Geoff Jackson, *The Empire on the Western Front: The British 62nd and Canadian 4th Divisions in Battle*

Steve Marti and William John Pratt, eds., *Fighting with the Empire: Canada, Britain, and Global Conflict, 1867–1947*

Steve Marti, *For Home and Empire: Voluntary Mobilization in Australia, Canada, and New Zealand during the First World War*

Douglas E. Delaney and Serge Marc Durflinger, *Capturing Hill 70: Canada's Forgotten Battle of the First World War*

Peter Kasurak, *Canada's Mechanized Infantry: The Evolution of a Combat Arm, 1920–2012*

Sarah Glassford and Amy Shaw, eds., *Making the Best of It: Women and Girls of Canada and Newfoundland during the Second World War*

Alex Souchen, *War Junk: Munitions Disposal and Postwar Reconstruction in Canada*

George Belliveau and Graham W. Lea, eds., *Contact!Unload: Military Veterans, Trauma, and Research-Based Theatre*

Tim Cook and J.L. Granatstein, eds., *Canada 1919: A Nation Shaped by War*

Arthur W. Gullachsen, *An Army of Never-Ending Strength: Reinforcing the Canadians in Northwest Europe, 1944–45*

Peter Farrugia and Evan J. Habkirk, eds., *Portraits of Battle: Courage, Grief, and Strength in Canada's Great War*

Andrew L. Brown, *Building the Army's Backbone: Canadian Non-Commissioned Officers in the Second World War*

Matthew Barrett, *Scandalous Conduct: Canadian Officer Courts Martial, 1914–45*

STUDIES IN CANADIAN MILITARY HISTORY

Published by UBC Press in association with the Canadian War Museum

Printed and bound in Canada by Friesens
Set in Minion and Helvetica by Apex CoVantage, LLC
Copy editor: Deborah Kerr
Proofreader: Caitlin Gordon-Walker
Cover designer: JVDW Designs
Cover image: iStock/borchee